Jewish Responses to Anti-Semitism in Germany, 1870–1914

ALUMNI SERIES OF THE HEBREW UNION COLLEGE PRESS

Jewish Responses to Anti-Semitism in Germany, 1870–1914

A Study in the History of Ideas

by

Sanford Ragins

Hebrew Union College Press
CINCINNATI, OHIO 1980

Library of Congress Cataloging in Publication Data

Ragins, Sanford.
  Jewish responses to anti-Semitism in Germany,
1870-1914.

  (Alumni series of the Hebrew Union College
Press ISSN 0192-2904)
    Bibliography: p.
    Includes index.
    1. Jews in Germany—Politics and government.
2. Antisemitism—Germany. 3. Centralverein Deutscher
Staatsbürger Jüdischen Glaubens. 4. Zionism—Germany.
5. Germany—Ethnic relations. I. Title. II. Series.
DS135.G33R33   305.8'924'043   80-13202
ISBN 0-87820-115-7

MANUFACTURED IN THE UNITED STATES OF AMERICA

This book is published under the auspices of the Rabbinic Alumni Association of Hebrew Union College—Jewish Institute of Religion. A quinquennial fund to which its members contribute is set aside for the specific purpose of encouraging members of the Association to pursue studies in Judaism with the prospect of publication.

ALFRED GOTTSCHALK
President, Hebrew Union College—
Jewish Institute of Religion

NORMAN KAHAN
President, Rabbinic Alumni
Association

WALTER JACOB
Chairman, Publications Committee
of the Rabbinic Alumni
Association

For Masayo, and for our children, Arona, Noam, and Yohanna

TABLE OF CONTENTS

PREFACE

In the last decades of the nineteenth century the Jewish community of Germany was precipitated into a crisis of major proportions. In 1871 the Jews of Germany had been granted the full civil emancipation for which their leadership had struggled for many years. In the wave of patriotic enthusiasm and economic prosperity which accompanied the unification of Germany and the establishment of the Reich, the Jewish community believed that the Jewish Question had been laid to rest for all time. Pockets of resistance to the full integration of the Jews into the German state and nation might linger on for a time, and some vestiges of pre-emancipation prejudices might abide, but, the Jews believed, the basic problem had been solved. Emancipation was a reality—politically, legally, and economically.

Yet within a decade a completely unanticipated development took place: in the late 1870's a powerful surge of anti-Jewish sentiment emerged and quickly grew to alarming dimensions. The anti-Jewish movement was complex and embraced a wide variety of groups and ideologies, including a new form of *Judenhass* bearing the neologism "anti-Semitism," which justified anti-Jewish antipathy on grounds of völkisch and racial distinctions.

Initially most Jews believed that the anti-Jewishness of the late seventies was merely a transitory sickness, one of the last reflex twitches of the old pre-emancipation hostility for which no remedy was possible or even required. Jews were disposed to regard anti-Semitism as a holdover from medieval times, which, with ever-continuing progress and the spread of enlightened attitudes, would soon shrivel up and disappear. Before long, however, it was clear to many that this blandly optimistic interpretation could not be sustained. Anti-Semitism clearly grew stronger, not weaker. It found advocates in high places and was propagated in speech and print by enthusiastic agitators who brought to broad groups within Germany their message that *"Die Juden sind unser Unglück."* At the height of the first wave of anti-Semitism, a petition calling for the repeal of Jewish emancipation was circulated and signed by a quarter of a million Germans before being submitted to Bismarck. Political parties campaigning on an explicitly anti-Semitic platform were formed and, within a decade, won seats in the *Reichstag* where their deputies made speeches on the Jewish menace to Germany.

Slowly, incredulously, the German Jewish community began to realize that anti-Semitism was a dangerous threat to their integration into Germany and could not be dismissed as an ephemeral phenomenon. As this realization grew, German Jewry began to mount its responses to anti-Semitism, hesitatingly at first, and then with growing vigor, activity and organization. The essay that follows is an attempt to describe and analyze these responses as manifested in the publicistic, intellectual, and organizational activities of the German Jewish community in the last decades of the nineteenth century and the first of the twentieth.

It must be borne in mind that a large number of German Jews had no active concern with creating a response to anti-Semitism. Although most of these did not deny their Jewishness, their involvement with Jewish affairs was minimal, and they remained largely indifferent to all communal enterprises, including that of *Abwehr*. Moreover, the numerous Jews in the Social Democratic party saw in socialism the most effective means of ending all social conflict, including that manifest in anti-Semitism. Although involved with anti-Semitism at times, these Jewish socialists did not deal with it out of any significant sense of Jewish identity. This study, however, is restricted to considering the responses of those Jews for whom Jewish identity was a matter of conscious concern (either positively or negatively), and the attitudes and activities of those of whom this was not true will be touched upon only in passing. Our scope is thus limited to the reactions created by those for whom being a Jew was, in some way, important enough to move them to respond *as Jews* to anti-Semitic hostility.

The major source used as evidence about these Jewish responses is the German Jewish press during the years under study, for in these organs of opinion the various wings and tendencies within the community expressed their attitudes about anti-Semitism and offered proposals for dealing with it. Likewise the speeches, autobiographies, and memoirs of those who were involved in the communal debate over anti-Semitism yielded valuable information, but non-Jewish journals (such as *Preussische Jahrbücher* and *Die Zukunft*) have been consulted only when, on occasion, they dealt with questions of Jewishness and anti-Semitism within the terms of this exploration.

The discussion below will attempt to show how the Jews responded to anti-Semitism and why they responded as they did. The basic arguments presented are that German Jewry reacted by mobilizing a spirited defense of the liberal tradition which had first been invoked to justify the granting of the emancipation at the end of the eighteenth century; that despite efforts to unify the entire Jewish community in a campaign of resistance to anti-Semitism, significant elements remained aloof or openly hostile to this enterprise; and finally that one of the groups which refused to participate in the liberal communal consensus—the German Zionists—created a new ideology which interpreted anti-Semitism and Jewish identity in ways that were radically at variance from those previously propagated. The ideas of the German Zionists will be given special treatment because, although they were numerically and organizationally insignificant during the period surveyed here, we will find in their approach to the issues of Jewish life clear evidence that the Emancipation Ideology which had dominated Jewish aspirations for many decades first began to crumble at this time, precisely when it was being articulated with clarity and defended enthusiastically.

In recent years the dilemma of German Jewry has attracted the attention of several younger students of Jewish history, and for a rather different treatment of many of the themes considered in this study the reader should consult the works by Ismar Schorsch and Jehuda Reinharz listed in the bibliography.

I wish to express my gratitude to the following individuals with whom I consulted at various stages of this project: Walter Laqueur; Martin Cohen and Fritz Bamberger of Hebrew Union College-Jewish Institute of Religion, New York; Joseph Guttmann of Wayne State University; Ernest Hamburger; and Henry Schwarzschild. I owe a special debt of thanks to Ellis Rivkin of the Hebrew Union College in Cincinnati, Ohio who first provoked my interest in Jewish history and has been a consistent source of insight and wisdom, and to Ben Halpern of Brandeis University for his abundant patience, generous advice, and penetrating subtle criticisms. I was assisted generously by the Leo Baeck Institute, the New York Public Library, the Weidener Library, and the library of Brandeis University. I am particularly beholden to Herbert Zafren of the Hebrew Union College Libraries, the late Edward Kiev of the College-Institute Library in New York, and their respective staffs, for their extensive help. A research grant from the Jewish Culture Foundation proved invaluable, as did the patience of the synagogues I tried to serve while completing this study: Leo Baeck Temple, Los Angeles, California; Congregation B'nai Jeshurun, Lincoln, Nebraska; and Woodlands Community Temple, Hartsdale, New York. I was blessed with the editorial guidance of Nancy Meyer who brought to her task great skill and wit. Finally, my wife Masayo, and my children, Arona, Noam, and Yohanna, receive my boundless gratitude for putting up with so much for so long.

CHAPTER ONE

The Background

THE EMANCIPATION

During the period from the mid-eighteenth to the late nineteenth century Jewish life in Western and Central Europe was radically transformed. Powerful forces were revolutionizing all Europe in those years. The growth of commercial and, later, industrial capitalism, the spread of nationalism, the emergence of new social classes out of the crumbling old corporate structures, the growing dominance of new modes of thought in religion, science, politics, and philosophy—all these irresistible currents were destroying, reordering, and challenging existing ideas, patterns, and institutions. A new Europe was being shaped to take the place of the old, and the ghetto, the locus of Jewish life and activity for centuries, was among the many structures which were transformed or destroyed.

Thus began the era designated by Jewish historians as the emancipation, a period during which the Jews of Western and Central Europe were brought from the periphery of society into its center, a time marked by "the transformation of despised ghetto-Jews without rights into citizens with equal rights, [and] of poor *Hausierers* [pedlars] into affluent merchants or academicians."[1] During the long and difficult process of emancipation, continuous debates raged among Jews and non-Jews about the significance of the changes that were taking place. Out of these debates came a new tradition of thought within Jewish life, one that may be called the emancipation ideology. This highly articulated and well-defined pattern of ideas, drawn largely from the intellectual heritage of the French Enlightenment, was used by advocates and defenders of emancipation to justify those changes that had already taken place and to argue on behalf of others which had not yet occurred. Virtually all significant issues in Jewish life at this time— religious reform, the definition of Judaism, the concept of Jewish identity, the questions of *Gleichberechtigung* (equality of rights) and

1

citizenship—were argued in terms of the emancipation ideology with its rationalistic and universalistic premises.

The emancipation ideology was not merely a restatement of the French Enlightenment, but an application of its premises and values to the concrete circumstances of Jewish life.[2] In the earliest discussions of the situation of the Jew in Germany the term "emancipation," which implied that natural rights had been illegitimately withheld, was not used. Those concerned with Jewish affairs wrote instead of *Verbesserung* (amelioration), with its clear implication that some sort of improvement was required to transform the status of the Jews.[3] Consider, for example, the classic discussion of the Jewish problem in eighteenth-century Germany offered by the Prussian historian Christian Wilhelm Dohm (1751-1820) in his essay *Über die bürgerliche Verbesserung der Juden.*[4] In that work Dohm adumbrated the basic themes that were repeatedly returned to in one form or another during subsequent discussions of emancipation.

Dohm conceded that the Jews ("these unfortunate Asiatic refugees") were clearly in need of *Verbesserung,* for in their present circumstances they pursued corrupt occupational practices, were morally degenerate, and constituted a burden and irritation to society. But Dohm argued that the evils in Jewry were solely the result of the conditions in which they had been forced to live for centuries and did not stem from anything inherent in the nature of the Jews or of Jewish life. He concluded that dramatic reforms and improvements among the Jews could best be effected by changing the conditions of their life. Change their unfortunate circumstances by removing the economic and political restrictions that had bound them for so long, grant the Jews citizenship, encourage them to become artisans, and remove the barriers that shut them out of agriculture and, he claimed, they will quickly become loyal and productive members of society. "The Jew is more of a man than he is a Jew," Dohm wrote, arguing that a sound, rational policy of benevolent reform would readily demonstrate the proof of this axiom. "In our firmly established states any citizen must be welcome who observes the laws and adds through his industry to the wealth of the state." Nothing in the nature of the Jews, neither their religion nor their acquired group character, constituted a cause for withholding from them the status which, as men, they had a right to expect. And in response to those who pointed out the obstacles to integration posed by Jewish religious teaching and custom, Dohm argued, "Either [the Jew's] religion contains nothing contrary to the duties of a citizen or such tenets can easily be abolished by political and legal regulations."[5]

Although hardly an original or profound thinker, Dohm crystallized the twin emphases that lay at the heart of the emancipation ideology: (1) As men, Jews have a right to be treated in the same manner as all other men, subject to no irrational limitations on their self-expression and activity; universal reason therefore requires the removal of all legal disabilities from Jews and the granting to them, as to all men, of full civil equality. (2) Partly as a result of civil emancipation, and partly as a means of accomplishing it, Jewish life must be reformed in order to bring the conditions of Jewish existence into congruence with the duties and opportunities inherent in membership in general society.[6] The claims for civil emancipation based on universal reason and the necessity for restructuring Jewish life in order to create a new kind of Jew who would be able to merit and enjoy emancipation were to be the poles between which all subsequent discussions of the fate of the Jews in Germany took place. Friends and enemies of Jewish emancipation continually made reference to these themes, and although the variations in emphasis and interpretation proved to be very rich indeed, the terms within which the Jewish question was to be debated for the next century had been set with great clarity. In the years that followed, defenders of emancipation essentially offered a lengthy series of footnotes to Dohm's discussion, while those who advocated the retention of restrictions on the Jews did so by referring, in denial or modification, to either or both of these premises. Before the nineteenth century had even begun, the ideological pattern limiting the discussion of Jewish emancipation had already been formulated.[7]

As the pace of modernization quickened in the late eighteenth and early nineteenth centuries, the emancipation ideology was embraced enthusiastically by a small but growing group of German Jews. As more and more Jews were drawn into the commercial, social, and intellectual life of German society, they found in the emancipation ideology a mirror of and a justification for the experiences of their life. Although most Jews continued to maintain their traditional patterns of life and thought, increasing numbers were educated in European culture and personally experienced "emancipation" as they were accepted as social and intellectual equals by their "enlightened" counterparts from Christian society.[8] The basic thrust of the time appeared to be toward increasing commercial and social integration of Jews into German life, and the emancipation ideology, accepted eagerly by the most advanced Jews, explained and seemed to legitimate that movement.[9]

There were setbacks, to be sure, and the period after the Congress of Vienna in 1815, in particular, was one during which Jewish efforts to achieve civil and legal status matching their economic and cultural position were repeatedly frustrated. Gains that had been made under

French occupation were nullified, and those emancipatory decrees which remained in force were often subverted in practice. Concepts of romantic nationalism gained currency, and the ideal of the Christian state was advocated as the most appropriate blueprint for organizing and governing Germany. Both these postures, one by emphasizing the mythic character of German nationhood and the other by asserting the Christian identity of the state, threatened to deny to Jews the full membership in Germany which they claimed on the basis of the emancipation ideology.

The Jews responded to these challenges by elaborating definitions of German and Jewish identity based on the premises of the emancipation ideology and expressed in terms of liberalism, the only political ideology which justified an end to Jewish restrictions. A Germany based on either völkisch or Christian principles would have no room for Jewish *citizens* and might, at best, offer the Jews some sort of tolerated or protected status at the periphery of national life. Only the establishment of a *Rechtsstaat* (constitutional state) based on law, not *Volk* or faith, could allow full Jewish participation in civil affairs, and it was a clear recognition of this fact that brought those Jews who were politically active into the ranks of the liberal politicians of Germany in Vormärz. [10] Along with other liberals, they struggled for the creation of a *Rechtsstaat* built on Anglo-Saxon and French models, and although the majority of the Jews in Germany remained aloof from political affairs and passively loyal, that union of Jewish and liberal political interests which was to prove so durable was established for the first time. [11]

These Jewish liberals assiduously avoided any policy based on specific Jewish minority group interests. The fight for Jewish freedom was identified with and subsumed under the struggle for the freedom and unification of Germany. As Johann Jacoby, one of the leading Jewish liberals of the era, wrote in 1837: "As I myself am a Jew and a German at the same time, so the Jew in me cannot become free without the German, and not the German without the Jew. Just as I cannot divide myself, so I cannot separate within myself the freedom of the one from the other." [12] Or as Gabriel Riesser put it in 1835: "If I were to be offered, in one hand, the emancipation that is the goal of my profoundest aspirations, and, in the other, the realization of the beautiful dream of German political unification and freedom, I would unhesitatingly choose the latter: for I am firmly and deeply convinced that it includes the former too." [13] These Jewish liberals saw the *Rechtsstaat* as the solution to *all* the basic problems of Germany, including the Jewish question. They never doubted that the fate of the Jews would be determined by the course of German liberal politics, and that Jewish emancipation would depend on the success or failure of the struggle to liberate all Germany from the medieval institutions and attitudes that prevented national unification, parliamentary rule, and rational economic policies.

The political ideal of Germany as a *Rechtsstaat* had its counterpart in the idealized image of German *Geist* that was accepted by Jews who aspired to be full participants in national culture as well as civil affairs. *Deutschtum* (German civilization) was identified by them with figures such as Lessing, Goethe, Schiller, Humboldt, and especially Kant. Jews found in these men the ethical idealism and humanitarianism, the universal vision and devotion to rationalism which were integral parts of their own emancipation ideology. These culture heroes were enshrined with sincerity and zeal by German Jewry and followed loyally, even after the German intellectual mood had changed and classicism was replaced by such less "enlightened" movements as romanticism and left-wing Hegelianism.[14] These new currents were intellectually fasionable, but they seemed to reflect the political reaction that was impeding the movement toward emancipation. Although entertained by individual Jewish intellectuals, they could scarcely be accepted by a community which was wedded by self-interest and growing cultural tradition to a specific, albeit somewhat passé image of German *Kultur.*[15]

The *Rechtsstaat* and classical *Kultur*—these were dominant images by which Jews viewed the society into which they were rapidly integrating. Although they knew that the real Germany in which they lived was marked by absolutism and pre-Enlightenment attitudes and values, the ideal Germany to which they were increasingly devoted was one defined by these dominant models, for, Jews felt, a nation and culture structured on any other principles could not include them. Yet the emancipation ideology made it clear that even a secular and rational Germany would have room for Jews only if the Jews themselves were reshaped in accordance with the requirements of life in a modern state. The refashioning of Germany had to proceed hand in hand with the restructuring of Jewish life from its old corporate status into a religion or *Konfession*. Hence, during the first half of the nineteenth century a whole series of reforms were introduced to create a new Jewish religious identity that would allow the adherents of Judaism to participate fully in the general society.[16]

Although there was no unanimity within the Jewish community as to the precise nature and extent of reforms, a clear perception developed, shared by traditionalists and modernists alike, that to be a Jew in Germany meant one was an adherent of a religion and nothing more. All conceded that an end at last to Jewish communal self-government, which had been steadily eroding for many years, was the fair price demanded for emancipation. Despite the bitter controversies which soon raged in many communities over one detail or another of proposed reform, all agreed that faithfulness to Judaism in no way conflicted with the duties of citizenship, because Judaism was construed as the Jewish confession. Jewish distinctiveness was not denied, and only a small group of German Jews actively advocated complete disappearance by absorption into German life.[17] But the differences that continued to separate the Jew from his fellow German of Christian faith were confined to matters of religion as defined in Western Christendom. Any suggestion that they might have a basis in Jewish nationality (*Volk, Stamm*) was categorically rejected. As the *Allgemeine Zeitung des Judenthums,* the authoritative spokesman for the Reform community, declared in 1848: "We are and want to be only Germans! We have and desire no other fatherland than the German! We are Israelites only according to belief; in all other matters we adhere in our depths to the state in which we live."[18]

The constriction of Jewishness to religious identity was accompanied by a drastic reduction of the positive content of Judaism to universalistic and rationalistic precepts scarcely different, if at all, from those held by all "enlightened" Germans. "Judaism," declared Abraham Geiger (1810-1874), the leading reformer, "must give up all outworn forms and, devoid of all its nationalist elements from the past, come forth in its eternal truth, in its lofty teachings and with its appeal to mankind to hallow all of life."[19] Geiger and others provided the rationale for cleansing Judaism of the "dross" and "superstitions" which had accumulated in earlier, darker times. Blatantly parochial values and traditions were either abandoned altogether or reinterpreted in accordance with the dictates of universal reason. A new being, the German of Jewish faith, began to replace the ghetto Jew as the dominant type, a change that was marked by David Friedländer's efforts to replace the term "Jew," with its negative associations, by "Israelite."[20]

As the economic and social status of Jews rose between 1815 and 1848, the continuing restrictions on Jews still maintained by most German states increasingly appeared absurd and irritating.[21] The Jews felt they had done their part in modernizing themselves; they had worked assiduously at divesting themselves of those habits and traditions which, it was claimed, made them unfit for citizenship. How could the state continue to withhold the civil status which the Jews, after fulfilling so extensively the expectations of the emancipation ideology, now had every right to expect?[22]

It became clear that the rate of transformation within Jewry had advanced much more rapidly than the willingness of the states to grant civil emancipation, and as awareness of this contradiction grew, the Jewish advocates of the emancipation ideology began to assert themselves with a new aggressiveness. The changed mood was expressed by Gabriel Riesser (1806-1863), who argued in 1831 that the Jews should no longer wait passively for new gains to be granted them but should organize themselves in order to gain emancipation by determined action. Riesser believed that Jews should confront Christians as self-respecting equals, without timidity or apology, and demand their full due. He was especially critical of those who left the Jewish community and assimilated by conversion to Christianity. He believed that by remaining loyal to his Jewishness the Jew made a contribution to a free Germany, and that those who had converted in order to procure advancement had hurt the cause of freedom and thus weakened their fatherland. Riesser denied that his stubborn Jewish loyalty was in any way incompatible with devotion to German welfare, and he founded a journal, provocatively titled *Der Jude,* to propagate his views and call for a coordinated campaign in which a flood of petitions for Jewish emancipation would be sent to the various German parliaments.[23]

Although Riesser added nothing to the emancipation ideology in the way of new concepts, his outspokenness and willingness to attack the bastions of reaction inspired a boldness, a sense of self-respect, and even a fighting spirit among some Jews, and a good number followed his lead by fighting for Jewish interests through political liberalism. Yet up to and through the Revolution of 1848 such liberal Jewish political activists were hardly representative of the Jewish masses who generally accepted the emancipation ideology but remained politically passive. Persisting in their traditional loyalism, the bulk of the community remained somewhat to the right of its most active members, and out of fear of revolutionary anarchy and anti-Jewish violence, they opposed the use of force. *Ordnung und Gesetzlichkeit* (law and order) and *Ordnung und Ruhe* (order and peace) were their slogans.[24]

During the decades after 1848, however, and especially in the 1860s, this configuration changed significantly. The conservative loyalism of the Jewish majority in Vormärz gave way to a greater acceptance of political liberalism, and as Jewish liberal politicans were accepted as pathfinders for the entire community, a basic transformation of Jewish political attitudes took place. Liberalism became the dominant creed, and a more or less complete attachment to it by both Jewish political leaders and the broad ranks of the community was forged.[25]

From this time, and especially after 1866, the Jews were largely identified with the National Liberal wing of liberal politics, not with the more progressive Fortschritt faction. The views of Jacoby and Riesser on the intimate link between German unification and Jewish emancipation were now accepted by the Jewish community as a whole, and most Jews supported Bismarck's foreign policy, which seemed to be leading to the realization of both goals. From these years, too, dates the increasingly widespread use of a phrase that expressed succinctly, albeit in a rather cumbersome manner, the self-image of the Jews in Germany: *deutsche Staatsbürger jüdischen Glaubens* (German citizens of the Jewish faith). This expression—a compromise formula declaring the dual aspirations of German loyalty and faithfulness to Judaism—became more and more popular as the Jewish community as a whole adopted the ideal of Jewish identity which it expressed.[26]

The first half of the formula achieved substantial realization in the emancipation decrees of 1869 and 1871 issued in the wake of Bismarck's triumphant wars of national unification. Although the united German Reich did not fully approximate, or even come significantly close to the liberal dream of a *Rechtsstaat* based on full parliamentary rule, its establishment was welcomed enthusiastically and with sincere patriotic fervor by the overwhelming majority of German Jews. Riesser's "beautiful dream of German unification and freedom" had only been realized in part, but Jewish liberals, and indeed almost all liberals, were willing to settle for that. And while the second half of the expression, *jüdischen Glaubens*, was invested by most Jews with no more than a rather pale content compounded of filial piety, philanthropy, and a vague sense of mission, few seemed bothered.[27] The struggle for emancipation, first the vision of a few and then that of the community as a whole, had now been realized. "Mankind *has* progressed; humanity *is* victorious," proclaimed one liberal Jewish paper. "The *she-he-che-yanu* [a Hebrew prayer of thanksgiving] has never been more appropriate than in our time," wrote another.[28] And the *Allgemeine Zeitung des Judenthums* summarized the jubilant sense of fulfillment of German Jewry when it declared: "The German Reich, the king of Prussia as Kaiser, the German Reichstag, a general right to vote, freedom of conscience and equality of rights, freedom of commerce and of movement have now become incontestable achievements."[29] Germany was one. The battle for emancipation had been successfully completed. To the Jews of Germany it seemed that the long struggle initiated decades before was ended at last and for all time. The Jewish problem had been solved.[30]

RESISTANCE TO EMANCIPATION BEFORE 1870

Accompanying the development of Jewish emancipation, and especially evident in the first part of the nineteenth century, was a movement of active resistance to the integration of Jewry into German state and society. Many of the most ardent gentile advocates of emancipation had not been motivated by philo-Semitism; rather, they defended the removing of Jewish restrictions out of a desire to realize the idea of the modern state, because of *raison d'état,* or out of a commitment to the concepts of the Enlightenment, but not from any special affection for Jews or Judaism. Indeed, as we have noted, the proponents of emancipation were highly critical of the existing circumstances of Jewish life and of traditional Jewish beliefs and practices, although their negativism on these topics did not lead them to advocate policies preventing the incorporation of the Jews into European society.[31] Yet many others did defend such policies. Accompanying the rising tide of emancipation, and growing with it in every phase, was a countermovement whose purpose was to retard, restrict, or deny Jewish integration. As the emancipation ideology with its principles of political liberalism was embraced by the Jews and their allies, that ideology was consciously rejected by several groups who, preserving the traditional prejudice against the Jew, expressed a variety of arguments against granting full civil rights to the Jews in Germany. The hope that antipathy toward the Jews would disappear with the advance of Enlightenment was not fulfilled, and anti-Jewish sentiments appeared to grow in some quarters.

The slow, sporadic process of modernization in Germany left major traditional institutions and groups with considerable power and influence. Altar and throne were continually challenged but not destroyed, and although elements of the urban bourgeoisie took hold, they never succeeded in gaining dominant power in state and society. Old class and institutional structures, such as the nobility and the established church, remained intact, and their spokesmen mobilized a powerful movement counterposed to the forces demanding change. The representatives of the new conservatism formulated, as an integral part of their general views about German affairs, a policy of opposition to demands for increased Jewish rights.

This conservative resistance to emancipation often had less to do with hatred for the Jew than with devotion to the old order. The integration of the Jew was for them a symbol of the destruction of old and cherished institutions and values, and as part of their overall struggle to retard or reverse the growing rate of change, they often singled out the Jew as a special target of abuse.[32] Their ideal was the organic, corporate state, rooted in tradition and based on Christian principles. In such a state there could be no room for emancipated Jews who shared in neither the medieval Germanic heritage nor the Christian faith.[33]

The thrust of the conservative arguments drew considerable emotional power from the traditional image of the Jew in earlier centuries, an image which was still widely accepted throughout Europe.[34] According to Christian teaching, as popularly interpreted, the Jew was fated to be a perpetual outsider in Christian society because of his refusal to accept Jesus. Although hostility to Jews in feudal Europe was often related to specific instances of economic or social conflict, it had always been rationalized in terms of the position assigned to the Jew by Christian theology. In some of its coarser expressions, the Christian religious mentality depicted the Jew as a deicide, a poisoner of wells, desecrator of hosts, or murderer of children, and in some rare, benevolent forms, that same attitude might even advocate tolerance for the Jew.[35] But whether framed negatively (the usual attitude) or positively, the image of the Jew was defined in terms of religious concepts. The term "Jew" had meaning as part of the Christian theological scheme, and centuries of Catholic and Protestant teaching had had the cumulative effect of infusing the European consciousness with a stereotyped picture of the Jew as radically different from the Christian in appearance, habits, morals, and faith. Thus, in their defense of the Christian state, the conservative opponents of emancipation could readily invoke and mobilize for their purposes the still-intact popular conception of the Jew.[36]

The Jews had long been accustomed to being seen by the Christian world in these terms, but in the early nineteenth century they increasingly believed that such clearly outdated medieval notions would soon be discarded as mankind progressively became enlightened. They felt that the Age of Reason had unleashed irresistible forces which would one day beat back the powers of darkness, that with declining religious fanaticism, all sorts of irrational traditions, superstitions, and bigotry would be swept away by advancing civilization. A new image of the Jew was emerging, one dictated by the emancipation ideology, and Jews confidently expected that the fact of the transformation of the ghetto Jew into the "German citizen of the Jewish faith" would soon be recognized by gentiles.[37]

These sanguine Jewish expectations did prove to be justified in large part, but, ironically, not quite in the way anticipated. With the weakening of religious faith and institutions during the nineteenth century, the old theological definition of the Jew did lose currency and a new secular image became prominent and, ultimately, dominant. But that image only perpetuated in a new form the traditional, negative posture toward the Jew. The image of the Jew was detheologized, and the Jew was less likely to be criticized or rejected because of his Judaism. Modern post-Christian ideologues, however, continued to reject the Jew and argue against his inclusion into German society on thoroughly secular grounds. Moreover, their target was increasingly not the ghetto Jew, but the new emancipated Jew, the one who had been shaped in response to the emancipation ideology.[38]

Secular arguments directed against the Jews had been fashioned in France during the eighteenth century by thinkers within the very Enlightenment invoked to support emancipation,[39] and the two leading German exponents of rational idealism, Kant and Hegel, had expressed negative views on Judaism in their philosophical systems.[40] But the most pointed anti-Jewish arguments, and those with the widest impact, came from romantic nationalists like Fichte who emphasized the inability of the Jew to participate in the unique German *Volksgeist.* Declaring that the Jew could never become a German citizen, Fichte wrote: "The only way I can see to give [the Jews] civil rights is to cut off their heads in a single night and equip them with new ones devoid of every Jewish idea. . . . To protect ourselves against them, again I see no means except to conquer their Promised Land and pack them all off to it."[41] Similar concepts were publicized widely in the flood of anti-Jewish pamphlet literature which appeared during the debate at the Congress of Vienna over the status of Jewish emancipation in the Rhineland. The persistent theme in these pamphlets was that, by virtue of their foreignness as a nation or the pernicious character of their economic activities, the Jews should be subject to severe restrictions or expelled altogether.[42]

The romantic nationalists thus did more than offer a modern version of the old theological anti-Jewishness, for among their arguments, as in Fichte's statement, there was frequently a new theme previously unknown in European discussions of the Jews. Christian religious tradition had always held that conversion by the Jew would end his status as pariah. By baptism Jews could, and occasionally did, qualify for full membership in Christendom. Individual Jews had long used sincere or opportunistic conversion as a means of integration, and Christianity persistently expected that one day the Jews as a whole would repent of their perfidy, accept Jesus as the Christ, and so bring a full end to their separatism. Hence, in addition to sustaining anti-Jewish hostility, Christian theology also supported the expectation that the position of the Jew as outsider and all of the disabilities inherent in that status could be terminated instantly and at will by the Jew who agreed to conversion. For Christianity, in short, the Jew was not ineradicably or perpetually doomed for exclusion and degradation.[43]

Some of the early secular treatises attacking Jewish emancipation continued this tradition of openness to the Jew willing to abandon his Judaism, and there were those who argued against removing Jewish restrictions without implying that the Jews could never, under any circumstances, qualify for membership in German society.[44] Yet, as the progressive detheologizing of anti-Jewish arguments continued during the years before 1870, this position of receptivity to the Jew who repented was increasingly abandoned, and it was more frequently assumed that the Jews were marked by something in their very nature which made them permanently incapable of being incorporated into German life.

These sentiments can perhaps best be described as proto-racist, for at this time, in the first half of the nineteenth century, anti-Jewish spokesmen invoked antagonistic *seelische Volkseigenschaften* (qualities of the völkisch soul) or a fundamental incompatibility between the Jewish and German *Geist*, as the factors which set Germans and Jews apart from each other. There was as yet no pretense to scientific argument, but more and more those ranged against the Jews pointed out what they believed to be inherent, unchangeable qualities making Jews and gentiles irreconcilable adversaries.[45] To cite but one example, Bruno Bauer, an exponent of radical-left Hegelianism, had declared in 1843 that the essence of Judaism as a non-historical conception of life made the Jew incapable of development and hence unfit for emancipation so long as he continued to cling to his Judaism. He had concluded that as long as the Jew remained faithful to his religion he could not be emancipated. But returning to this subject in 1859, after he had become active in conservative circles in Prussia, Bauer argued that Jewish isolationism was a manifestation of *racial*, not religious or historical factors. He claimed that the Jewish essence was determined by blood factors that were not subject to amelioration; the Jew was a "white Negro."[46]

By the time the Jews had finally been emancipated in all of Germany in 1871, a well-defined tradition of *modern* anti-Jewishness had been developed and stocked with a rather elaborate arsenal of arguments. There was as yet no modern "anti-Semitism," and indeed that term had not yet been coined. But within a decade of the emancipation edicts, the secular arguments would be formulated systematically and "scientifically" into an ideology of exclusion, and popular movements, led by agitators preaching racial anti-Semitism, would emerge.[47]

The Jews had not been oblivious to the resistance they met in their struggle for civil emancipation, and they had frequently responded with counter-arguments and pointed refutations when attacked.[48] But they generally regarded the continuing hostility as a regrettable legacy from pre-enlightened times which would certainly, they believed, disappear with time and more progress.[49] Virtually all Jews shared Eduard Bernstein's assessment of the prospects for the future: "There were enemies of the Jews but no anti-Jewish movement; the exclusion of Jews from certain state offices had not yet disappeared, but it was diminishing and not increasing. Also the lot of the Jews in those lands where they had not yet obtained civil equality appeared to become increasingly better with the spread of liberalism."[50]

THE EMERGENCE OF MODERN ANTI-SEMITISM

Within a rather remarkably short time after the unification of Germany, a powerful and completely unanticipated surge of counter-reaction to the recently gained emancipation burst upon the German Jewish community in a form that can be called modern anti-Semitism. The anti-Semitism which emerged after 1870 was complex and embraced a rich variety of personalities, social groups, and ideologies. It included and appealed to Germans of widely different backgrounds and commitments, and although only a very few ever voted for the candidates of the specifically anti-Semitic political parties, the net effect of the events and propagandistic activities of this period was the resurrection of that very Jewish problem which, the Jews believed, had been solved for all time.[51]

German unification had brought in its train a swift acceleration in the rate of industrialization, and this concentration of fundamental political and economic changes had a profound impact on the social structure of the nation. A great, rapid transformation was set in motion, and a land of farmers and independent artisans was reshaped into a modern state of factory workers and white-collar employees. International commerce grew in importance, population increased, and multitudes migrated from the countryside into newly industrialized towns which quickly swelled into large urban centers. There was a great deal of financial speculation and occasional corruption, and some profited greatly from the changes taking place. But old, relatively stable social groups like the peasantry and the *Mittelstand* (lower middle class) were now faced with disaster as the conditions which had sustained their positions in society were destroyed. Faced with the threat of proletarianization, and highly vulnerable to the swings of the economic cycle, these victims of industrialization were exposed to acute social distress.[52]

The proliferation of anti-Semitic ideologies and organizations after 1870 must be understood against this background of upheaval. The admission of the Jews to German civic life had taken place just as the nation was entering a deep and abiding period of tension.[53] The emancipation ideology, which the Jews believed should command the respect and allegiance of all moderns, could have little appeal to the

Mittelstand and the peasantry. Political and economic liberalism were clearly associated with the very forces that had precipitated them into such great distress, and they looked for other, more credible doctrines that might better interpret the evil times in which they lived. Many remained largely apolitical of course, but some were recruited to Social Democracy, which grew in power during the next decades. And many found in anti-Semitism what seemed to be a highly compelling analysis of the reasons for their misfortune.

The ideologies of anti-Semitism that were now elaborated in Germany used the basic concepts that had been first expressed during the struggle for emancipation, redefining them with somewhat greater erudition and more attention to theoretical consistency. As a result of this process of amplification, the established German tradition of *Judenhass* (Jew hatred) was modernized into anti-Semitism. Hence, conservative Protestant thinkers revived the ideal of the Christian state and with it the theological mode of anti-Jewishness, theoreticians of nationalism presented anew their case against the Jews, and the proto-racism of earlier decades was developed into full-blown racial anti-Semitism. These three types of anti-Semitic ideology were predominant now as they had been earlier, although there was often overlapping between categories, and mixed expressions of theory were not uncommon.

Conservative Protestant thinkers, for example, brought new life to the ideal of the Christian state propounded earlier by Stahl and the von Gerlach brothers. Acting as spokesmen for the landed nobility, and using the *Kreuzzeitung* as their organ, they taught that church and state were two limbs of one organism, and that in a properly constituted Christian state, Jewish emancipation was unthinkable. They claimed, moreover, that the refusal of the Jews to accept salvation through Christianity had monumental effects because it prevented the realization of the final redemption promised in the New Testament. This argument sustained the still popular image of the Jew as the enemy of salvation and was even invoked in blaming the Jews for those realities of daily life which, it was claimed, proved that the ultimate fulfillment had not yet arrived (e.g., high prices, too much snow). Although the conservative Protestant thinkers generally rejected the theory of racial anti-Semitism, their revival of the idea of the Christian state helped crystallize and spread in the highest strata of state and society the anti-Semitic sentiments which were becoming more modish throughout Germany.[54]

Conservative Christian hostility to Jews and Judaism was, of course, not new. But the Jewish community was severely shaken at the end of the 1870s when an unforseen enemy arose from a different, and supposedly friendly, quarter—German nationalists. Anti-Semitism was given sanction at one of the highest levels of social and intellectual respectability when the historian Heinrich von Treitschke, professor at the University of Berlin, gave his support to the anti-Semitic movement. Treitschke was a liberal with impeccable credentials and had long been opposed to the conservative concept of the Christian state. He rejected both the theological and the racial attacks upon the Jews and wrote that "there can be no talk among the intelligent of an abolition or even a limitation of the emancipation. That would be an open injustice, a betrayal of the fine traditions of our state."[55] But in 1879 he published an article delivering a withering assault on the Jews because of the danger they posed to the strength of the German nation, and a major cause célèbre was born.[56]

For many decades Treitschke had been concerned with building a powerful, unified state as the means for guaranteeing the fulfillment of the destiny of the German nation. In his voluminous historical writings and in his lectures attended by masses of students at the university, he stressed the primary importance of national unity, for only through cohesiveness could the German nation achieve the security and power it merited. These basic concerns shaped his criticism when he turned his attention to the Jews and attacked them for retarding the development of German national solidarity. The Jews, he claimed, refused to become fully Germanized and persisted in maintaining *national* traits that were alien to the German character. The raucous anti-Semitic agitation was "only a brutal and spiteful but natural reaction of the German national consciousness against an alien element which has usurped too much space in our life."[57]

Underlying Treitschke's argument was a rejection of the Jewish understanding of the terms of the emancipation. For the Jews, entering German civil society meant being accepted as full and equal participants in a secular state in which religious affiliation and belief were completely separated from the duties, rights, and privileges of citizenship. A secular state was one that had been dechristianized and was fully neutral with regard to religious matters, and in such a state, the Jews believed, they could legitimately preserve and express their separate religious identity. Treitschke, however, disputed this understanding of Germany, and while arguing against the conservatives that Jews should have equal rights in the *state*, he maintained that membership in the German *nation* was a different matter.

I am not an adherent of the doctrine of the Christian state. The state is a secular organization and should act with justice and impartiality toward non-Christians also. But without any doubt we Germans are a Christian nation. To spread our universal religion among the heathen, our ancestors shed their blood; to develop and perfect it, they suffered and battled as martyrs and heroes. At every step, as I progress deeper in understanding of the history of our country, it becomes more and more clear to me how deeply Christianity is entwined with every fibre of the German character. . . . Christian ideas inspire our arts and sciences. Christian spirit animates all healthy institutions of our state and our society. Judaism, on the other hand, is the national religion of a tribe which was originally alien to us.[58]

For Treitschke the claim of the Jews that they were able to become fully German and yet retain their Jewish identity and communal organizations compromised the Christian character of German nationhood and dangerously weakened Germany as a whole.[59]

Treitschke's attack on the Jews was essentially a restatement of the attitudes of the romantic nationalism of the early nineteenth century, and his proposed solution to the Jewish problem also drew on an old theme from the emancipation ideology. "The only way out," he wrote, ". . . is for our Jewish fellow citizens to make up their minds without reservation to be Germans."[60] The Jews were not unassimilable, merely as yet unassimilated. Until that process of acculturation had been concluded, they must, as appropriate for a small minority, assume a more modest and circumspect manner of conducting themselves in cultural, economic, and personal affairs. Failure to become more fully Germanized would be tantamount to an arrogant demand by the Jews for national status within Germany and would destroy the legal basis for the emancipation. "For the fulfillment of such [national] desires there is only one means: emigration, foundation of a Jewish state somewhere abroad, which may then see whether it can get recognition from other nations. On German soil there is no room for double nationality."[61]

Treitschke's assault was particularly serious, partly because it came from one of the most prestigious figures in German academic circles, but even more so because it was an attack on the *emancipated* Jew mounted from *within* liberalism. Treitschke's target was not the ghetto Jew nor Judaism as a theological system, but the *new* Jew, the *deutsche Staatsbürger jüdischen Glaubens* who had been shaped in response to the promise of the emancipation. On the foundation of the premises of liberal German nationalism, Treitschke charged that even the modern Jew would be alien so long as he did not become fully acculturated to his Christian surroundings. Implicit in his argument was a demand that the Jews of Germany must give up their separate religion and their position as members of an organized Jewish community.[62]

Moreover, Treitschke's attitudes were not those of an isolated or eccentric thinker whom the Jewish community might have been able to ignore as unworthy of response. He was in truth the spokesman for a major tendency within German liberal Protestant circles. These writers and political leaders agreed with the Jews that there should be a separation of chuch and state, but they emphasized that this did not mean the removal of Christian influence from public affairs. Christianity still had to be the foundation of the state by acting as a moral and educational force suffusing all areas of life with religious self-consciousness. The separation of church and state was defended by them as a means of strengthening Christianity, of deepening it and allowing its influence to pervade the life of every citizen. With Treitschke, they understood Germany to be a *Kulturnation,* an organic, historic entity with deep roots in a unique Germanic, Christian tradition which had reached its most vivid expression in the Lutheran Reformation. From their point of view the Jewish expectation to perpetuate Judaism, no matter how acculturated its forms or content, was an intolerable anachronism; Germany, as they defined it, could not tolerate such separatism. Jewish emancipation had to mean total absorption into the German state and nation, and also the end of all separate Jewish activities, whether social, cultural, educational, or religious.[63]

Not all Protestant liberals supported these contentions, and there were some from the Freisinnig faction who agreed with the Jews that there should be no interference by religion in the state in any way.[64] Yet even those who were not interested in a strong Christian presence, and who defended the Jews from the agitation mounting against them, agreed that there was no basis for continued Jewish distinctiveness.[65] These liberals included some of Jewry's most outspoken and consistent defenders; but even when they took issue with Treitschke for his intemperate language and for encouraging mob passions that had best be controlled, they agreed with him that equality did not mean, as the Jews held, the right for German citizens to be different one from the other, but rather the necessity for homogenization.[66] For example, while the most illustrious representative of this position, the historian Theodor Mommsen, attacked Treitschke, he also demanded that the Jews recognize their persistence in separatist activities stimulated anti-Semitism. It is the obligation of the Jews, he declared, "to put aside [their] peculiarity" and "to cast down with determination all barriers between themselves and the other German fellow citizens."[67] Hence the Jewish interpretation of the emancipation was denied not only by conservatives, reactionaries and racists, but also by these modern liberals of the right and left wings, and the Jews met ideological antagonism from those political and cultural elements in Germany with which they felt their greatest kinship, the Protestant liberals.[68]

After 1870 yet another major change in the discussion of the Jewish problem took place. For the first time science was invoked to support antipathy toward the Jews. It was an era of great enthusiasm for science, and the concepts of Darwinism, now being popularized, enjoyed a tremendous vogue, as did the swiftly developing disciplines of anthropology and ethnology.[69] The proposition that the forces governing man's nature and behavior could best be understood by examining his biological makeup and genetic inheritance became modish, and the concepts and terminology of avant-garde scientific research were invoked to explain human history as a racial phenomenon.[70] Objective laws of race and racial behavior were sought and found, and it was claimed that man's will and intelligence were helpless when opposed to the irresistible power of blood. Considered in this way the Jewish problem was clearly rooted in neither religion nor nationality but race. The Jews were members of one race (the Semitic), the Germans of another (the Aryan), and all instances of friction and incompatability between the two groups were reducible to these hard, biological realities.[71]

The self-conscious modernism and areligiosity of this racial ideology was expressed in the very term "anti-Semitism," which was coined at this time and quickly came into general usage.[72] The racial ideologists took as their target the Semite, a creature defined by race, not the Jew as the believer in Judaism. To the extent that Judaism figured in their thinking at all, it was strictly as an expression of the racial nature of the Semite. Moreover, they were critical of Christianity, an off-shoot of Semitic Judaism, because of its role in alienating men from the realities of matter, nature, and blood and seducing them to involvement with Jewish monotheism, morality, spirituality, and universalism. True racial progress, they claimed, required transcending the influence of both Judaism and Christianity by achieving once again the elemental fellowship of those who are united through blood.[73]

By insisting on the primacy of race, these anti-Semites introduced a dramatically new and, from the Jewish viewpoint, ominous element into the debate over the Jewish question. For the first time it was argued on scientific principle that Jewish emancipation was utterly unworkable in theory as well as practice. The evils of the Jews—their rapacity, their internationalism, their subversive influence on culture and morals, the parasitism of their economic ventures—were all determined by Semitic racial traits that could under no circumstances be controlled or reformed. Whereas the traditions of Christian thought and romantic nationalism had combined anti-Jewish criticism with clear proposals that left room for Jewish acceptance, provided certain steps were taken (conversion, full Germanization), racial anti-Semitism permitted no possibility of a response by which the Jew might alleviate or correct the evils for which he was castigated.[74] As one delegate elected to the Reichstag as an anti-Semite declared in his maiden speech: "Changed circumstances will not change the Jew."[75] The slogan of racial anti-Semitism was: *"Was der Jude glaubt ist einerlei; in der Rasse liegt die Schweinerei"* ("it matters not what the Jew believes; the filthiness inheres in [his] race"), a watchword which located the essential nature of the Jew in his fixed racial makeup.[76]

In racial anti-Semitism the ultimate antithesis to the emancipation ideology had been created. The indelible nature of race was counter-posed to the belief that men could be changed by altering the conditions under which they lived, and the claim that the Aryan race was superior to the Semitic was set against the Enlightenment faith in the equality of man.[77] According to racial anti-Semitism, reforming religion and mores, granting citizenship, restructuring occupational pursuits, even baptism and intermarriage were useless. Even the converted Jew transmitted the evil to his offspring, and if the Aryans were to defend themselves properly, they would have to take stern measures. As Paul de Lagarde wrote in 1887, "One would need a heart as hard as a crocodile hide not to feel pity for the poor exploited Germans, and—which amounts to the same—not to hate the Jews and not to hate and despise those who—for reasons of humanity!—defend these Jews, or who are too cowardly to trample this vermin to death. One does not negotiate with trichinae and bacilli, nor does one educate trichinae and bacilli; they are exterminated as speedily and as thoroughly as possible."[78] According to Lagarde's logic, therefore, the only way to end the danger which the presence of the Jew created would be to remove him from Germany, either by transporting him to his own territory or by annihilation.

Thus, within a decade after German unification, a whole arsenal of ideological weapons directed against the Jews had been developed and refined. These theories and arguments were immediately put to use in the service of a new political movement led by a number of dedicated agitators. Political anti-Semitism was launched with the creation of Court Chaplain Adolph Stöcker's Christlich Soziale Partei (Christian Social Party) (1878), and soon a whole array of anti-Semitic organizations was formed: Wilhelm Marr's Antisemiten Liga (Anti-Semites League) (1879), Ernst Henrici's Soziale Reichspartei (Social Imperial Party) (1880), Liebermann von Sonnenberg and Bernhard Förster's Deutscher Volksverein (German People's Association) (1881), and Theodor Fritsch and Otto Boeckel's Deutsche Antisemitische Vereinigung (German Anti-Semitic Confederation) (1886).[79]

Although a mass organized effort was able to gather about a quarter of a million signatures for an anti-Semitic petition presented to

Bismarck in April 1881, the various parties were plagued with friction and competition between themselves, much of it due to a prolonged ideological dispute between Stöcker's Christian movement, which dominated the anti-Semitic movement in the 1880s, and the racial anti-Semites, who took the lead in the 1890s.[80] All efforts to elect candidates to the Reichstag in the elections of 1881 and 1884 failed, and only in 1887 did the anti-Semites manage to elect their first delegate (Boeckel). At their moment of maximum political strength, in 1893, only a small fraction of the electorate voted for the anti-Semitic parties, and even then the anti-Semites elected did not act in concert in the Reichstag.[81] A clear measure of their failure is shown by the fact that, at a time when legislation had been enacted and enforced against a series of minorities in Germany (Catholics, Poles, Social Democrats), not a single law directed against the Jews was passed.[82]

Although the political power of the anti-Semitic movement was never great in any objective sense, its impact on the public mood was considerable. The pamphleteering campaigns of the early century were insignificant compared to the broad popularization and vulgarization of anti-Semitic ideas between 1870 and 1914. Fries and Bauer had had only a limited audience, largely confined to sections of the intelligentsia; but in an age of rising literacy and increasingly effective mass communication, ideologies could be propagated widely. Through the efforts of the agitators and their followers, public attention was focused on the Jews of Germany and the subject of Jewish activities was made a topic of political discussion. Mass meetings were held, broadsides, pamphlets and newspapers were published and distributed widely, and speakers—some of them dramatically effective orators—appeared. Some of the anti-Semitic leaders were opportunists pursuing their trade for personal profit, but the majority appear to have been dedicated missionaries and true believers driven by conviction.[83] Through them the ideologies of anti-Semitism were brought to the attention of broad groups, as in informal beer-hall meetings and the like the Jewish question became part of the daily experience and conversation of many.[84]

Propagated in this way, the anti-Semitic ideologies changed significantly, and while gaining in appeal and political effectiveness, they lost a good deal of their theoretical consistency and intellectuality. The agitators were naturally concerned with building the strength of their movement and had to take into account the special sensitivities and interests of their audiences. In their practical political work, therefore, the party leaders generally did not call for a repeal of Jewish emancipation because they knew that such a demand would not be accepted by German public opinion or by the majority in the

Reichstag.[85] Because racial theories were still somewhat exotic and unacceptable to a populace so strongly influenced by Christian institutions and education, the implications of racial theory were usually muted or absent altogether from their public statements.[86] Instead, an amalgam of racial and traditional religious motifs was forged and widely used, and the anti-Semites often stressed, especially in the first years of the movement, that their goal was to purify Christian society from Jewish domination.[87] Beginning in the 1880s, and increasingly through the next decade, the ancient blood libel was revived in Germany, and the anti-Semites charged that ritual murder was a racial trait of the Jews.[88] And to make their candidates even more appealing to potential supporters, racial concepts were synthesized with class consciousness, as when the *Mittelstand* was identified as the true bearer of the Aryan race and the repository of Nordic, aristocratic superiority.[89]

After 1880 anti-Semitism was thus politicized and popularized and, for the first time, made into a mass phenomenon as the Jews were blamed with responsibility for a variety of social ills. Anti-Semitism now gave expression to diverse resentments among both rural and urban groups groping for a way of articulating their discontent. By uniting a call for social reform with their attacks on the Jews, the racial anti-Semites in particular were successful in establishing a rather credible public image of anti-Semitism as a progressive movement concerned with social justice.[90] And while the agitators were usually devoted to anti-Semitism out of conviction, and disgruntled factions of the masses listened to it with interest because it appeared to have coherence and relevance, the movement was cynically used on occasion by established leaders, especially among the Conservatives, who saw in it an instrument that might be manipulated for political purposes even though they found the ideological excesses repulsive.[91] The willingness of respected political figures, originally only on the right but later on the left as well, to entertain electoral alliances with anti-Semitic groups and candidates was of great importance. It showed clearly that political anti-Semitism could have an impact well beyond the narrow confines of those who were its committed adherents, and that the strength of the movement was greater than indicated by its puny showing at the polls.

During the last decades of the century, therefore, a distinctly cool and occasionally hostile posture toward the Jews became widespread in Germany. As a result of the writing of men like Treitschke, anti-Semitism had become respectable in cultured liberal circles, and the efforts of Stöcker and the racial agitators had created a place for it in the spectrum of political parties. Moreover, another phenomenon both closely related to the intellectual and political mood became increasingly evident: social anti-Semitism grew as the exclusion of Jews from clubs, associations, and resorts, and even from casual daily intercourse, became widely practiced. Those areas of society from which Jews had always been shut out, such as the higher bureaucracy and the officer corps, seemed more inaccessible than ever, and some sectors which had only recently been opened to Jewish participation (Masonic lodges, for example) were now closed once again.[92] Even after 1900 when it seemed clear that anti-Semitism as a political movement was in decline, public opinion was saturated with anti-Jewishness, and negative attitudes were widely accepted.[93] Latent, unofficial anti-Semitism had become established throughout much of German life, involving even those who were likely to condemn the excesses and crudities of overt anti-Semitism. Anti-Semitism had become *salonfähig* (socially acceptable), but the Jews had not.[94]

In a remarkably short period of time the expectation of the Jews that the emancipation would be fully and speedily consummated had been dashed. A broad front of opposition had sprung up to challenge the Jews and their aspirations in many areas and on the basis of a number of different concepts, some venerable and others strikingly modern. Ranged among their enemies the Jews found not only old expected foes but former allies and, in the racial anti-Semites, an utterly new kind of adversary. Beginning with the end of the 1870s, German Jewry entered a period of great challenge.[95]

CHAPTER TWO

Jewish Responses to Anti-Semitism, 1879–1893

The surge of anti-Semitism in the late 1870s took German Jewry completely by surprise, and for some time their response to it was marked largely by a continuation of the buoyant optimism with which they had greeted the Emancipation Edict. Though occasionally recognized, the signs of the growing tension in German-Jewish relations were consistently underestimated or dismissed altogether. In an age of enlightenment, it was believed, isolated incidents of hostility were without abiding significance. The Jewish community was counselled by its leadership not to create problems where none existed by reacting with excessive sensitivity to minor expressions of prejudice. Again and again, in reporting on instances of anti-Semitism, the Jewish press emphasized the powerlessness and the transitory nature of the new agitation and claimed that the anti-Jewish movement had already reached its limits. Hence the Jews of Germany were generally inclined to wait out the storm which, they thought, was bound to pass quickly.[1]

Yet it did not, and especially as a result of the rash of anti-Semitic activity around 1880, the mood of some within the leadership and part of the community began to change as it became more and more evident that some kind of reaction was called for. Even as this awareness grew, however, and as Jewry began to grope for some way of coping with the new hostility, three major factors were at work conditioning and retarding the development of a Jewish response. These factors help account for the disorganized, fumbling, and hesitant way in which the organized Jewish community reacted to anti-Semitism before 1893.

PRECONDITIONING FACTORS INHIBITING REACTION

First of all, the leadership had to reckon with a deeply rooted mood of indifference within the Jewish community. The years of eager adaptation to the requirements of German life had had their effect. Believing themselves fully Germanized, and with a highly attenuated sense of Jewish identity, many Jews professed to be unconcerned with anti-Semitism and wished only not to be seen or considered as Jews. They could not understand why they should be exposed to hostility because of a Judaism in which they did not believe with any conviction. Eduard Bernstein recalled that the Reform community in Berlin was the gathering place of liberal Jews, the greatest part of whom "were complete doubters or coarse unbelievers in religious matters." Because of family ties or social position they could not sever their relationship with Judaism. "They were, however," Bernstein said, "not much more than an ethical society of members of a certain *Volkstum*, who preserved certain memories of this *Volkstum* and of its cult, who on the other hand continued to hold onto the beliefs which lay at the foundation of this cult only in so diluted a form that their power on the heart could be only evanescently slight."[2] Such Jews now evinced little will or desire to defend a Jewishness that was so insignificant a part of their self-consciousness.

Even among those who accepted Jewishness as a positive value there was often little sense of deep alarm. As late as 1890 Heinrich Steinthal, the philosopher and cofounder of *Völkerpsychologie*, spoke for many in expressing the basic confidence of the first generation of emancipated Jews. "I do not understand this [Jewish] question," he wrote to his former student Gustav Glogau, "and therefore I am indifferent towards it. Treitschke says that a Jew cannot be an *Unteroffizier* [noncommissioned officer]; well then, he cannot. What, then, can he be? No one can keep him from being a decent human being. Hence he may strive to become such." Brushing aside the whole question of race, Steinthal declared: "Which nation I belong to is totally my affair." And those who refused to recognize him as a German troubled him, he claimed, only because of their manifestly un-German behavior.[3]

Steinthal's attitude of confidence blended with indifference was characteristic of broad elements within the Jewish community. The anti-Semites were frequently dismissed as scoundrels unworthy of being dignified by a reply or refutation.[4] They were ignored, or watched with some anxiety, but—with the single exception of Treitschke—not engaged. The long struggle for emancipation and the virtually unquestioned emancipation ideology had molded the mentality of a whole generation, and when that generation was suddenly confronted with the emergence of anti-Semitism, their first reaction could not go beyond incredulity. Nothing in their experience or thinking had prepared them for what happened, and so the initial response was bounded with quietism.

Secondly, German Jewry's reaction to anti-Semitism was severely limited by the long-established ideological commitment to liberalism, the political mode through which the emancipation ideology was expressed. German liberalism had been the creed which had sustained the fight for emancipation, and it was the only available system of ideas that could be invoked to defend the status of the Jews. Yet, fatefully, at precisely the moment when German Jewry was most in need of its support to guarantee the emancipation, liberalism was in the midst of a serious ideational and organizational crisis. We have already taken account of the hostilities toward the Jews within German liberalism, and by themselves these manifestations would have compromised severely the power of liberalism as an instrument of Jewish defense. But other developments in German political affairs had an even more devastating effect.

In its pure form European liberalism was marked by a basic concern for the individual and worked to protect the individual from interference by despotic authorities. In religion and politics, in economic enterprise, and especially in the expression of opinions, liberalism fought to establish safeguards which would insure a maximum expression of individuality and prevent arbitrary restrictions on individual freedom.[5] The political apparatus liberalism advocated (parliamentary government and constitutional law) was important as an instrument for creating and maintaining the freedom of the individual; and for a liberal true to his principles, any act which compromised the freedom of one was an attack on the freedom of all. Within Germany this pure, idealized liberalism had been expressed cogently by Gabriel Riesser in 1848 when he argued against a proposed amendment offered in the National Assembly which would have excluded the Jews from equality of rights. "Do not suppose," Riesser had said, "that discriminatory laws can be passed without a fatal crack being made in the whole structure of freedom, without the seed of destruction being sown in it."[6]

As liberalism developed in Germany, however, it underwent a unique evolution in the course of which liberal values were repeatedly compromised and employed to serve rather than challenge established, traditional authorities.[7] Even in its earliest manifestations German liberalism was characterized by an air of academic irrealism and by a tendency to separate thought from action. The political weakness of the bourgeoisie, the classic carriers of liberalism in other

Western lands, fostered an urge to self-expression in humanistic culture, aesthetic pursuits, and philosophy, rather than in political action.[8]

Furthermore, German liberals had long been concerned not only with preserving individual liberty but also with the task of unifying Germany, and the enormous obstacles they faced in establishing a united nation demanded much, if not most, of their attention and energies. As a result German liberalism bore within itself a deep and ultimately unreconcilable dualism: it advocated both *Freiheit* (liberal values as established by the *Rechtsstaat*) and *Einheit* (German national unity). After 1848, when it increasingly seemed that only one of these ideals could be attained, the majority of the liberals chose national union over constitutional rule. As one of them wrote in 1867:

If Germany is faced with the choice between *Einheit* or *Freiheit,* it must, in accordance with its history and its position unconditionally choose the former. . . . It must not retreat in terror before either the path of conquest or that of dictatorship and not even before the military dictators. It must willingly follow the despotic *Führer* who is able to secure for it the possessions of its members, its existence, its position of equality among nations and therewith its future. [If the realization of the national idea is accompanied by that of the liberal idea, good, but if not] . . . then the liberal idea must give way to the national idea . . . the realization of the national idea dare not be frustrated by the liberal idea.[9]

When a unified Germany was finally delivered by Bismarck with only pseudo-parliamentary rule, it was not only accepted but welcomed enthusiastically by most liberals.[10]

By accepting Bismarck's successes with only a few puny objections, German liberalism had made a major capitulation. The extent of its surrender was confirmed in the next years when liberals supported the chancellor in one instance of suppression after another in which the power of the state was employed to crush dissident minorities and enforce *Einheit*. On the question of the annexation of Alsace and Lorraine, on the issue of Polish national rights in Posen, in the Kulturkampf, and on the anti-Socialist law, the majority of liberals backed Bismarck, and in so doing showed a willingness to subordinate their liberal principles to *raison d' état*. Moreover, the Jewish delegates voted overwhelmingly along with the other National Liberals on these questions. Heedless of Riesser's strictures on the unity of freedom, Jewish political leaders voted for *Sondergesetze* (special legislation) directed against other minorities, and thus helped establish precedents which seriously compromised the integrity of liberalism and which could, some day, serve as the basis for measures directed against the Jews.[11]

By 1880, then, German liberalism as actually practiced could no longer claim the high ideological consistency and coherence which its spokesmen continued to declare in their rhetoric. The tension between *Freiheit* and *Einheit* had been resolved in favor of the latter, and much of what remained of the fervid idealism of 1848 had been eroded by the long series of concessions and capitulations made by liberals in the Reichstag and in their press. The premises of liberalism which had only recently been invoked to justify the removal of Jewish restrictions had now been deserted with rapidity, precisely at the moment when they were most needed by the Jewish community. Jewish emancipation depended on *Freiheit*, not *Einheit*, and the legislation passed against Catholics, Social Democrats, and Poles constituted an implicit threat that such laws could also be passed against Jews. [12]

If the liberal ideology was a shambles, so was its political structure after 1878. In that year a major political reorientation took place as Bismarck abandoned the liberals, his former primary support in the Reichstag, and set about creating new alliances with the conservative parties and the Catholic Center. In the elections of 1878 the liberal majority in the Reichstag was erased; the National Liberals saw their strength reduced from the 152 seats they had held at the height of their power to 98, and the Fortschritt (Progressive) Party was reduced from 49 to 26. In the election of 1881 the National Liberals lost more seats, so that within only seven years they slipped from first to fifth place in parliamentary strength. [13] In the wake of that campaign debacle, the National Liberal Party split as a group of left-wing secessionists broke away and joined with the Fortschritt Party to form a new Deutschfreisinnig Party. [14] The National Liberal remnant, powerless and liberal in name only, was now willing to give its support to the conservative majority when asked. [15]

The crumbling of the National Liberal Party and its power had profound effects on the Jews of Germany, for that had been their political home for well over a decade. As the party splintered, so did the formerly united Jewish political loyalties, and while a few remained with the National Liberals, others went to the right and many went to the left. Some supported the Catholic Center or found their way into the ranks of the Social Democrats. [16] The Center was too narrowly confessional for most Jews, however, and Social Democracy was stigmatized as the party of revolution and anarchy. [17] Hence the most attractive political group proved to be the Freisinnigers in which the Jews saw the only loyal defenders of liberalism and the only party that would consistently oppose anti-Semitism with vigor. With the Conservatives cynically manipulating anti-Semitism, and the National Liberals at best neutral, the majority of the Jews came to the Freisinnig

Party as a last resort, because they felt they had no other choice.[18]

The allegiance given by Jews to the Freisinnig Party staved off political isolation and provided them with a parliamentary defender, albeit one that was quite weak. As a result, the Freisinnig Party was quickly labelled as *Judenpartei*. The former affiliation with the dominant National Liberals had been a mark of Jewish integration into German political life, but after the shift to the new oppositional party, the Jews were vulnerable to the charge, immediately raised by the anti-Semites, that they were actually pursuing their own narrow group interests through the Freisinnig Party. This development amounted to a considerable setback for the Jews who, since the period of Riesser's leadership, had consistently maintained that they had no specific Jewish political concerns and that Jewish interests would be well served by the process of settling Jewish issues in terms of the general public welfare. They continued to reiterate that claim but, granted the new circumstances, it seemed considerably less credible.[19]

Not only did the Jews thus have a greatly weakened organizational apparatus through which they could respond to anti-Semitism in the political arena, the circumstances within the Jewish community were no better. There had been no coherent institutional structure leading the fight for emancipation, and now there was none in existence which might defend it.[20] The Jews had reshaped themselves into a religious community in order to merit German citizenship, and the existing Jewish communal institutions were organized exclusively for purposes consistent with the new confessional status. There were Jewish organizations devoted to education, philanthropy (including occupational training), and religious affairs, but not a single one that might be readily adapted to the needs of the new situation. Religiously, Jewry was split into three separate sub-denominations, Neo-Orthodox, Conservative, and Reform, each with its own synagogues, seminaries, and publications.[21] In addition, localism persisted, and there was no overall organization that could purport to represent or appear in behalf of all the Jews of the Reich.

In 1869 the *Deutsch-Israelitischer Gemeindebund* (German-Israelite Communities League) had been founded, but despite its name, it did little more than coordinate the flow of information and funds between local communal bodies which preserved full autonomy. Moreover, the Gemeindebund was severely handicapped by the refusal of the Orthodox community to participate in its affairs, despite the fact that its constitution excluded all involvement in religious matters. Political questions also could not be dealt with lest its juridical status be impaired, and thus the Gemeindebund was concerned solely with educational and philanthropic activities. At most it could deal with anti-Semitism in an oblique fashion, as when, in 1889, it commissioned and published a volume entitled *Grundsätze der jüdischen Sittenlehre,* an apologetic work designed to refute the charge that Jewish religious teachings were morally perverse.[22]

Each of these factors—the indifference of the mass of German Jews, the ideological and organizational decay of liberalism, and the limited nature of the existing Jewish institutions—influenced the nature of the Jewish response to anti-Semitism that soon emerged. Each posed a serious obstacle which had to be dealt with and, if possible, somehow overcome.

MORITZ LAZARUS SPEAKS OUT

Because the Jewish community lacked both the institutional apparatus and the will to offer a coordinated response to anti-Semitism, the field of action at first was left to well-meaning Christians and to a few isolated Jews who acted as individuals.[23] Many of the latter were men like H. B. Oppenheim, Levin Goldschmidt, and Ludwig Bamberger, all Jews who were politically active but had heretofore demonstrated little interest in Jewish affairs. The first comprehensive response from one within the leadership of the established community came from Moritz Lazarus in 1879.[24]

A leading figure in Berlin Jewry, Lazarus had achieved a respected position as an *Honorarprofessor* at the University of Berlin after a long and distinguished academic career and, with Hermann Steinthal, had pioneered in the development of the new *Völkerpsychologie.* A devoted German patriot, Lazarus also maintained an active interest in Jewish communal affairs and had served as president of the synods convened in Leipzig (1869) and Augsburg (1871) where liberal Jewry had validated the accommodation of the Reform synagogue practices to German nationalism. Probably no other German Jew embodied so fully and with such authority the dominant outlook within Jewry at that time, and in an erudite lecture, *"Was heisst national?,"* delivered on December 2, 1879, to a general meeting of the Hochschule für die Wissenschaft des Judenthums, he expressed his reaction to the recent agitation.[25]

There were no new concepts in his discourse, nor were there as yet any suggestions for some sort of organized Jewish reaction to oppose anti-Semitism. Rather, Lazarus offered an eloquent restatement of the emancipation ideology and, in particular, of the Jewish understanding of German nationalism. National identity, he argued, is not determined by objective factors. A nation or *Volk* is a "purely spiritual entity," and membership in a nation is not fixed by blood ties or ancestry. National identity is created by those subjective realities—language, a sense of common history and destiny, a consciousness of participation in the *Geist* of a people—which shape the consciousness of an individual and nurture in him deep national sentiments.[26]

After establishing the nature of national identity in a general way, Lazarus answered directly the question raised by the anti-Semites:

> To which nationality do we [Jews] belong? Gentlemen, we are Germans . . . we belong to only one nation, the German . . . The land in which we dwell, the state which we serve, the law which we obey, the science which instructs us, the education which enlightens us, the art which elevates us—they are all German. Mother tongue and fatherland are German; both engender our inner being.[27]

And brushing aside the current emphasis on race as a product of "gross-minded materialism," he declared:"Blood [*Blut*] means bloody little [*blutwenig*] to me; when it is a matter of the worth and value of man, individually or collectively, *Geist* and historical culture mean almost everything to me."[28]

Lazarus also argued that continued adherence to Judaism clearly did not compromise the full Germanness of the Jew. "There is no *German* religion," he said. *"Judaism is German in exactly the same sense that Christianity is German."*[29] Every nationality, he pointed out, includes several religions, just as every religion is involved with a number of nationalities; like German Catholics and Protestants, Jews are linked to their fellow-Jews in other states only through *"Religionsgeschichte"* (religious history). Those agitators and ideologues who cannot understand these axioms and preach other conceptions of the German national idea do great damage to the entire nation and its lofty ideals, not merely to Jews and Jewish interests. In fighting them, Lazarus suggested, the Jew works for the highest values of his country. Resistance to anti-Semitic agitation with its manifold distortions constitutes a labor of service to Germany and an expression of the finest German patriotism.[30] Likewise, the Jew who remains faithful to his Jewishness serves his fatherland: "In order to be complete Germans in the highest degree, we not only may but must be and remain Jews. We are not only entitled but also dutybound to preserve that which we possess as a *Stamm* by way of spiritual uniqueness and as a religion in the form of ancestral virtues or wisdom in order to place it in the service of the German national *Geist* as part of its strength."[31]

Lazarus thus reaffirmed Jewry's long-established self-perception of the compatibility of Jewish identity with full German identity, and he also introduced a theme which was to underlie all subsequent justifications of Jewish self-defense, namely the claim that in resisting anti-

Semitism the Jews were acting not only on their own behalf but for all Germany. Yet at this point, in late 1879, that argument was not invoked to support *organized* Jewish defense work. As offensive as the anti-Semitic movement was to Jewish sensibilities, and as dangerous as it was believed to be to the stability and honor of Germany, neither Lazarus nor any other Jewish community leader yet called for opposing anti-Semitism with concerted countermeasures by Jews acting either behind the scenes or through a public organization. Although a sense of concern had begun to grow, the Jewish leadership was still wedded to the idea that, in principle and practice, the interests of their community would best be served by working through the established modes of response and not by developing anything that might be construed as separatism.

APPEALS TO THE GOVERNMENT

The development of an independent Jewish response was further retarded by the expectation that the anti-Semitic movement might be suppressed by government action. In late 1878 the anti-Socialist laws had been passed in order to crush another movement which was, like anti-Semitism, subversive of the public order; and the willingness of the Bismarck regime to take stringent repressive measures against elements that were undermining the security of Germany fostered the hope in Jewish circles that they might be able to prod the government into action by judicious petitioning. Hence when Stöcker had mentioned the name of the Jewish banker Bleichröder (a close associate and supporter of Bismarck) at a mass meeting in the summer of 1880, Bleichröder wrote to the Kaiser to alert him to the revolutionary dangers of the Christian Social Movement. Stöcker's movement, he wrote, was different from Social Democracy only in that it was "more practical and therefore more dangerous." "I know," he continued, "that the high authority of the state would come to my protection in the final and most acute catastrophe, but . . . the use of force against me, to which men are being incited . . . could not remain isolated [and] it would necessarily be only the beginning of a horrible and disastrous social revolution."[32]

Besides Bleichröder's action, the leadership of the Berlin Jewish community had lodged protests about the agitation on three separate occasions with Prussian Minister of the Interior, Count Eulenberg. As early as October 1879 they had contacted him, calling upon the government to take steps to suppress the anti-Semites, but had received no reply until June 1880. When it finally came, the response was hardly encouraging. Eulenberg simply informed Meyer Magnus, the chairman of the Berlin community's governing board, that in the government's view the Berlin Jewish leadership had no right to speak for all Prussian Jewry and that the activity of Stöcker's party was not illegal.[33]

The failure of these attempts to gain government support for the suppression of anti-Semitic agitation must be understood in light of the explorations then being made by Bismarck and the Conservative Party to determine whether they might reap some practical advantage from a tactical alliance with popular political anti-Semitism. The possibilities of creating a mass movement from the right were already being realized by Disraeli in England, and the German Conservatives, looking for new parliamentary support now that the old coalition with the National Liberals had been abandoned, began to flirt with the opportunities offered by Stöcker's movement. Through careful manipulation, they thought the Christian Social Movement might be used to win votes for the Conservative Party among the working class—at the expense of the Social Democrats.[34] Hence the Jewish appeals fell upon deaf ears, and even the protest of the influential Bleichröder evoked from the Kaiser, after considerable delay, only a mild admonition to Stöcker.[35]

The fall of 1880 brought a renewed and particularly vigorous burst of anti-Semitic activity in Berlin. A rash of ugly incidents took place in the streets, at public restaurants, and in the university, all accompanied by widespread circulation of anti-Semitic leaflets.[36] A number of leaders of the Berlin Movement began circulating an anti-Semitic petition which included among its demands a call for severe restrictions on Jewish civil rights and the exclusion of Jews from employment as judges or teachers in primary schools.[37] When a Freisinnig delegate rose in the Reichstag in late November to ask the government about its attitude toward the petition, a full-fledged *Judendebatte* lasting several sessions was provoked. Instead of the expression of rebuke the inquiry was intended to elicit, the government answer, offered by the vice president of the Prussian cabinet, referred only to the constitutional guarantee that all religious denominations were equal and said that no change in the legal situation would be permitted. This response— "correct and cool to the core," as one observer remarked—was taken by the anti-Semites as a sign of the government's resentment at the question posed by the liberals. The organizers of the petition were encouraged rather than disheartened and continued their drive for more signatures.[38]

The shock of this parliamentary debate, coming in the wake of Treitschke's articles on the Jewish question which had appeared earlier in the year, and in the midst of the renewed and increasingly vigorous agitation, was enormously discouraging to the liberal Jewish leadership. "[I have] lived and labored in vain," wrote Berthold Auerbach, an author and delegate to the Reichstag, the day after the debate. "That is the growing impression which I have of this two-day debate in the house of delegates. Even when I say to myself that it is perhaps not entirely so bad, the horrible fact remains that such crudity, such untruthfulness, and such hatred are still possible. . . . The consciousness of what is still preserved in the German man and what can explode unexpectedly—that is indelible."[39]

THE DECEMBER COMMITTEE: FIRST ORGANIZATION FOR SELF-DEFENSE

Against the background of these events, and in a mood of depression caused by the absence of effective assistance from those quarters where it had been sought, Moritz Lazarus once again spoke out on anti-Semitism. In the changed circumstances of late 1880, however, his method and his proposals were different from the purely academic lecture he had delivered the previous year. For about a year small groups of community leaders had been meeting from time to time to discuss whether some sort of action on their part was called for, but although a shared sense of concern united them, no agreement had been reached and hence nothing had happened. In April of 1880 a group of some twenty-five had gathered to consider a course of action, and on that occasion Lazarus had urged them to act on behalf of their common special interest. Again, however, nothing had happened, at least in part because of a fear that any Jewish response would only increase the agitation and make it spread even further.[40] Finally, at the end of a depressing year, and little more than a week after the parliamentary debate on the status of the Jews, Lazarus acted on his own authority and invited a large number of prominent Jewish figures from the Berlin community to gather with the express purpose of determining whether or not the time had come to take action together.

Some two hundred Jewish notables, most of them men of prominence who had previously demonstrated little concern with specifically Jewish interests, responded to Lazarus' invitation and were addressed by him. Their assembly was, he pointed out, not secret but confidential in that press publicity was neither sought nor welcomed. "Seeds must be covered in order for them to sprout," Lazarus said. "When the plant has grown up it enters the free light of the day." Moreover, although the meeting was a Jewish gathering, those who came were there, Lazarus reminded them, as "patriotic, enthusiastic sons of the German fatherland" who felt compelled to protect the honor of the German *Geist*.[41]

Attempting to win their support for his proposals, Lazarus repeatedly stressed that any act of Jewish self-defense would be less an expression of Jewish group interest than a way of defending German honor by working to remove from it the shameful stain of anti-Semitism. The mere fact that the Jewish question exists and is a matter of open discussion, he told them, is not only an offense to Jewry but also to the German nation as a whole. "We are hurt in our heart more as Germans than as Jews, and we are sensitive to the shame of the German nation before the eyes of the world."[42]

Lazarus noted that the policy of inaction and letting things take their course had been tried for some time without any effect on the continually growing agitation which had now, he underlined, reached alarming proportions. Keeping silence, isolated one from the other and capable only of sporadic individual actions, lacking an address or focus of resistance, the Jews were weak and defenseless before the anti-Semites. Jewish passivity had created a vacuum which was exploited by the anti-Semites and which provoked frustrated, individual Jews, acting in thoughtless anger, to take indiscreet or irresponsible steps.[43] Hence Lazarus had convened the present meeting not merely to discuss anti-Semitism but to propose the formation of some sort of a body which would end Jewish disunity and inactivity and prevent the Jewish public from being embarrassed by ill-considered responses that might be taken as representative of the whole community.[44] Such a body would be used to carry on carefully thought-out, circumspect defense on behalf of Jewry.

Since the existing communal bodies were prevented by their very nature from assuming this vital function, Lazarus called for the creation of a committee "whose purpose is to be a central point for the ideal tasks of the Jews in Germany, for those ideal tasks which they themselves have to accomplish as Jews in service of the fatherland, for the benefit of the German nation." In a terse, three-point program, Lazarus defined those tasks as follows: "(1) Defense against the agitation which is carried on against us and against tolerance and humanity; (2) elevation of Judaism in the eyes of Jews and non-Jews . . . (3) elevation of the Jews." Although he did not specify in detail how he proposed to accomplish the first point, Lazarus made it clear that the response proposed in points two and three would demand a good deal of work *within* the Jewish community. "Elevation of Judaism" would require bringing increased knowledge of the greatness of Jewish tradition to the highly assimilated and deeply ignorant who are "Jews by the grace of Stöcker." Although he added a disclaimer lest he be taken as saying that the Jews were in need of some special improvement, he emphasized that everything done by the Jews in their own behalf must also be a force for moral elevation within Jewry and increased self-respect and pride.[45]

That night the first Jewish defense organization in Germany was founded as *Das jüdische Comité vom 1. Dezember, 1880,* and a group of twenty-eight notables was established to direct its activities.[46] A fortnight later another, larger meeting with six hundred present was held and again addressed by Lazarus. On this occasion the meeting closed with those assembled adopting unanimously a resolution declaring the convocation's opposition to the efforts of the anti-Semites to make Jewry responsible for the acts of individual Jews, and also against "the unworthy efforts to represent German Jews as a separate nationality standing outside the totality of the German Volk." It concluded with a reaffirmation of the unshakable loyalty of the Jews to the German fatherland.[47]

Beyond these two meetings, however, little came of the December Committee. Lazarus had had to struggle with tremendous inertia within the Jewish community just to bring about the formation of this elitist organization committed only to the most circumspect and vaguely defined tasks of self-defense. Although the liberal Jewish leadership had, for a moment, perceived the necessity for some kind of specifically Jewish reaction to anti-Semitism, it still lacked the determination and sense of urgency to put together either a durable institutional framework or a tactic of response that could be coherently administered. Deeply embarrassed by the need to mount any Jewish response at all, they had brought the December Committee into being as a last resort. Built on a constituency of notables—most of whom had only the most tenuous ties to Jewish communal life but a deep sense of German loyalism—the posture of the committee was disposed toward Jewish activity in reaction to anti-Semitism only because it seemed for a time that no other avenue was open to them. Hence it proved to be an ephemeral structure which emerged in a moment of acute distress and then quickly faded into insignificance once the circumstances that had called it into being changed for the better.[48]

POLITICAL LULL AND ANTI-SEMITIC STORM

The change seemed to come with the parliamentary elections of 1881 in which the ability and willingness of the German electorate to reject anti-Semitism were tested. In those elections the Conservative Central Committee, the political arm of Stöcker's Berlin Movement, put forward six candidates, four of whom were well-known anti-Semites.[49] The campaign was marked with extensive anti-Semitic propaganda as Stöcker and his associates sought to win support from the educated elements in the *Mittelstand* (teachers, civil servants, professionals), as well as from shopkeepers and artisans. Linking the Freisinnig Party with Jewry, they called for an end to Jewish supremacy and to the rule of mammon, and they demanded "healthy social reform, built on Christian foundations."

In the election, however, all six seats in Berlin were won by the Freisinnig candidates, and Stöcker himself won re-election to the Reichstag only because he had also been a candidate in a safe Westphalian district. The election figures in Berlin revealed the continued strength of the Freisinnig party there:[50]

Year	Freisinnig Party (votes)	Conservative Central Committee (votes)
1878	86,000	14,000
1881	89,000	46,000

In Germany as a whole, the same pattern prevailed:

Year	Freisinnig Party (votes)	(Reichstag seats)	Conservatives (votes)	(Reichstag seats)
1878	607,339	39	749,494	59
1881	1,181,865	115	830,807	50

While the anti-Semites were heartened by the fact that they had grown impressively stronger and had even surpassed the Social Democrats, Jewish voters drew considerable reassurance from the continued power of the Freisinnig Party.[51]

Following the election, the sense of Jewish isolation and powerlessness abated, and the tempo of anti-Semitic agitation fell off drastically in the next decade. The anti-Semitic ranks were torn by factional disputes among the leadership, and as the economic slump of the 1870s gave way to a moderate recovery and a more stable political alignment in support of the government was forged, the movement went into decline. One of the leading agitators, Theodor Fritsch, wrote that by 1885 the anti-Semitic movement had "by all appearances come to a complete standstill, indeed an undeniable retreat."[52] The inactivity of the anti-Semites fostered a return to quietism in the Jewish community. Discussion of Jewish resistance and defense work ceased, and the next few years brought only a few sporadic literary efforts, such as the publication in 1884 of a declaration by one hundred and three rabbis against the defamation of Jewish moral teaching.[53]

The lull ended in the 1890s with a recrudesence of anti-Semitic agitation marked by two significant changes. For the first time radical, racial anti-Semites predominated while Stöcker and the moderating influence he represented declined. Moreover, the increased expression of explicitly racial anti-Semitism was accompanied by a greater measure of tactical consolidation within the movement as the various social groups began to coordinate their activities.[54] Although an attempt at unifying all the splinter groups failed, two of the major competing factions agreed to cooperate in the elections of 1890, and this new tactic led to the first significant political success for anti-Semitism. The first anti-Semite had been elected to the Reichstag in 1887. But in the elections of 1890 an additional four were victorious, and after a by-election two years later, they were joined by Hermann Ahlwardt, a new figure in the movement who exemplified the new radical emphasis. Ahlwardt had been catapulted into notoriety by his publication of a series of writings which exceeded in vehemence and absurdity anything yet seen by the public, and he had been elected in a runoff over a Freisinnig candidate with the support of his defeated Conservative opponent.[55]

Encouraged by their initial campaign successes, the anti-Semitic groups had also launched a vigorous propaganda campaign after 1890. At one point they sent out three to four thousand pieces of literature from one office in order, in their words, "quietly to enlist new friends of the ideas of the anti-Semites."[56] Moreover, in 1891-1892 German Jewry was shaken by a trial in the town of Xanten in the Rhineland where a local Jewish butcher named Buschhoff was accused of ritual murder. There had been ritual murder trials earlier in the century, at Damascus in 1840 and at Tisza-Eszlár in Hungary in 1882. But the emergence of this frequently discredited medieval accusation *in Germany* more than twenty years after legal emancipation had been achieved was, to say the least, a profound shock to Jewish sensitivities. Buschhoff was acquitted in the summer of 1892, and the final judgment was greeted enthusiastically by the liberal Jewish press, which found in it confirmation of the hope that, "despite all aberrations and darkenings," the German national spirit "would surely fulfill its great world mission of humanity."[57]

But in addition to these assertions of optimism, by now almost an established ritual in the Jewish press when commenting on anti-Semitic episodes, signs of a rather less sanguine mood had also begun to appear, as had new calls for greater activity in behalf of Jewish self-defense. As early as 1890, after a tumultuous *Judendebatte* in the

Berlin city council and in the Reichstag, during which Jewish delegates had generally remained silent, voices were raised arguing that the Jews had to take their defense into their own hands and not rely on noble-minded Christians to fight their battles for them. In the spring of 1892, with the Buschhoff case as yet unresolved and the scandal over Ahlwardt's latest publication still raging, the mood in some quarters of the Jewish community approached despair. "Are we Jews outside the law?" asked the Orthodox *Jüdische Presse*. "Can our personal, our civil, our religious honor really be dragged in the filth, be ridiculed and derided in this way without hindrance or penalty? Has some law removed us Jews from the protection of those paragraphs which bring the disrupters of civil peace and the besoilers of religious sanctities to punishment? . . . Is the insulting of Jews and Judaism a privilege which guarantees immunity to its perpetrator even when he treasonously exposes the most vital interests of the state, its defense capability, [and] its esteem in the judgement of the nations, in a senseless passion for slander?"[59] Anti-Semitism had reached such absurd excesses, the paper declared, at least partly because of Jewish inactivity and passivity. After analyzing and dismissing the rationalizations offered for doing nothing in self-defense, it asked: "How much longer? To what desperation must conditions come to in order to startle the indolent? Has the confidence in the 'protection of the authorities,' the boasting of our so-called 'equal rights' not yet been shaken?" Concluding on the sustained note of urgency that informed the whole article, the *Jüdische Presse* called for an end to Jewish quietism by rallying all Jewry to unified self-defense.[60]

A NEW COMMITTEE FOR THE ELITE

Under circumstances remarkably like those of 1880, with anti-Semitic agitation increasing and a new Jewish disposition to take counter-measures, a group of Jewish notables once again established a special committee, the *Comité zur Abwehr antisemitischer Angriffe* (Committee for Defense Against Anti-Semitic Attacks).[61] The Committee was formed in Berlin on the initiative of Julius Isaac on June 30, 1892, and, like its predecessor and model, the December Committee, it was made up of a small group of some twenty to twenty-five distinguished persons. In fact, of the eighteen men listed as members of the Committee, at least six had also been members of the directing group of the December Committee; hence it was, in a sense, a reconstitution of the earlier body.[62] However, since the Committee also included Rabbi Hirsch Hildesheimer, publisher of the *Jüdische Presse* and a major figure in German Orthodoxy, it presented a somewhat broader image than had its predecessor.[63] The effective leadership of the group was in the hands of three men: James Simon (a Berlin merchant, philanthropist and patron of the arts), Dr. Edmund Friedemann, and Paul Nathan.[64]

Nathan (1857-1927) was representative of most of the membership of the Committee, both in his background and in his approach to anti-Semitism. Descended from a line of distinguished Berlin bankers, he had found his way into liberal politics as a journalist and protégé of Ludwig Bamberger, one of the founders of the Freisinnig Party. He served for two years as editor of the weekly *Die Nation*, regularly writing political commentary. Raised without religious tradition, his interest in Jewish affairs was minimal, and he became involved with work against anti-Semitism because he regarded it as part of the general struggle for law and justice. He was less concerned with the defense of specific Jewish group interests than he was with right and Kultur, and he offered his energy and journalistic skill to the Committee in order to weaken anti-Semitism by spreading truth, the sure antidote to hatred based on lies and calumnies.

Nathan had reported extensively on the ritual murder trials at Tísza-Eszlár and Xanten,[65] and under the auspices of the Committee he soon published two extensive scientific studies, one on Jewish criminality and another on the participation of the Jews in the military. In them he used abundant statistical data which he interpreted deftly to demonstrate that the amount of Jewish criminality corresponded exactly to the Jewish socio-economic position, not religion or race, and that Jews had participated in all German wars since 1813 in accordance with their proportion in the general population.[66] These carefully worked publications typified the approach of the Committee, which remained a small elite group of influential Jewish figures working quietly to spread enlightenment through serious presentations of factual information. Like the organization established by Lazarus, it neither sought mass participation by the Jewish community nor attempted to carry out counter-agitation or legal defense against anti-Semitism.[67]

THE VEREIN: CHRISTIAN ASSISTANCE

The only effort to establish anything approaching a public organization to fight anti-Semitism on a mass basis during this period was carried through by two distinguished non-Jewish, left-wing liberals, Rudolf von Gneist and Heinrich Rickert.[68] In November 1890, acting with other political figures and intellectuals, they founded the *Verein zur Abwehr des Antisemitismus* (Association for Defense Against

Anti-Semitism). At the start of the next year they published a proclamation signed by five hundred and thirty-one prominent citizens urging opposition to anti-Semitism, and within two years its membership had grown to over thirteen thousand.[69] Although many Jews joined and lent financial support, they did not control the affairs of the Verein, which preserved its non-Jewish identity.[70]

The nondenominational character of the organization gave it special appeal to liberal Jews who had long preferred to protect Jewish interests, to the extent they were conceded to exist at all, through general German organizations and institutions. By joining and supporting the Verein, such Jews could participate directly in the struggle against anti-Semitism as Germans, without calling attention to or emphasizing their own Jewish identity. Moreover, granted the elitist character of the Committee, the Verein was the only organization posed to fight anti-Semitism which welcomed broad public support; there was as yet no other group through which those worried about the anti-Jewish movement could express their concern. Hence the Verein received a good deal of support from the Jewish public and press. The *Allgemeine Zeitung des Judenthums,* for example, warmly greeted the emergence of the Verein by reprinting on the front page the full text of its initial proclamation, and readers were repeatedly urged to join and support the organization.[71] Wishing the new group well, the *Allgemeine Zeitung des Judenthums* said: "By means of the triumphant power of enlightenment and truth, may you succeed in reaching your goal of disarming hatred, fanaticism, and prejudice wherever it appears in our glorious German fatherland."[72]

The establishment of these two organizations, the Committee and the Verein, reveals that the major patterns of response first given institutional expression by the December Committee in 1880 were still intact in the early 1890s. Even though Jewish spokesmen expressed apprehension over the renewed activity and growing strength of the anti-Semites, their concern had not yet led them to institutional arrangements or tactics which were significantly different from those developed earlier. The nature of the defense groups organized in the first years after 1890 demonstrates that the established community was still predisposed to respond to anti-Semitism essentially as it had a decade before—by founding an elite committee that would work quietly and with circumspection, by spreading truth in order to bring enlightenment, and especially by working through nondenominational channels whenever possible.

The last tendency was of major importance. The Jewish communal leadership conceded only with great reluctance that some sort of action on its part was necessary, and even when a few had become convinced that some form of Jewish self-defense was necessary, they had to argue against the enormous inertia congealed in a community which had long been accustomed to eschew all activities implying that Jewish interests were in any sense separable from those of Germany as a whole. The notables in the December Committee, for example, were so deeply committed to avoiding Jewish separatism that they allowed their organization to wither away as soon as possible. So long as anti-Semitism was moderately quiet and the Freisinnig Party had some semblance of strength, the impulse for an independent Jewish response was stunted, and the range of the Jewish reaction to anti-Semitism in the period before 1893 remained highly limited, both in terms of organization and tactics.

THE B'NAI B'RITH AND THE KARTELL CONVENT: FRATERNAL RESPONSES

Although there was a lull in political anti-Semitism during the 1880s, the social consequences of anti-Semitism continued to be felt in an acute form in many areas, and among those most exposed to continuing anti-Jewish pressures there was an undercurrent of dissatisfaction with the dominant communal practice of restraint. In the period before 1893, therefore, there were some significant responses to anti-Semitism resulting in the formation of durable institutions and a spirit of greater self-assertiveness. Significantly, these came not from the German Jewish elite appealed to by Lazarus and the Committee, but from the ranks of a younger and less established generation.

In the 1880s Julius Fenchel, a Berlin merchant, reacted to anti-Semitic insults he had suffered in his Odd Fellow Lodge by tendering his resignation and organizing the first German lodge of the American B'nai B'rith. The rapid spread of the *Unabhängiger Orden* B'nai B'rith—within three years there were twenty-nine lodges with a membership of three thousand—showed that at least some Jews had abandoned the expectation of a speedy end to discrimination within Freemasonry to the extent that they were willing to revert to the practice followed early in the century and establish their own masonic clubs.[73] Although the German B'nai B'rith lodges were not primarily concerned with fighting anti-Semitism, their very emergence and growth at a time when the first defense organization was fading away shows that at least some Jews, albeit not those in the most prestigious circles of community leadership, were prepared to embrace permanent Jewish institutions as an expression, in part, of their response to anti-Semitism.

For the first time, in 1886, the idea of active Jewish self-defense was broached and given organizational expression by a group of students at the University of Breslau. Despite the decline of political anti-Semitic agitation, anti-Semitism had continued and even increased in the universities during the 1880s, a circumstance reflected in the manifesto issued by these students. "Anti-semitism seems to be dying," it began, and there followed a survey of the decline of Adolf Stöcker and the movement he had guided. But, the students warned, it would be a grievous error to assume that the effects of the anti-Semitic movement had ceased to be felt:

The undergraduates at the universities who ought to be the guardians of ideals, have absorbed the anti-Semitic doctrines with the greatest enthusiasm and are eagerly at work to bring them to life. . . . We feel depressed and humiliated, but the consequences of these doctrines are serious and a threat to even wider sections of the population. The young people at the universities are looked upon as the future leaders of the nation who will influence the life of their country to a very great extent. The education of generations will be in their hands . . . no end to this movement can be foreseen. Racial hatred will become a tradition and will increase from one generation to the next. The tension accumulated in this way may one day explode with elemental force over our heads.[74]

Expressing special concern that an atmosphere so charged with anti-Jewish hostility would have a disastrous effect on the youngest Jewish students who had just left the gymnasium, the manifesto proposed the establishment of a Jewish student organization whose essential purposes would be self-defense and the preservation of Jewish self-esteem in the hostile university community.

Soon the first Jewish student fraternal organization, Viadrina, was established at the University of Breslau, and shortly thereafter a number of similar groups were founded at other universities. In 1896 these clubs joined together to form the *Kartell Convent jüdischer Verbindungen* (Confederation of Jewish Fraternities). The Jewish fraternities consciously imitated the patterns of the *Burschenschaften*, with their ceremonial drinking, singing, and the wearing of a distinctive colored cap and ribbon. They also adopted and emphasized the practice of fencing and physical education in order to prepare their membership for active self-defense against anti-Semitism, through duelling if necessary.[75]

Although middle-class Jewish society was taken aback at first by the emergence of these openly Jewish student associations practicing such aggressive self-defense, the Kartell Convent was firmly wedded to the emancipation ideology.[76] While the students had been driven by the hostility of their environment to a style of response not sanctioned by the established community, their attachment to the ideology of their elders had not been shaken. They exercised the flexibility of their youthfulness by forging new tactics to serve the old ideology. Hence their manifesto called for self-defense, but it also declared:

We uphold . . . the principle that we can be Jews and good Germans at the same time, and we shall prove it by our behavior. We intend to educate ourselves to become men who will fulfill all demands that the state makes upon its citizens, with enthusiasm and a sense of duty. We want to work at the great tasks of our times together with our Christian countrymen. A union of Jews does not in any way mean seclusion; we shall not stop meeting our Christian fellow-students. We do not fight the Christians, but only anti-Semitic interference. . . .[77]

The Kartell Convent appeal for membership ended by recalling to Jews the tragic fate of their medieval ancestors who had to fight a losing battle for freedom of conscience against the intolerant spirit of their times:

We descendants are in a happier position; we can fight for our rights in the spirit of our time, in the spirit of the century that acknowledges the Rights of Man.

We march unerringly through darkness to light. The genius of the century carries its torch before us.[78]

That same restiveness and disposition to greater activism found expression in a polemical pamphlet, *Offene Antwort eines Juden auf Herrn Ahlwardt's 'Der Eid eines Juden,'* published in 1891 by a young poet, Ludwig Jacobowski (1868-1900).[79] Unlike the circumspect apologetic pamphlets issued by the established community, that of the twenty-three-year-old Jacobowski did not extol the virtues of Jewish religious teachings or offer factual information to correct anti-Semitic distortion. His essay was a spirited counterattack on the anti-Semites epitomized by Ahlwardt. "Throughout the decade," he wrote, "we have borne the muddy breakers of anti-Semitism patiently, without uttering a sound. There has been enough patience and forbearance. *Now the battle comes!"*[80] Like the new student organizations, however, Jacobowski's attack on the anti-Semites was based on a reaffirmation of the values of the emancipation ideology. He charged Ahlwardt with being un-German, with using outlandish logic ("*Kinder-und Kellnerlogik*"), with concocting false generalizations that violate all canons of rationality, with using dishonorable means of combat, and with being a Social Democrat. But these judgments were suffused with a degree of righteous indignation and anger heretofore unusual in polemical works by Jewish liberals. While Jacobowski concluded his remarks with a declaration of eternal resistance to all that oppresses "free, beautiful and true humanity," he also noted:

A young Jewish generation is being prepared which is German and feels German as [can] only a blonde with blue eyes, [one] which, however, will not tolerate those brutal attacks by street ruffians merely because it has not tasted holy water. It is a generation *which has learned for itself from an honorable anti-Semitism* that has no part in many of its father's sins, which has been raised in the presence of blood and fumes and tears, of curses and threatening, clenched fists.

This young generation has not yet stirred. But signs have already appeared!

It will come.[81]

Before 1893, then, there were signs of increasing concern among some Jews, particularly those of the younger generation, that the growing power of anti-Semitism was not being challenged adequately. A new mood of militancy had emerged and was expressed in terms of the emancipation ideology. A sense of dissatisfaction with the style and content of the quietistic defense work sanctioned by the community leadership had begun to become manifest, and there seemed to be a readiness in some circles to entertain new forms of activity.

CHAPTER THREE

The Centralverein

In December 1892 there occurred the first in a series of events that were to alter the framework within which all previous Jewish responses to anti-Semitism had taken place. In that month, at the Tivoli Hall in Berlin, the Conservative Party held its first convention since 1876. As we have seen, an awareness had long been growing among conservative political leaders that the key to power in an age of elections depended upon their ability to attract the votes of substantial masses. Now, in 1892, with Bismarck no longer in office and the new chancellor, Caprivi, following policies hostile to their interests, the aristocrats felt impelled once again, as they had over a decade before, to find ways of reaching out to other groups in Germany with whom they might forge a mass movement from the right. At the Tivoli conference the Conservative leadership formally recognized the tactical importance of anti-Semitism as an instrument for creating that necessary popular base.

Just a fortnight before the conference, in a by-election in a district in the heart of *Junker* territory, Ahlwardt, the anti-Conservative, radical anti-Semite, had defeated a Conservative candidate by winning twice as many votes as his opponent. This event, along with the growing appeal of political anti-Semitism clearly reflected in the elections of 1890, gave credence to the claim long made by Stöcker and Wilhelm von Hammerstein, editor of the *Kreuzzeitung*, that if anti-Semitism were advocated under Conservative auspices, vast numbers of voters could be gained for their party. At the convention a few moderate *Junkers* still resisted this tactic and proposed a plank which said, "We condemn anti-Semitism." But the proposal was struck out by the assembled delegates after securing only seven votes, and the final program adopted by the party on December 8, 1892, included these declarations:

State and Church are institutions decreed by God; their cooperation is necessary as a prerequisite of our people's moral health.

We fight the multifarious and obtrusive Jewish influence that decomposes our people's life.

We demand Christian authority and Christian teachers for Christian pupils.
. . .[1]

Thus the Conservatives became the first major political party in Germany to endorse the anti-Semites' call for a struggle against Jewish influence as an official part of its platform.

The cynical motivation behind this development was expressed by Count Otto von Manteuffel, chairman of the Conservative groups in the Reichstag and of the Tivoli convention, who said: "We could not avoid the Jewish question unless we wanted to leave to the demagogic anti-Semites the full wind of a movement with which they just would have sailed by us."[2] And the weighty significance of the change was summarized by Helmut von Gerlach, an aide of Stöcker who had been active in managing the convention. Anti-Semitism, he said, "made the greatest gain in prestige it could hope for when it became part of the Conservative party's program. Previously it had been represented only in various small splinter parties; now it became the legitimate property of one of the biggest parties, of the party nearest to the throne and holding the most important positions in the state. Anti-Semitism had come close to being accepted at the highest level of social respectability."[3] Almost immediately the principles of the Tivoli conference were translated into action as the Bund der Landwirte (Farmer's League) was established to spearhead the drive to gain popular support for the Conservatives among the small landholders.

FORMATION OF THE CENTRALVEREIN

In January 1893, in the aftermath of the Tivoli convention, the Jewish community was swept by a sense of alarm which led to a number of proposals for action. Although the *Allgemeine Zeitung des Judenthums* suggested that anti-Semitism was merely a "transitory surge" sure to be dissipated because there were circles within Conservatism working against it, the general mood was now beyond finding comfort in such interpretations.[4] Eighty-nine prominent Jews signed a proclamation headed *"Zur Abwehr der Antisemitismus"* in which they called for contributions to support the publication of leaflets and brochures and to finance the work of roving speakers who would be active in counteracting the lies propagated by the anti-Semites. They insisted that all legal means must be used to defend the principle of equality of rights in Germany and the security of those public institutions on which all Germans depended for their well-being.[5]

The same themes were argued at greater length by a writer using the pseudonym F. Simon in a pamphlet entitled *Wehrt Euch!!—Ein Mahnruf an die Juden (Defend Yourselves!!—A Warning to the Jews).*[6] Simon argued that determined Jewish self-defense, including point-by-point refutation of anti-Semitic charges, would win over some of those misled by the agitation and gain respect for the Jews, even in anti-Semitic circles. Excessive Jewish circumspection had led to the belief that the Jews were cowardly, but the time had now come, he said, for *"ruthless energetic defense, with all the means which law and propriety permit, against shameless insults to [our] honor or brutal physical attacks! Defend yourselves!"* "Keen and resolute defense," he wrote, will show the enemy that Jews are not outlaws (*vogelfrei*), and this reality will bring him to his senses so that he will lose the desire to engage in public attacks. Simon called for setting up a watch upon the anti-Semitic press in order to be able to instigate lawsuits whenever justified, and he suggested that the Jews could learn a good deal from the organizational arrangements of the anti-Semites, especially from their use of provincial affiliates and traveling agitators. He closed by urging his readers not to allow themselves to become embittered by anti-Semitism, nor to allow it to weaken their loyalty to the Kaiser and the Reich, "for whose establishment Jewish blood has also been shed [and] Jewish hearts have throbbed. Germanness and Judaism shall be blended harmoniously in us. We want to be *Germans* and remain *Jews, loyal citizens of the new Reich, reverent followers of the old God."*[7]

In the tense weeks following the Tivoli conference the single most controversial proposal was the suggestion entertained by the governing body of the Berlin Jewish community, led by *Justizrat* Hermann Makower, to send a deputation to the Kaiser asking him to take the Jews under his protection.[8] The proposal unleashed a vigorous public debate which led the *Allgemeine Zeitung des Judenthums* to publish prominently an admonition for unity, reminding its readers that decisions made by the elected communal leadership must be respected, and that an army made up only of generals was sure to perish.[9] On January 9, 1893, in the midst of the controversy, there appeared a slim pamphlet, *Schutzjuden oder Staatsbürger,* which proved to be the actual impulse that precipitated the formation of the Centralverein.

Though published anonymously, its author was soon revealed to be Dr. Raphael Löwenfeld (1854-1910), a Jewish intellectual with no established position in the Jewish community. Löwenfeld was a member of the *Ethische Gesellschaft* (the Ethical Culture Society, founded in America) and was imbued with universalistic humanism. He believed that shared ethical concerns and a common devotion to homeland and state should unite all citizens and enable them to transcend the regrettable divisions wrought by differing religious beliefs.[10] Löwenfeld attacked the plan to approach the Kaiser for protection as practically useless and, what is of greater moment, morally reprehensible. Only someone who lacks civil rights needs to beg for royal protection, he said. The Jews, on the other hand, were complete citizens with full citizens' rights. Therefore, "whoever wishes to fight [anti-Semitic statements] should enter the lists with the weapons of the spirit and not call for help from outside. If we do more, we *degrade* ourselves. [Calling for help,] we would silently renounce the means which our rights guarantee us and fall back into the medieval misery which made our ancestors *Schutzjuden* [Jews protected by special privilege]."[11] Because the Jew is a German, he wrote, with the same privileges and means of self-protection as any other German, any move to invoke special consideration from the crown would constitute an act of self-renunciation, by the Jew, of his citizenship status. Thus Löwenfeld called for a unanimous protest against the governing body's impending action. "Let us help ourselves out of our own strength! We do not want to be *Schutzjuden* but citizens. . . ."[12]

Löwenfeld also argued that the notion of approaching the Kaiser was proof of the woefully inadequate and chaotic state of Jewish defense arrangements, and he emphasized that the greatest danger such anarchy bred was that self-appointed but unrepresentative spokesmen would act in the name of the entire Jewish community. Hence, when a German publication had recently sought out an authoritative Jewish opinion, they had turned to Rabbi Hirsch Hildesheimer, the Orthodox leader. While conceding that Hildesheimer was an honorable man, Löwenfeld denied that he, or any other representative of Orthodoxy, could serve as a spokesman for Jewry.[13]

Löwenfeld then delivered a scathing attack upon Orthodox Judaism and upon the Talmud in particular. He suggested that rather than responding to attacks made by anti-Semites on Talmudic Judaism with refutations of their criticisms, the German Jewish majority should declare openly and clearly that they have nothing to do with the Talmud and its teachings.

Who of all of you knows the Talmud? Who has ever read it? Who of you has leafed through it, in fact, who has ever even seen it? One in a thousand . . . for most of you [it] is not a binding book. Does a different law or ethic from that of our Christian fellow-citizens govern our action? Is our education different? Have you not all taken the great ideas of the national poets fervently into yourselves? Is not your moral philosophy the same as that of your neighbor of different faith? Why, in cowardice, play the defender of an obsolete book whose worth or lack of worth has no relationship to our actions? Why not acknowledge courageously that we know nothing of this book, and though it was once the ethical code of our cousins, it is not ours? Are you afraid of the outcry of the obscurantists who would rather exercise their subtle intellect on an antiquated sophistry than swim with the stream of modern thinking and feeling? Are you afraid of the judgment of a blind minority which feels itself bound through moldy laws and separates itself from living together pro-ductively with an enlightened totality in order not to share food and drink with it?[14]

If Orthodox Jews had reservations about their full participation in German life, Löwenfeld argued, then the only course remaining for those who were completely devoted to German Kultur was to proclaim "openly to all the winds that the majority of the German Jews have nothing in common with the views of those Orthodox who have understood neither the spirit of the time nor our position in the state."[15]

Like his criticism of the Berlin communal leadership, Löwenfeld's opposition to the Orthodox was rooted in his conviction that an effective response to anti-Semitism had to be based both on resistance to the agitation and on stringent disciplining of all Jewish actions and behavior. Any practices or dealings which compromised the full Germanness of the Jew served to confirm the anti-Semitic assertion that Jews were foreigners. Hence he asked whether one who con-tinued to pray "next year in Jerusalem" is a citizen. "He who still says these words ardently should go where his heart or his religious enthusiasm pull him; he who only blabbers them because they have been spoken for centuries, generation after generation, is a fool!" But the "better part" of the German Jews had nothing in common with "the dishonorable band of businessmen without a fatherland," and the spokesmen for the latter should no longer be allowed to act on behalf of the community. "Do we educated Jews stand closer to the fanatics of Talmudic wisdom than to the enlightened Protestants whose educa-tion and upbringing are also ours?" he asked. "Do we stand closer to the French Jews than to the German Catholics? No!"[16]

In order to demonstrate to the large mass of Germans who were neither philo- nor anti-Semites that the Jews were truly German, Löwenfeld called for public dissociation from all those Jews who refused to be Germanized. An effective response to anti-Semitism therefore had to involve increased discipline within the Jewish com-munity so that all unpatriotic and unrefined elements were either reformed or cast off. To accomplish this, Löwenfeld called for a new Jewish leadership which would be more representative of the educated majority of Jews and would act as a spokesman for "modern educated Judaism" without constant regard for those who have lagged behind. By driving out all "bad elements," other Germans might once again be convinced of the patriotism of the Jewish community.[17]

In an appendix to his brochure, which later became the basis of the formal principles of the Centralverein, Löwenfeld listed six theses which he proposed be recognized as the basic views of the majority of Jewish citizens:

1. We are not German Jews but German citizens of the Jewish faith.

2. As citizens we need and demand no other protection than that of constitutional rights.

3. As Jews we belong to no political party. Political opinion, like religious, is an affair of the individual.

4. We stand firmly on the basis of German nationality. We have no other common interest with the Jews of other lands than the Catholics and Protestants of Germany have with the Catholics and Protestants of other lands.

5. We have no other morality than that of our fellow-citizens of other faiths.

6. We condemn the immoral behavior of the individual, no matter what his faith may be. We reject any responsibility for the behavior of individual Jews and guard ourselves against generalizations through which careless or malevolent critics charge the totality of Jewish citizens with the behavior of individual Jews.[18]

Löwenfeld's demand that the Jewish community demonstrate its national consciousness and full commitment to the German fatherland was hardly unusual, and protestations of patriotism had formed a constant theme in virtually all appeals made for resistance to anti-Semitism during the preceding decade and a half. The emancipated Jewish community, including the Orthodox groups, were unanimous in their self-conscious German nationalism. But Löwenfeld's aggressive attack on the Orthodox, his comments about the Talmud, and his suggestion that the failure of the Orthodox to become completely Germanized was one of the main causes of anti-Semitism were, to say the least, highly provocative. Rabbi Hirsch Hildesheimer, editor of the *Jüdische Presse,* had been one of the first to call for Jewish self-defense and was a member of the Committee; hence Löwenfeld's attack on his religious faction was a serious threat to any possibility for establishing a broad Jewish consensus against the anti-Semites. Löwenfeld was willing to strengthen his appeal to the most highly assimilated elements in German Jewry for participation in defense by sacrificing the Orthodox and creating a kind of separatist liberalism. But for those who responded to his call for organized Jewish resistance to anti-Semitism and who wished to conduct it on as broad a foundation as possible, the Löwenfeld pamphlet was not only an important impetus to action but also a source of acute embarrassment which had to be neutralized as quickly and judiciously as possible.[19]

Löwenfeld had concluded his pamphlet by urging all those who shared his views to write his publisher. He soon contacted a number of those who wrote and invited them to participate in a series of discussions on ways in which his suggestions might be implemented. These meetings were held at first in Löwenfeld's quarters, and then at the home of Julius Isaac, a member of the Committee in whose home, six months earlier, that organization had come into being. Among those participating in these preliminary discussions were two veterans of Jewish defense work who had been members of the original December Committee as well as of the Committee: Professor Emanuel Mendel, the neurologist, and Hermann Stern. Mendel assumed the leadership of the group in these first phases of development.[20]

On February 5, 1893, barely a month after Löwenfeld's pamphlet had appeared, the organizing group arranged a larger meeting—again in the home of Julius Isaac—which was attended by some two hundred respected figures from the Berlin community. After considering the possibility of implementing Löwenfeld's call for self-defense through the existing Committee, it was decided that a new organization should be established for the purpose of carrying on public resistance to anti-Semitism, and that the Committee would remain intact, carrying on its work quietly as before. The new organization was to serve as a central point from which the defense of Jewish civil rights would be directed and carried out in full public view (Öffentlichkeit).[21] An executive committee was chosen, and, in addition to Löwenfeld, its eleven members included both Mendel and Stern.[22] At the Committee's first meeting, on Sunday, March 26, 1893, the new organization was formally constituted and given the name Centralverein deutscher Staatsbürger jüdischen Glaubens (Central Organization of German Citizens of the Jewish Faith).[23] Since Professor Mendel was unable to continue as executive officer, a committee of three was established to share the leadership; its members were Dr. Martin Mendelsohn, Dr. Eugen Fuchs, and Dr. Heinrich Meyer-Cohn (who had also been a member of the Committee). Of this inner group, Fuchs soon emerged as the major spokesman for the Centralverein and the formulator of much of its ideology.

During the spring of that year, however, as the executive committee met to develop plans for the establishment of the full organizational apparatus and to agree upon the articulation of their leading principles, the political scene in Germany was dominated by preparations for the forthcoming parliamentary elections. By the time the first public meeting of the Centralverein was held later in the fall, the elections had already taken place, and their disastrous results gave tremendous impetus to the growth of the new organization.

On the very eve of the election, in May, an incident of relatively minor significance in German affairs but of major importance for the Jewish community took place: the Deutsche Freisinnige Partei split into two separate factions over the issue of an army bill, and the resulting fragments established their own party structures. The left-wing Freisinnige Volkspartei was led by Eugen Richter, and the right-wing Freisinnige Vereinigung by Heinrich Rickert. The party that had been the political home of the majority of the Jews since the collapse of the National Liberals in the 1880s was thus rent asunder just one month before a vital election in which the power of German liberalism to defeat anti-Semitism would again be tested. The Jews approached the elections with considerable trepidation and, to their dismay, their worst fears were realized.[24]

The election of 1893 was an enormous victory for the anti-Semitic parties. The 47,500 votes and five Reichstag seats they had won in 1890 now increased spectacularly to 263,861 votes and sixteen seats, enough to allow them to function as a separate parliamentary group.[25] Although the Conservatives raised their votes from the 895,103 they had won in 1890 to 1,039,353, their total delegate strength decreased from seventy-three to seventy-two; of the eleven new seats gained by the anti-Semites, eight had been at the expense of the Conservatives.[26] The Social Democrats also made impressive gains, but the splintered progressive parties suffered a severe defeat, falling from the sixty-seven seats they had won in 1890 to only thirty-seven in the new legislature (divided between thirteen for the Freisinnige Vereinigung and twenty-four for the Freisinnige Volkspartei). Moreover, no Jews were elected to the Reichstag except on the Social Democratic ticket.[27]

Perhaps almost as disquieting for the Jewish community as the election results were the tactical alliances with anti-Semitism that had been made by a number of candidates during the campaign. The Bund der Landwirte had made support of its program a condition for receiving its endorsement, and especially in districts where a strong Social Democratic showing was expected, National Liberal candidates as well as Conservatives accepted this condition and the endorsement of anti-Semitism that it implied.[28] Worst of all, even the Freisinnig parties had failed to oppose anti-Semitic candidates in all instances, and in some contests where they were confronted with a choice between an anti-Semite and either a Social Democrat or a National Liberal, they too had endorsed anti-Semites.[29]

The impact of the chain of events unleashed by the Tivoli conference on attitudes in the Jewish community was great. Within a few months the anti-Semitic movement which had been watched with apprehension for over a decade, reached fearful dimensions in political prestige and parliamentary power. Moreover, at almost the same time, the party in which the Jewish community had found a political home and through which it had opposed anti-Semitism underwent a schism and then suffered a disastrous election defeat.

The change in the mood of the Jewish public was reflected in the *Allgemeine Zeitung des Judenthums,* the judicious and sober organ of the Reform segment. A year earlier, in July 1892, the paper had noted the increased agitation and observed: "Today only one hope, one consolation remains to us: namely, that anti-Semitism *will destroy itself* [through internal dissension]." Certain that the authorities would not permit conditions to reach the state of a civil war, it advised that Jews should confidently expect an end to the conflict: "As surely as the sun must rise on the morrow, so certainly will the sun of humanity rise over Germany again, and before its luster all the specters of the night will fade away! Until then, we agree with the German poet who declared . . . life's deepest wisdom: endure, bear patiently, be silent!"[30]

Then, in March 1893, the *Allgemeine Zeitung des Judenthums* reprinted an article on the founding of the Centralverein which pointed to the presence of a strong movement for action among the Jews, remarking, "One feels that conditions have become intolerable for us, a way out is being sought; a deed is expected." Finally, after the elections in June, the paper called for unified defense activity in the Jewish community. "For us a time of earnest defense now begins," it said. Noting that defense activities had prevented the spread of anti-Semitism in several election districts, whereas in others the indolence of local Jewry and their failure to counteract the agitation had led to considerable gains for the anti-Semites at the polls, it concluded: "Now we know that resistance helps. We are permitted to hope that *energetic, systematic defense activity* will succeed in damming up the anti-Semitic stream and—in years of assiduous work—in draining its sources."[31]

The rather dramatic shift in attitude charted by the *Allgemeine Zeitung des Judenthums* had taken place in broad areas of the Jewish community. The concatenation of alarming developments, coming as they did one on the heels of one another, convinced many Jews their long-cherished hope that anti-Semitism would prove to be ephemeral was without basis. Likewise, the established tactics of fighting anti-

Semitism through organizations or parties that were not overtly Jewish, or through disseminating "enlightening" *(aufklärender)* litera- ture, were questioned. The old counsels of avoiding action lest the flames of Jew-hatred be fanned by Jewish activity and of expecting Christian liberals to combat anti-Semitism no longer seemed credible to many. Anti-Semitism was too strong, and the forces opposing it too weak and disorganized, for Jews concerned about their rights and the honor of Germany to remain inactive or to engage only in circumspect defense work, publishing statistics and carefully documented in- formation in order to refute anti-Jewish slanders. Demagogic anti- Semitism operating effectively in the public arena with the support of major political allies required, so it now seemed to many, a more aggressive Jewish response, one that would oppose anti-Semitism publicly and with determination.

Against this background of alarming political events and their profound impact on the mood of the Jewish community, the Cen- tralverein began to develop beyond its initial stage into a full-fledged organization committed to uniting all German Jews in public defense against anti-Semitism, on the basis of the emancipation ideology. This program was succinctly expressed in the slogan: *Selbstverteidigung im Lichte der Oeffentlichkeit* (Self-Defense in Full Public View). The eman- cipation ideology, of course, had long been the basic principle of German Jewish life, and as we shall see, the Centralverein did not bring about any substantial innovations or radical changes in that pattern of thought, although it did restate and defend it with vigor. The essential uniqueness of the Centralverein lay rather in the two features which set it off from its predecessors: its devotion to coordinated *public* defense carried on with aggressiveness, and its aspiration to become a *Gesamtorganisation,* a mass organization uniting all Jews of the Reich into one powerful group which would be the authoritative defender of and spokesman for Jewish interests expressed on the basis of German patriotism. We turn now to a consideration of both these factors and to an examination of the way in which the Centralverein approached political activity and Jewish self-reform as responses to anti- Semitism.[32]

AIMS AND LIMITATIONS OF THE DEFENSE CAMPAIGN

By establishing a Jewish organization to fight anti-Semitism pub- licly, the founders of the Centralverein appeared to have broken with the assumption that Jewish interests were best served by acting through the general channels of German affairs. German Jewry had long held to that premise, and there were many Jews who refused to follow the lead of the new organization and opposed it on the grounds that it was fostering separatism.[33] But the Centralverein consistently argued that the creation of an organized public Jewish response to anti-Semitism in no way implied the pursuit of *Sonderpolitik* or an attenuation of their dedication to the primary values and goals of the emancipation ideology. "We are Germans, and we want to remain Germans," declared Eugen Fuchs. "We do not want to fight to gain a special justice or a separate position; rather we defend that which the law and the constitution pledge for us."[34] In particular, the new tactic of aggressive Jewish defense action was justified as a means of protecting and implementing the values of the Enlightenment and the emancipation ideology. Through defense, Jewish integration would be preserved, not undermined.

Underlying this justification of defense were three assumptions made by the Centralverein about the nature of anti-Semitism. First, anti-Semitism was regularly interpreted by the Centralverein as a danger to Germany as a whole, not merely or even largely a threat to the Jews. "So-called anti-Semitism is nothing but a special form of anarchism," said Curt Pariser at a meeting of the organization, "and it is no separate battle in which we find ourselves; rather this battle against anarchism is only a part of the general [battle] and is related to the civil unity of the fatherland like any defense against another nuance of this same spiritual depravity."[35]

By generalizing the nature of the anti-Semitic challenge and refusing to see it only as a threat to narrow Jewish interests, the defense efforts of the Centralverein became imbued with significance for the well-being of all Germany. Since anti-Semitism was anarchy, or a form of revolution, or an attack on the *Rechtsstaat* as a whole, or, as Alphonse Levy, editor of *Im deutschen Reich,* held on one occasion, an "un-German" imitation of French chauvinism, resistance to it was, Levy declared, "the duty of every patriot." It followed that those Jews who now banded together to oppose anti-Semitism did so out of concern for their nation and in order to make a contribution to the welfare of their fatherland. In their dedication to defense, Jewish citizens gave proof of their patriotism and deep devotion to the national interests of Germany.[36]

That same German national consciousness was evident in the second premise by which anti-Semitism was interpreted, namely the refusal of the Centralverein to consider or deal with anti-Semitism as an international problem. Members of the Centralverein were certainly aware of the difficulties experienced by Jews in other lands in the late nineteenth century, but there was never an attempt by the leadership to formulate the Jewish question in any framework other than that of German political and civil affairs. Their focus was upon anti-Semitism as a German issue and upon defense in Germany.

Finally, the whole value of the defense program was predicated on the Centralverein's conviction that anti-Semitism was not a permanent danger but a movement subject to control if not eradication. There is a general tone of realism in the Centralverein's discussion of anti-Semitism, and the leadership was no longer inclined, as had been the fashion, to speak of it as merely a perpetuation of medieval prejudice and ignorance which would disappear of itself in the course of continued progress. After fifteen years, anti-Semitism had not withered away as hoped, and Centralverein leaders like Fuchs were forced to concede that the Jews would have to prepare for a more bitter and protracted struggle than they had thought would be necessary a decade or so earlier.[37] Yet they always believed that this struggle would eventually be crowned with success, and they refused to grant that anti-Semitism was in any way a necessary or unavoidable aspect of life for the Jews in Germany. Even when they recognized that anti-Semitism was nourished by economic distress and found advocates in influential places, and even when they acknowledged the possibility that it might, if left unchecked, endanger the status of the Jews in Germany, it was an article of faith for the Centralverein and all other Jewish liberals that anti-Semitism could be successfully brought under control and finally destroyed *in Germany*. The very existence of a defense campaign was itself testimony to this belief.[38]

Yet in establishing that defense effort, the Centralverein faced a number of serious difficulties. One of the most important was the variegated nature of the anti-Semitism they were pledged to fight. How might one combat a movement which found dedicated adherents among the farmers and the *Mittelstand* and was also supported by intellectuals, clergymen and aristocrats? How could a refutation be found for a doctrine of exclusion that was formulated now in terms of traditional Christian theology, now on an appeal to organic national identity, and now on the basis of racial differentiation? And how could one struggle against subtle discrimination exercised through the impersonal bureaucratic decisions or entrenched in the folk attitudes and institutions of a nation with an established aristocratic tradition, a nation which had never allowed Jews to occupy high positions in those areas of state service which brought the greatest prestige and social eminence?

The continued Jewish commitment to the emancipation ideology limited the possibilities of defense even more. With their faith in the power of enlightenment, Jews had long held that when clear facts were calmly considered in rational discussion, all rational men would have to agree that there could be no sound reason for denying Jewish membership in the German *Rechtsstaat*. Other liberals might be reached and convinced by Jewish appeals to statistics and truth, for they generally shared the same presuppositions about the nature of man and the power of rational discourse. But how could such rationalism be effective in converting or even refuting those, like the advocates of the Christian state or of völkisch nationalism, who made very different primary assumptions about the nature of society? The concepts of the Christian nation, or the organic state, or the racial community were taken as articles of faith by their advocates and were thus impervious to critical reason. Such ideological commitments were beyond the challenge of any defense program based on the principles of the liberal faith.

This Jewish adherence to the emancipation ideology and its liberal corollaries set limits to the defense program in yet another way. It was not infrequently recognized by Jewish liberals that anti-Semitism had its roots, at least in part, in deep economic and social tensions which were themselves the product of great transformations affecting the underlying structure of the German economy and society.[39] Recognizing the importance of these structural factors, the Social Democrats argued that anti-Semitism could be ended only by a revolution which would so transform capitalist society as to end, once and for all, the sources of social conflict.[40] But the Jews, with most other liberals, were convinced of the essential rightness of the existing political and economic institutions in Germany.[41] Even when they conceded that there were serious economic problems which contributed to anti-Semitism and sustained it, they could not accept a radical solution to the Jewish question such as that indicated by the Social Democrats. A good many Jews found the Socialist analysis convincing, and later, especially after the Freisinnig parties had joined the Bülow block in the elections of 1907 and gave their support to anti-Semitic candidates, increasing numbers were drawn to the Social Democrats.[42] The great mass of Jewish liberals, however, were bound by their faith in the essential health of the established order and by their antipathy for the antipatriotic internationalism of the Socialists to another, more moderate remedy for anti-Semitism, namely defense, carried on within the limits of the law. No other tactic of combat was allowed by their ideological commitments, and as a result they were unable to deal with the deepest ideological and social roots of anti-Semitism.[43]

Within these rather severely circumscribed limits, a self-defense campaign could still accomplish a good deal, and the record of the Centralverein's defense program shows how its energies were effectively concentrated into those specific areas where actions could, and did, make a difference. Although neither the ideological underpinnings of anti-Semitism nor the underlying social tensions which nourished it were subject to control or even significant influence by Jews working within the limits of the emancipation ideology, there was one area where a concerted effort might have results: a defense campaign might keep public opinion from being influenced by the anti-Semitic agitation to the point where the Jewish position would become endangered.[44] In the age of mass politics, the attitudes of the recently enfranchised multitudes had become a factor of the greatest moment, and the leadership of the Centralverein was aware that anti-Semitism had grown because of its ability to use demagogic methods which appealed, without restraint, to the passions of the masses.[45] "We live in a time," one of them wrote, "when the greatest political results will be achieved through the power of lies, when the art of shrieking has been cultivated to the highest level of virtuosity. Hence it would be inappropriate if, out of falsely conceived discreetness, Jewish citizens were to keep silent."[46] With anti-Semitic agitators operating so effectively in the public arena, a strong counterposing force was required, and that is what the Centralverein attempted to establish with a two-pronged defense campaign. The nature of that campaign was defined by Eugen Fuchs in these terms:

Legal protection and enlightenment are thus [the] means and goal of our organization: legal protection as a repressive, enlightenment as a preventive means. Since political power is denied to us, we can protect our economic and social position only with the weapons of the Enlightenment.[47]

By "weapons of the Enlightenment," however, Fuchs clearly meant something which would have much greater impact on public attitudes toward the Jews than the circumspect methods used by the Committee.

THE LITERARY FRONT

The publication of apologetic and defense literature was a well-established tactic in the Jewish community, and although the Centralverein continued to use it as a "preventive" means of nullifying the impact of anti-Semitic lies, it now emphasized the mass circulation of such writings.[48] The work of producing extensive, detailed apologetics was left to the Committee, while the Centralverein concentrated largely on printing and distributing large quantities of briefer pamphlets, leaflets and broadsheets devoted to dealing with specific issues or defining for the public in a general way the goals and loyalties of

German Jewry.[49] In July 1895 its own monthly journal, *Im deutschen Reich*, began to appear and was sent regularly to Christian parliamentarians, high officials in government service, and army officers. The name of the publication had been carefully chosen to underscore the German national consciousness of the Centralverein, and individual issues occasionally carried factual material designed to refute anti-Semitic assertions.[50]

A good deal of this "preventive" activity was devoted to dealing with the problem of "scientific anti-Semitism" in the writings of established German scholars. During the last decades before World War I, a number of scholarly works were published dealing with Judaism and the Jews, both ancient and modern, in highly prejudicial terms. The work of Harnack in theology, of Paulsen in ethics, of von Luschan in anthropology, and of Sombart in sociology posed a special kind of threat to the Jewish community. Although their publications were not directed to a broad reading public and they avoided the absurd excesses of *Radau-* or "gutter" anti-Semitism, their critical judgments of Jewish life and belief were couched in scientific terminology which made them acceptable in circles where the vulgar anti-Semitism of the street agitators would never have been entertained.[51] Moreover, scientific anti-Semitism was unique in that it attacked the Jews by using the same modes of discourse—objective consideration of data and dispassionate, rational argument—employed to defend the emancipation. Jews held that when the truth about Jewry and Judaism was presented with clarity, free from bias and reflected upon soberly, anti-Jewish prejudice would be proven without foundation. Hence studies that scientifically analyzed the facts of Jewish life only to reach conclusions that called into question the worth or nobility of Judaism and the Jews were highly embarrassing. They challenged, at its very roots, the Enlightenment belief that truth would lead to Jewish liberation.

At the same time, this scientific anti-Semitism was also the only form of anti-Jewish bias which was, in principle, vulnerable to the classical defense tactic of using *aufklärerische Schriften* (enlightening writings) to convert the unenlightened. Because those scholars were at least ostensibly committed to rationality, their studies could be scientifically refuted by challenging their lines of argument, offering alternative interpretations of data, or citing overlooked facts. The Centralverein therefore mobilized a small staff of collaborators to carefully watch learned literature for instances of scientific anti-Semitism, and *Im deutschen Reich* dealt with the general question of scientific anti-Semitism and with specific instances of it on numerous occasions.[52] In some cases representatives of the Centralverein even succeeded in convincing publishers to change offending passages or to remove certain books from the market.[53]

LEGAL DEFENSE

While the Centralverein's work on behalf of enlightenment was, in effect, a modernized version of traditional Jewish apologetics adapted to the needs of an era of mass literacy, in the other aspect of the defense campaign, "repressive" defense through legal action, the Centralverein struck out boldly into new territory. Turning from private intervention with the German administration by Jewish notables, like that of Bleichröder in 1880 and of Berlin communal authorities in 1893, the Centralverein now concentrated on public action through the courts. Legal defense was seen as the most effective way to disarm the agitators and prevent the anti-Semitic movement from operating with total freedom in stirring up the passions of the people.[54] In order for this legal action to be most effective, a carefully organized structure was established.

A special *Rechtsschutzkommission* (Legal Protection Commission) was created with Fuchs as its head, and an office was opened in Berlin to which Jews who had suffered anti-Semitic insults might apply for assistance in obtaining legal redress. In addition, the attorneys on the executive committee of the Centralverein were organized into a standing *Rechtsschutzabteilung* (Legal Protection Department) to advise the commission on its work. The executive committee considered the reports of the commission and then decided whether or not to take legal action in specific instances.[55] Each member of the executive committee was further charged with the responsibility of reading carefully a particular anti-Semitic publication to detect statements that might offer cause for bringing suit.[56]

Possible cases were then divided into three categories: (1) those requiring action without regard to chances for conviction because an important issue was involved; (2) those inappropriate for action because legal measures would be fruitless or because a relatively insignificant matter, on which the squandering of energy would be of no value, was at stake; and (3) those deemed of considerable moment and deserving of action but which were best left to "the enlightenment and edification of the masses through word and writing."[57] In general, action was taken on behalf of an individual Jew only if, in his case, the interests of Judaism as a whole had been injured, or if he had suffered damages solely because of his adherence to Judaism.[58] In short, the Centralverein agreed to prosecute a case only when "not merely Mr.

Cohn or Mr. Levy was offended, [but] when *the* Jews, all Jews *without exception*," had been stigmatized.[59] Following these guidelines, the *Rechtsschutzkommission* functioned as an active clearing house for proposed suits against the anti-Semites, sorting out and evaluating complaints, and in many instances initiating legal action.

The work of the *Rechtsschutzkommission* evoked from the anti-Semites the charge that the Centralverein was a *"Denunziantenverein"* (an organization of informers), and even within the Jewish community there was criticism of these activities on the grounds that the authorities had the primary responsibility of initiating action against the anti-Semites.[60] Defending the commission, Fuchs asked:

Should one always preach caution and patience? Should one console the Jews by holding out hopes for a future when the social question will have been solved? And should one, in the meantime, stand by in idleness because in favorable cases a petty fine results and in the majority of cases the wrongdoer is acquitted? Should one graciously leave in peace the broadsheets which awaken and stir up the fanaticism of the masses and continually try to convince the people that the Jews commit perjury for religious reasons, adulterate foodstuffs, and slaughter Christian children? Is it any wonder if these accusations are raised again and again without a hand or a voice moving against them, that then the people finally believe these fairy tales?[61]

Mounting a concerted challenge to anti-Semitism through the courts, Fuchs maintained, would have the double impact of helping to stifle the publication of anti-Semitic slanders and of strengthening the Jewish attachment to the German *Rechtsstaat*. By fighting anti-Semitism through the established instrumentality of the legal system, the power of the *Rechtsstaat* to protect the Jews would be demonstrated and the Jews, both individually and as a community, would be shown that German justice could be invoked in their behalf. "To advise the Jews to give up the battle for justice as hopeless," Fuchs wrote, "would mean to despair in the *Rechtsstaat* and humanity."[62]

Although there were numerous setbacks in this legal effort, and the German authorities were, especially at the beginning, recalcitrant and slow to cooperate in the prosecution of cases brought by the Centralverein, a good measure of success was achieved.[63] One veteran racial anti-Semite, Willi Buch, ruefully conceded the effectiveness of these efforts to obtain convictions bearing "sentences which were often very hard. To the best of my knowledge, not a single anti-Semite who was at all active in the interests of Germandom, either through the spoken word or through writing, got away without paying fines or going to jail."[64] The imposition of jail sentences and fines on anti-Semites damaged those, like Stöcker, whose primary appeal was to groups committed to law and order and concerned with public respectability. Other agitators, like Ahlwardt, were able to turn these convictions to their own advantage by pointing out to their followers the perverseness of the Jews who had invoked the letter of the law to cut off their enemies. To the extent that these anti-Semites appealed to groups which had little esteem for the law, a conviction for slander could be used to prove the virtuousness of the defendant and also the wily trickiness, infamous behavior, and "dirty fighting" of the Jews.[65]

Nonetheless, the convictions had an undeniable impact in restraining the anti-Semitic oratory and press. Since most of the agitators rarely had access to substantial funds, the fines imposed were frequently a severe burden for them.[66] Anti-Semitic papers were forced to be considerably more circumspect in their statements lest they risk prosecution; individual Jews could no longer be accused in print without substantial evidence being offered for their alleged wrongdoings, and if the anti-Semites made charges without offering names, they were less likely to be believed, except by those already committed to the movement.[67] The Centralverein took a justifiable measure of pride in its ability to inhibit the worst verbal excesses of the agitation through the *Rechtsschutzkommission*. At an observance commemorating the tenth anniversary of the Centralverein's founding, Eugen Fuchs observed: "The outrageous attacks, the brutal defamation against individual Jews named by name has disappeared. The attack on the Old Testament has disappeared; the assertion that ritual murder exists has disappeared."[68]

The anti-Semitic movement was not ended through the *Rechtsschutzkommission*, of course, and neither were the entrenched anti-Jewish attitudes which sustained informal social discrimination. But in a period where action to combat anti-Semitism was so rarely crowned with any kind of visible success, these small victories in dozens of minor lawsuits were in themselves sufficient reason for the Centralverein to feel its efforts had been worthwhile. Moreover, with each judgment in their favor, the intense German loyalism of the Centralverein was reinforced. Despite the many ominous signs which suggested the contrary, the work of legal defense had tested the functioning of the *Rechtsstaat* and found it strong.

POLITICAL ACTIVITY

Since the emphasis placed by the Centralverein on defense was consistent with its understanding of the Jewish problem as essentially one of justice (*Rechtsfrage*) rather than of politics (*Parteifrage*), the organization was officially nonpartisan and aloof from all political affairs. Yet it was very difficult to honor this stance in practice, and strong pressures increasingly worked to draw the Centralverein into the area of election campaigns where the anti-Semites were enjoying considerable success. And although legal defense activity significantly hampered the work of the anti-Semitic press and had an indirect impact on the political campaigns, a fully effective struggle against the anti-Semites could hardly be conducted without some sort of direct participation in the electioneering process. Furthermore, after 1893 the assertion of the Centralverein that it was possible for a Jew to belong to any party of his choice could not be seriously sustained; in truth, the range of political parties which a Jew could support had narrowed rather drastically. The anti-Semitic parties, including the Conservatives, were ruled out of course. The Social Democrats, although opposed to anti-Semitism, were still stigmatized as an unpatriotic party devoted to internationalism and revolution and therefore unacceptable to most Jews with their strong sense of German nationalism. And the Catholic Center was also beyond consideration because it was so clearly identified as a confessional party. Although individual Jews did participate in and support these groups (with the exception of the anti-Semites), for the majority the choice among major German parties had been narrowed to the two Freisinnig splinters. They were regarded as the only philo-Semitic parties in which Jews might participate, and while preserving the rhetoric that the Centralverein was impartial, many of its members supported the Freisinnig parties and many of its directors preserved close ties with the major figures in the progressive camp.[69]

When, on rare occasions, the Centralverein did participate openly in an election struggle, it did so in a highly circumscribed way. Up to 1898, the Centralverein managed to avoid all direct political involvements, and intervening in a campaign in that year for the first time, it took a position on only one candidate in one district. It supported the election of a Jewish delegate to the Prussian house of delegates on the grounds that full defense of Jewish interests in the legislature demanded the presence of a representative who might be specially informed and willing to act on their behalf. Defending this intervention, Eugen Fuchs argued that the election of a Jew to represent Jewish communal interests was no more inconsistent with full devotion to the German state than the election of expert representatives of agriculture and industry to defend those interests. By supporting the election of a Jewish delegate, he said, the Centralverein was not advocating or expressing Jewish political separatism but only acting to protect the Jewish position in the *Rechtsstaat* and hence making a contribution to the general interest of the nation.[70]

In the elections of 1903 the Centralverein once again took open political action, but this time, too, only in a highly limited way. In that campaign the Centralverein actively opposed the anti-Semitic candidates for the first time and urged its membership to support any candidate other than an anti-Semite who appeared to have the best chance of victory. Recognizing that this might force Jews to support candidates or parties with whom they were not fully in sympathy, the Centralverein urged its members to bear in mind that the anti-Semites were, in every case, to be regarded as the greater evil.[71]

Although it was occasionally accused of being a "Jewish Center" comparable to the Catholic political organization, that was clearly not the case, and before 1906 the political involvements of the Centralverein remained confined to these two narrowly defined instances. Jewish political interests continued to be expressed almost entirely through the Freisinnig splinters, and the continuing power of this urge to work through general, rather than Jewish, political modes is further revealed in the fact that every attempt during this period to forge a Jewish political structure which, like the Catholic Center, might be able to operate independently, ended in failure. In January 1893, for example, the same month in which the Löwenfeld pamphlet delivered the impetus for launching the Centralverein, Eduard Kashtan wrote an article for the *Allgemeine Zeitung des Judenthums* in which he called for independent Jewish action patterned on that of the Catholics. Kashtan's article created considerable controversy at the time, and the slogan of a "Jewish Center" was hotly debated; but soon after the Centralverein was founded in March of that year, he backed off from his own proposal and nothing further came of it at that time.[72] Renewed attempts by some Jewish communal leaders to create a strengthened structure for the defense of Jewish interests in addition to the Centralverein then centered on a move to strengthen and expand the *Deutsch Israelitischer Gemeindebund* in 1898 and on Martin Phillipson's call for a *Judentag* (Jewish general assembly) in 1900. Again, despite much public debate, nothing resulted from either effort.[73]

The only tangible result of these attempts to build a new organ for advocating Jewish interests was the formation of the *Verband der deutschen Juden* (Alliance of German Jews) in 1904. The Verband was created after the elections of 1903 in which the Freisinnig parties had not only suffered another defeat but had also begun to make campaign agreements for mutual support with Social Democrats and anti-Semites. This development was tantamount to the final collapse of the Freisinnig splinters as a Jewish political base, and some Jews argued that Jewish political interests would have to find another mode of expression. When the Verband was established, it was endorsed by *Im deutschen Reich*, which noted that "the liberal parties no longer have the power to be able to battle for Judaism with real effectiveness" and that—though one may still choose to belong to the political party of his choice—"the Jews must defend their own cause."[74] Although strained greatly, the link between large numbers of Jews and the Freisinnig parties remained intact, and the Verband never became the independent political factor which some had hoped it would be.[75]

Then, in 1906, Chancellor Bülow dismissed the Reichstag and in preparing for the new elections formed a block which included all parties except the Social Democrats and the Center. This meant that Freisinnig candidates appeared on a common list with anti-Semites and Conservatives and were bound to support these enemies of the Jews not only in the campaign but also, in the event of victory, in the ruling coalition in the Reichstag. The long process of increasing political isolation now seemed to have reached its final phase. German Jewry faced the dilemma of choosing between one of four highly unpalatable political options: support of the Center, support of the Social Democrats, abstention from the elections, or the formation, at last, of a specifically Jewish party. Careful research by Jacob Toury has revealed that the last possibility was seriously explored, and that at the end of 1906 secret negotiations were undertaken between Zionist and Centralverein leaders, with the participation of representatives from the B'nai B'rith, for the purpose of creating an overall Jewish political organization. The negotiations collapsed at the last moment, however, because of the inability of the participants to agree upon the political orientation of the proposed party. Thus the formation of an autonomous Jewish political body remained an unrealized possibility in the period before 1914, and in the wake of 1906, Social Democracy gained enormously in its appeal for Jewish voters, although some supported the Center and others were politically passive.[76]

The highly limited nature of the Centralverein's political activity and the failure of attempts to achieve some form of independent Jewish political representation in Germany demonstrate clearly the continuing power of Jewish aspirations for integration into German life and affairs. An independent Jewish political organization would have been tantamount to a declaration that Jewry had become formally constituted as a minority group with special interests, and that was an abhorrent prospect for a community which had given itself so devotedly to the task of achieving full incorporation into Germany as a confessional group. The massive acculturation process of the past century had done its work, and for most Jews the notion of instituting and maintaining separate Jewish political representation in Germany was an utterly unacceptable fantasy.[77]

INNER MISSION

The defense activities of the Centralverein were predicated on the assumption that anti-Semitism was an *unjustified* attack upon the Jews. Based upon medieval or modern myths, addressed to the lowest passions within man, and addicted to irresponsible generalizations or outright fabrications, the anti-Semitic movement was regarded by Jewish liberals as an affront to logic as well as a danger to the public order. Anti-Semitism was the epitome of anti-enlightenment, and hence the Centralverein attempted to demonstrate through its preventive and repressive defense work the baselessness of the anti-Semitic assertions.

Related to this posture, however, and not at all incompatible with it, was another of a quite different nature. In addition to organizing a public campaign in order to prove the falseness of the anti-Semitic charges, the Centralverein and other liberal Jewish groups also conceded that at least some of the responsibility for anti-Semitism was lodged in the nature of Jewish life itself, and that there were real, objective characteristics in Jewry that contributed to the causes of anti-Semitism and helped sustain it. Having acknowledged this, it followed that a campaign for Jewish inner reform was a necessary supplement to *Abwehr*. Successful defense against anti-Semitic lies had to be accompanied by changes in Jewish life in order that anti-Semitic truths might be laid to rest or at least deprived of all objective reality.

In form, this line of thought came rather close to that formulated by the Zionist thinkers of the same period. Zionists like Leo Pinsker and Theodor Herzl argued that the anti-Semitic movement was an ugly but logical response to the fundamental abnormality of Jewish life, namely the lack of a Jewish national homeland. Hostility to the Jews was an expression by the gentile nations of their awareness of the presence of a foreign nation within their midst. The Zionists concluded that a radical change in the circumstances of Jewish life—i.e., an end to Jewish homelessness—was the only way to end anti-Semitism.[78] The German Jewish liberals, of course, rejected the concept of Jewish nationhood, and they also gave considerable emphasis to the irrational component in anti-Semitism. But, like the Zionists, they too admitted that there were aspects of Jewish life which were contributing causes of the hostility they experienced. And, again like the Zionists, they acknowledged, for the most part, and these were located in the circumstances of Jewish life and behavior, not in Jewish teaching and religious doctrine. Not Judaism, but Jewry was in need of reform.[79]

In making these concessions the Centralverein was following, once again, patterns established by the emancipation ideology. Ever since Dohm it had been taken for granted that the removal of anti-Jewish restrictions would have to be accompanied by the reworking of Jewish life. Now that the emancipation was a reality to be defended rather than a dream to be pursued, both emphases continued. While the Centralverein worked to prevent the re-establishment of external barriers to Jewish integration into German life, at the same time it was concerned with eradicating those residual attributes in Jewry which retarded or obstructed a full consummation of the promises of the emancipation ideology. Since even the most Orthodox had accommodated their traditionalism to allow for German loyalism, it was believed that the necessary reforms in religious attitudes had already been successfully carried out.[80] However, some remaining defects in the distribution of occupational pursuits and in behavior still needed remedy, and in dealing with them under the slogan "Inner Mission," the Centralverein proceeded in full accordance with its basic integratory posture: it steadily maintained that the imperfections of Jewish life could be corrected in Germany within the limits imposed by German citizenship and national identity.

Occupational Reform. In their propaganda the anti-Semites frequently emphasized the concentration of the Jews in narrow areas of the economy, especially in the retail trade, the free professions, and journalism. Jews were accused of dominating these fields and using them to spread a pernicious influence on German life. Because Jews refused to engage in so-called "productive" occupations, they were charged by the anti-Semites with being exploitative parasites living off the labor of the German farming and artisan groups. To protect Germany this Jewish control had to be ended, and one anti-Semite, Eduard von Hartmann, proposed that the Jews be reformed by closing the professions to them and forcing them to do manual labor as artisans, farmers, and factory workers.[81]

The Jews could not deny their obvious proclivity for certain fields of endeavor, and the statistical evidence about Jewish occupations bore out the contentions of the anti-Semites. Invoking the arguments of economic liberalism, the Jews often denied that the effort of an individual to express his talents in whatever sphere he could was in any sense detrimental to society. All were enriched and benefitted when men were free to pursue their chosen occupations without interference. The alleged unproductivity of commercial and professional pursuits was also denied, and the contributions made by Jews to Germany through these activities were defended.[82]

While arguing thus, Jewish spokesmen conceded the truth of their opponents' charges when they revived plans for occupational redistribution offered in the first phases of the emancipation. The earliest suggestions that Jews ought to be distributed more broadly in the occupational structure of the economy had been made in the eighteenth century by thinkers, like Dohm, who were strongly influenced by French physiocratic doctrines, and during the early years of the struggle for civil emancipation a number of proposals for inducing greater Jewish participation in farming and artisanry had been broached with, albeit limited, results.[83] In once again summoning up the call for occupational reform, a new motivation was added to the original aim of achieving greater Jewish integration into the Germany economy: occupational redistribution was now justified as a means of preventing anti-Semitism. As one advocate of these plans argued:

If the Jews do not post a contingent in *all* types of occupations, if there are not soon more waiters and letter-carriers, miners and factory workers in the lower classes, court clerks and minor officials of every sort in the middle classes, and artisans and farmers in greater numbers among the German Jews, then we cannot complain about the hostile reproach that we constitute a *Volk* within the *Volk* and do not assimilate ourselves sufficiently. . . . It is my firm conviction that one Jewish roofer contributes more to the practical solution of the Jewish question than ten bankers, one Jewish farm laborer more than ten attorneys, and one Jewish canal worker more than ten merchants.[84]

And as another exhorted: "Jews, become farmers; then anti-Semitism will abate. With sickle and scythe you will cut it down before thousands of organizations, speeches, and writings. Become farmers!"[85]

In 1880 a *Verein zur Verbreitung der Handwerke unter den Juden* (Society for the Promotion of Crafts Among Jews) was founded in Düsseldorf, and within the decade it had established *Lehrlingsheime* (Dormitories for Apprentices) in that city and in Cologne to offer apprenticeship training to young Jews.[86] Similar institutions were also founded in Berlin, but the most important foundation for accomplishing occupational reform was that created by Moritz Simon (1837-1905). Simon was a well-to-do banker and a life-long bachelor. During a visit to America he had been moved by the poverty of the newly arrived Jewish immigrants and had resolved to take steps on behalf of occupational reform in Germany when he returned home.[87] After an attempt to introduce vocational training into the curriculum of the Jewish teacher's seminary in Hanover had failed, he and a few colleagues started the *Israelitische Erziehungsanstalt* for training Jewish youth in horticulture and manual skills at Ahlem, near Hanover, in 1883.

Although Simon's motivations were self-consciously philanthropic, he also made it clear that he expected his institution to help prevent the increase of anti-Semitism.[88] Simon had witnessed the failure of the immigrants to America to disperse throughout the country as farmers and manual laborers and their concentration in the cities as impoverished pedlars. As a result, he believed, Jewish customs had been rendered conspicuous and offensive to the native Americans, and anti-Semitism—previously unknown in the United States—had been evoked. Conceding that occupational reform would not destroy all ill will toward the Jews in Germany, Simon argued that "a large part of those persons who now sympathize with the anti-Semites but are not themselves professional or racial anti-Semites will be healed of their prejudices as soon as they see how a number of Jews also participate in physically taxing labors."[89]

The ideas of Simon and his co-workers were followed closely and endorsed by the Centralverein. Simon himself addressed a meeting of the organization in Berlin in 1904, and Maximilian Horwitz, the Centralverein's chairman, emphasized the close relationship between his organization and the *Verein zur Förderung der Bodenkultur unter den Juden Deutschlands* (Association for the Furtherance of Agriculture Among the Jews of Germany) in their common effort to disarm the anti-Semitic charge that the Jews are disinclined to engage in working the land.[90] In a form of argument parallel to that used to defend the defense campaign, the Centralverein declared that active occupational self-reform by the Jews was both a means of defeating anti-Semitism and of strengthening Germany. It was, therefore, an expression of the union of Jewish and German interests assumed by the emancipation ideology.[91]

Beyond expressing verbal support for Simon's work, however, the Centralverein's interest in occupational reform was never translated into any concrete program of action. Moreover, the actual number of young people trained at Ahlem and the other institutions was quite small, and although the Verein zur Förderung der Bodenkultur unter den Juden Deutschlands had, at its height, over two thousand members, its budget did not exceed four thousand marks.[92] Compared to the effort that would have been required to carry through a major restructuring of Jewish occupational distribution, the work undertaken was insignificant. Occupational reform was largely a utopian scheme which was dealt with in public discussion without ever reaching the stage of substantial implementation. Although justified as an effective technique for fighting anti-Semitism, and even advocated by some of its partisans as a means of defense far more powerful than reasoned apologetics or legal action, extensive occupational reform was never attempted. To have done so would have required a fundamental structural change in German Jewry, and that was a prospect beyond the power of the liberal temperament.

The full implications of what occupational reform would have meant had it been undertaken were spelled out by Ernst Tuch in 1901.[93] Tuch's father, Gustav, was deputy chairman of the Verein zur Förderung der Bodenkultur unter den Juden Deutschlands and had served on the board of the institution at Ahlem; Ernst was active in carrying on his father's interests, both organizationally and by propagating the idea of agricultural and manual training for Jews.[94] Ernst argued that anti-Semitism was a result of the precarious economic circumstances into which the German *Mittelstand* had been forced in recent years. Trapped by a number of developments (especially the establishment of large warehouses and department stores) which had made many of their number superfluous, the small and medium-sized store owners were fighting for their existence. In their struggle to survive, they reached out for any instrument that seemed to offer salvation, including anti-Semitism with its promise to drive Jewish merchants out of a declining market in which there were too many competitors. Anti-Semitism was thus a "means of defense" whose usefulness was sustained by basic, apparently irreversible economic trends. Offering one of the rare critiques of Jewish defense presented by a non-Zionist, Tuch maintained that Jewish resistance to anti-Semitism had been misdirected against the superficial symptoms of deep economic distress. "The direct battle against anti-Semitism," he wrote, "whether through political measures or through enlightenment, will certainly bring much good as a result; it cannot, however, be considered a radical cure." Yet, Tuch argued, a remedy that could deal with the basic circumstances which had created anti-Semitism was available and could be implemented by Jewish action: "With calm consideration we must perceive that that with which the anti-Semites want to bring about our economic ruin would be in reality our good fortune, our progress. Yes, the anti-Semites are right: we must get out of the mercantile class to which, by far, our majority belongs. Not, indeed, because it is agreeable to the anti-Semites . . . but because it has become an economic necessity for us." In Tuch's view the Jews should recognize that their membership in a declining class would lead to disaster, and hence, as an expression of their own self-interest and out of dedication to their self-preservation, they must leave that class en masse and turn to agriculture and primary production. "The slogan for the economic redemption of Germany Jewry," Tuch said, "thus must read: Get out of the merchant class [*Los vom Kaufmannstande*]!"[95]

Tuch's analysis was remarkable in that it was one of the few instances in which a German Jew who was neither a Zionist nor a Social Democrat treated anti-Semitism as a symptom of profound structural disorder and offered a radical solution which the Jews might carry out to correct that malady. Yet even Tuch's prescription for radical Jewish action was in the tradition of the emancipation ideology in that his goal was to secure the integration of Jewry into the fabric of Germany. Although he perceived that the hostility facing the Jews was more than a continuation of medieval prejudice or an artificial enmity stirred up by a few agitators, he, like the Centralverein and other Jewish liberals, continued to believe that the Jewish question could be solved within Germany.

The Germanization of Jewish Behavior. In addition to the recognition that Jewish occupational activities sustained anti-Semitism, there was an awareness in some liberal circles that much anti-Jewish sentiment was occasioned by other aspects of Jewish behavior, in particular by Jewish personality traits and manners. Not infrequently, leading Jewish liberals described the conduct of their fellow Jews in highly critical terms, echoing closely the content and tone of anti-Semitic literature. In his address at the founding assembly of the December Committee, for example, Moritz Lazarus had called for "elevation of the Jews" by self-reform of objectionable characteristics, especially "the lack of pride and self-assurance." These defects were revealed in the Jewish inclination to "vanity and ostentation, [and] pushing into higher social circles."[96] In the pamphlet that had given impetus to the formation of the Centralverein, Raphael Löwenfeld had attacked the "insolent parvenus, arrogant about their wealth; the tasteless showiness of uneducated Jewish women, and the loud pushiness of shop boys in public places."[97] And Martin Philippson acknowledged openly the direct relationship between certain acquired defects in Jewish life and the anti-Semitic movement:

The extent, depth and duration of the anti-Semitic movement also have, however, factual foundations within the Jewish community. The harsh violence of its destiny during so many centuries has brought uncertainty, a lack of proportion, and coarse contradictions into its *Stammescharakter* ["racial" character]. Therefore the disquietude; the formlessness, the loud, rash nature; the running after external distinctions and the approbation of others . . . therefore alongside of the most inward family love, the most public charity; [alongside of] truly ideal readiness to sacrifice, limitless egoism and sensuality. Above all the disrespect and enslavement which continued for so long have caused a certain deficiency in firm sense of honor in many circles of those parts of the Jewish *Stamm* which have only recently struggled up to emancipation.[98]

To be sure, none of these liberals believed Jewish defects beyond amelioration, and Philippson's statement shows how even when such undesirable traits were acknowledged, they were related to the negative historical circumstances that had shaped the Jewish character and not, as the anti-Semites often claimed, to inherent racial factors.

The high degree of embarrassment revealed by Jewish spokesmen over these forms of Jewish behavior, and their willingness to accept the anti-Semitic charges as justified, are closely linked to the acculturation process by which the Jews had become Germanized. Germanization was widely taken to mean not merely adoption of German citizenship and language but also of German Kultur, including a whole set of manners and mores and an expected style of conduct. The standard by which the Jew evaluated his behavior and that of his fellow Jews had been internalized by him from the society in which he was so eager to be at home, and the ideal image he sought to embody was that of the cultured, urbane German gentleman—well-mannered, calm and dignified. It was believed that Jews who failed to approximate that model betrayed not merely their boorishness or lack of manners but their incomplete Germanization. Persistence in un-German habits of speech, gesture, and decorum like those described above was seen by Jews and anti-Semites alike as a sign of the Jewish failure to become fully accommodated to the cultural expectations of the emancipation and proof of a continuing attachment to the mode of life which had been characteristic of the ghetto. Hence, when gentiles responded to such Jewish behavior with antipathy, Jewish liberals agreed that there was a legitimate basis for that aversion, a justifiable kernel of truth in the anti-Semitic accusations.

Accompanying this high degree of sensitivity by Jews to evidence of incomplete Germanization in manners and mores was a profound identity dilemma which lay heavily upon many of the most assimilated Jews in Germany. The novelist Jakob Wassermann (1873-1934) expressed the tortured ambivalence of a good part of emancipated Jewry when he wrote of his struggle to resolve the problem of the relationship between his Jewish and his German identity: "Are you a Jew or are you a German? Do you want to be a Jew or a German? . . . I found myself compelled to decide in one direction or the other, even though I did not see the way by which I should go in one direction or the other. . . . I looked for a model and example, for encouragement and confirmation among those who had gone before me, in one direction or the other, but the search was without result."[99] Wassermann did not find his being German problematic; that part of himself was richly defined for him by his cultural and national loyalty. But he struggled in vain to relate that dominant German identity to his residual sense of Jewishness. He testified to feeling bound to a Jewish religious community even though he no longer professed Jewish religiosity nor participated in communal affairs. "Strictly considered," he said, "one was a Jew only in name and by virtue of the enmity, strangeness, or aversion of the surrounding Christian world . . . To what purpose, therefore, was one still a Jew, and what was the meaning of that? This question became increasingly more urgent for me, and no one could answer it."[100] The inner confusion which afflicted Wassermann was characteristic of many, in Eastern Europe as well as in the West, who had undergone pervasive westernization without divesting themselves of Jewish identity. Having adopted the values and cultural ideals of the non-Jewish world, they were left with what one Hebrew essayist called a "rent in the soul," a sense of inward dividedness—in short, an identity dilemma.[101]

Before examining the way in which the Centralverein offered a means of resolving that dilemma (and also of answering the criticism of Jewish behavior delivered by the anti-Semites), and in order to understand it more fully, we will consider first two other forms of resolution. Both were proposed by Jews standing well out at the margins of the Jewish community who responded to anti-Semitism and the problem of their own Jewishness in ways quite different from those developed by the participants in communal affairs. Their proposals for handling anti-Semitism were well beyond the consensus of opinion expressed by members of the Centralverein, and hence were rejected out-of-hand. Yet, inasmuch as the men who offered these proposals spoke out of the same highly acculturated background as did many of those in the Centralverein, their solutions illuminate the nature of the Jewish alienation and ambivalence out of which that organization developed, and also the significance of its approach to Jewish identity and the task of "Inner Mission."

The first proposal appeared in the year 1900 in the prestigious *Preussische Jahrbücher*, the same journal in which Treitschke had published his attack upon Jewry in 1879. Once again this organ of Prussian classical liberalism brought to its readers a statement on the Jewish question, this time, however, one written by a Jewish attorney from Halle named Weisler, who used the pseudonym Benediktus Levita.[102] In an article entitled *"Die Erlösung des Judenthums,"* he argued that the solution to the Jewish problem lay only in the "complete union" of Jews and Germans, a union which could be consummated only through the full disappearance of Jewry through conversion to Christianity. In arguing for this course of action, Weisler expressed with great candidness some of his inner turmoil to find peace as a German and a Jew. He also furnished one of those rare instances in which a rationale for conversion as the answer to the Jewish question was offered by a Jew.

Weisler wrote that German Jewry was divided into three groups, only one of which was ripe for the necessary solution. The Orthodox, detached not only from the Christians but even from most Jews in physical constitution, speech, and manner of thinking and living, did not want fusion with the German people and constituted a foreign but harmless clan. Also unprepared for amalgamation were those non-Orthodox Jews who continued to see value in their Judaism, who claimed religious differences were unimportant for German civil affairs, and who denied the existence of a Jewish question. As for the third group, "Those . . . who are detached, religiously and nationally, from Judaism, who see in it only a heavy, superfluous burden, and wish to be absorbed in the current of German *Volksthum* are ripe, overripe. I belong among these, and I speak in their name."[103]

After surveying the recent setbacks the anti-Semitic movement had brought in the efforts to be absorbed into German society, Weisler pointed out that all barriers to the acceptance of a Jew disappear the moment he agrees to undergo baptism. "In order to gain complete equality of rights, the Jew must first demonstrate that he is an unprincipled scoundrel." In his insistence on conversion, Weisler disagreed with the liberals' claim that German society is, or should be, indifferent to religion. On the contrary, he said, "religion is a much greater power than the freethinkers wish to concede; it is a part of national life." One simply could not imagine a German without his Sunday, his Christmas, Easter and Pentecost.[104]

Weisler challenged the claim of consensus Jewry that Judaism in Germany was only a religion, and a thoroughly denationalized one. He argued that "in Judaism religion is nothing but the form in which national life expresses itself," and then sketched the opposition between Jewish and German religio-national patterns:

Certainly, anyone who still tolerates the chattering and sing-song in his synagogue instead of grasping the treasures of German church music, who replaces the joyous ceremony of baptism with the disgusting circumcision and the flowers and colors of Christian funerals with the dismal blackness of his four planks, [anyone] who does not kindle the Christmas tree or ring the Easter bells—such a person must certainly appear as an alien to the German. We cannot become at home in the German *Volk* if we do not become one with it in the basic elements of its religious feelings.

We have already come so close to the German *Volk* that only baptism is lacking in order to disappear completely within it. This absurd social prejudice is for us an invaluable proof of the fact that the antithesis of race, culture and *Weltanschauung* has been overcome. *Only religion continues to separate us from the German Volk.*[105]

The Jews for whom he speaks, Weisler noted, are almost completely alienated from Judaism but not anti-religious. They profess "religion in general" and recognize the importance of dogma, ethical ideals, and remembrances in every religion. Although most elements of Judaism—especially the ceremonial laws with their nationalistic forms—no longer had an effective claim on their loyalties or emotions, Weisler's marginal Jews still fully accepted monotheism, "the essential dogma of Judaism." Recognizing that Jewish morality was the oldest, he argued that it was certainly not the highest and had been surpassed by Christian morality which had deepened and heightened ethical demands incomparably. "We love it, this earnest, deep *Weltanschauung* . . . [and] we reject the moral ideal of Judaism because we have found a better one."[106]

Some of Weisler's strictures on Judaism were identical with those leveled against the "legalism" of rabbinic law by the Reformers within the Jewish community. Yet Weisler found even Reform Judaism unacceptable:

Nothing is accomplished by abolishing the ceremonial law, by transferring the Sabbath to Sunday, by introducing German language or by generally modernizing Jewish affairs. One should have begun the reform by deepening the moral law. Judaism must cease to ignore the world-historical phenomenon of Jesus. . . . How could a true reform be possible without being connected with the great reformer of Judaism. . . ? His teachings should have formed the foundation of the new structure. But then Judaism would have ceased, for whoever recognizes the moral ideal of Jesus is a Christian. We repudiate a reform on a Jewish foundation: *we are no longer Jews.*[107]

But, Weisler asked, can we become Christians? The aspects of Christian religion devoted to morals and religious remembrances presented no obstacles, but the whole area of dogma in Christianity was rather more problematic. Although Weisler and his compatriots were so marginally Jewish they considered themselves outside the pale of Judaism, the doctrine of the trinity posed an insurmountable obstacle to entering the Christian world fully.

Not only its incomprehensibility repels us, but above all its incompatibility with our concept of God. It is unimaginable how greatly the doctrine of the incarnation is offensive to our sensitivities. . . . On this point we are and remain *Stockjuden* [typical Jews]. To place a being equal to God . . . is an abomination to us. . . . We will not allow ourselves to be robbed of, or even disturbed in, our belief in a single, incorporeal, imageless God. Our fathers poured out rivers of blood for this belief, and should we be forced today to kneel down before the crucifix, the same thing would happen.[108]

To be fully German, one must be a Christian; but to become a Christian, one must affirm the trinity—an impossible demand. Even modernized, undogmatic Protestantism persisted in using the traditional trinitarian confession of faith. As long as even the "new Christianity continues to hold on to the old formula," Weisler wrote, "we can certainly admire its ethical ideal, but *we cannot become Christians.*"[109]

What was to be done? Weisler, and those like him, professed to thirst for religion and believed to have found it in a Christianity which, despite its attractiveness, they were unable to enter. "A formula, a slip of paper separates us from it." Establishing a new "Jewish-Christian" sect, with its "inevitable Jewish national reminders," would only compound current divisions. So they were adrift and homeless:

And we are weary, oh so weary of our Judaism which separates us from our *Volk* without giving us in return religious exaltation. The priceless possession which nature places in the cradle of the most humble man—a *Volksthum*—remains denied to us. We cannot come into *Deutschtum*; we do not want to go back into Judaism. We must continue to wander our disconsolate way alone. The great crime of the crucifixion is visited upon us to the thousandth generation. The malicious cry of our ancestors is dreadfully fulfilled on us: "His blood be upon us and our children."[110]

But what, he asked, of the children? "Since we are no longer Jews, we have no right to raise our children as Jews. Since we have recognized Christianity as the right religion, then we must raise our children in it." And, Weisler concluded: "The eternal Jew dies. Our children will be Christians."[111] In fact, Weisler carried out this program in his own family. He remained a Jew and had his children baptized.[112]

Weisler's agonized analysis, culminating in a call for full Germanization by means of conversion, was a restatement of themes that had been first discussed in the earliest period of the struggle for emancipation. At the turn of the century David Friedländer, a disciple of Mendelssohn and an active proponent of religious reform in Judaism, had advanced the suggestion that a number of leading Jews would agree to embrace Christianity, and even go through the ceremony of baptism, provided they were not required to profess belief in the divinity of Jesus.[113] Throughout the nineteenth century there had been a steady trickle of conversion to Christianity by Jews, sometimes done out of religious conviction, but also, and perhaps most often, as a means of entrance to German society. With the achievement of emancipation and the legal recognition of Jewish confessional status, Jewish communal leaders could argue that it was no longer necessary to convert in order to enjoy the opportunities of participation in German life. Yet, as we have seen, German liberals, from Treitschke on the right to the Freisinnig spokesmen on the left, remained unsympathetic to all aspirations for continued Jewish communal and religious life, an attitude which found its fullest expression in their concept of Germany as an *Einheitskultur* (unified culture). Weisler's proposal was essentially a restatement of Friedländer's call for conversion, blended now with the liberal ideal of the *Einheitskultur*. Weisler accepted without modification the claim that German culture was deeply Christian in nature, and he concluded, with the liberal critics of Jewishness, that any continued expression of Jewish identity, even in the form of religion, was a declaration of separation from the German nation. Expressing views that were fully compatible with those of the liberal Protestant journal in which his article appeared, Weisler called for an end to all Jewishness as the only way to end the continuing tension between Germans and Jews, a tension which raged in his own being.

Another form of solution, also based on the belief that only full Germanization of Jewry could solve the Jewish question, was offered in 1897 by a young man who would later become one of the most powerful figures in German industry and government—Walther Rathenau. A few months before the first Zionist Congress convened in Basel, he published an article entitled *"Höre Israel"* in Maximilian Harden's literary journal *Zukunft*. [114] An apostate from Judaism, Harden had become established as one of the most formidable figures in German intellectual affairs, and during Bismarck's rule his publication had been used by the chancellor as a quasi-official organ through which the government's views might be made known to the general public. [115] In carrying Rathenau's essay, the *Zukunft* propagated in the highest intellectual circles a statement on Jewry of a highly provocative nature.

Rathenau began his discussion with the following comment:

Whoever wants to hear their [the Jews'] speech can go through the Thiergartenstrasse at noon on a Sunday in Berlin or glance into the foyer of a theatre in the evening. A strange sight! A separated alien tribe in the midst of German life, effervescent and vulgarly decorated, with hot-blooded, animated gesticulations. An Asiatic horde on Brandenburg sand. The forced cheerfulness of these people does not reveal how heavily old, unsated hatred bears down on their shoulders. They do not realize they are protected from that which their fathers suffered only by an age which holds all natural powers in check. In narrow cohesion among themselves, in strict seclusion outwards: thus they live in a semi-voluntary, invisible ghetto; not a living member of the *Volk*, but rather an alien organism in its body. [116]

It was pointless, Rathenau argued, to investigate who should bear the blame for this state of affairs. The irrefutable fact remained that the "best Germans" feel a deep antipathy against this Jewish reality. Even those Germans who were indifferent toward the economic issues on which "so-called anti-Semitism" is based were vitally concerned to the point of an "almost passionate aversion" to the cultural aspects of the Jewish question.[117]

For Rathenau the root of the problem lay in the failure of the Jews to live up to their side of the emancipation agreement. "The state made you citizens in order to educate you to be Germans. [But] you have remained aliens and [yet] demand that the state should grant full equality? You speak of fulfilled duties: military service and taxes. But here there was something more than duties to fulfill, namely trust."[118] Continued separatism, the refusal to become fully accommodated to German manners and mores, the persistence in alien habits and behavior—these characteristics of German Jewish society were responsible for the unresolved Jewish question. For, Rathenau implied, even if all the economic and commercial tensions that created the organized anti-Semitic movement were to be resolved successfully, the real problem, the *Kulturfrage*, would remain, a result of the Jewish unwillingness to become acculturated to German life.

To be sure, he said, there were some individual Jews who were pained and ashamed to be "aliens and half-citizens" and who yearned to come out of the "ghetto closeness into the German forest and mountain air." At first thought, conversion to Christianity might seem the only logical step for such Jews with deep German yearnings. And why not? Rathenau asked. "There is no difference between the deism of a liberal evangelical clergyman and that of an enlightened rabbi," and therefore in most cases becoming a Christian is not an affair of religious belief or conscience. Nonetheless, Rathenau argued, baptism cannot bring an end to the Jewish question. Some individuals might create better circumstances for themselves through conversion, but the totality cannot do this: "Even if half of all the Jews were converted, then nothing less than a more passionate 'anti-Semitism against the baptized' could arise, which, through spying and accusations on the one side, and through *Renegatenhass* and untruthfulness on the other side, would have an effect even more unhealthy and immoral than that of the present movement. The half left behind [i.e., the unconverted Jews], moreover, bereft of its elite, would shrivel up into an uneducable mass."[119]

Since conversion to Christianity was not the solution, what then must be done?

An event without historical precedent: the conscious self-education of a race to adapt to foreign demands. Adaptation . . . in the sense that group characteristics, irrespective of whether they are good or bad, which are shown to be hated by the other residents of the country, will be laid aside and replaced by more proper ones. . . . The goal of this process will be not imitated Germans, but rather Jews formed and reared as Germans. And indeed, first of all an intermediary position must be formed, which, recognized by both sides, will represent a separating and joining member between *Deutschtum* and *Stockjudenthum:* a Jewish patriciate, not of property, but of spiritual and bodily culture. By virtue of its roots this class will perpetually absorb new nourishment from below to above and in time assimilate all transformable, digestable material that is present.[120]

In Rathenau's view, few outsiders realized that this Jewish aristocracy already existed, and that if nothing intervened to retard it, the process of dissolution of individual parts would continue apace. A degree of self-awareness had begun among the masses, and, he said, "it is gratifying that even there the appellation 'Jewish' [applied] to personal traits and ways of acting has taken on an embarrassing coloration."[121]

Since the heart of the Jewish problem lay in the failure of the Jews to become German socially and culturally, the Jewish aristocracy had the special responsibility to work at reforming and re-educating the Jewish masses. This aristocracy, of which Rathenau considered himself a part, carried the burden of noblesse oblige, and under current circumstances that meant setting new and higher standards of behavior for those Jews who persisted in "alien, south-eastern" ways so repulsive to the northern peoples.[122]

Much of the remainder of Rathenau's essay was devoted to a detailed critique of current Jewish behavior patterns. Marked by high shoulders, clumsy feet, soft, roundness of form and other signs of bodily degeneracy, Jews should work at their physical regeneration for a few generations. Jews have only a superficial understanding of the forms of urbane intercourse, and Jewish conversations are a battle. They persist in using peculiar linguistic expressions. They should not be so eager to receive public honors, even when they feel they are entitled to them. They should be more restrained in talking about how they spend their money, and they should especially be modest in matters of philanthropy, realizing that "true compassion is modest, and whoever wears it for show prostitutes himself." They should let their exotic cousins from other countries stay where they are and remember that "the charge that you are international will be made against you as long as you are related by marriage with all the foreign Cohns and Levys." And they should not be ashamed if their children learn to speak German before French. "Whoever loves his fatherland can, and should, be a little chauvinistic." For Rathenau an increased Jewish awareness of these "defects" was not an end in itself but an important first step leading to inner reform and self-education. He was confident that once the Jews had begun to work at improving themselves, they would be entitled to knock at the gates of the state—"and they will be opened."[123]

Turning to official anti-Semitism and its effects, Rathenau conceded that the current policy of excluding Jews from the army, civil administration, and universities in order to prevent the "Judaization" of public life amounted to pursuing a legitimate goal with improper means. Judaization should be prevented, he thought, but the blanket exclusion of Jews from positions of standing was counterproductive. It drove some Jews into hypocritical conversions of convenience while others were forced toward the left-wing socialist and progressive parties. The effects of the present policy were the promotion of latent Judaization (because of dishonorable conversions being favored) and the powerful strengthening of the "destructive" political parties. If the state had a more precise knowledge of Jewish life, it would be aware of the differences and gradations within Jewry and abandon the slogan, "A Jew is a Jew."[124]

Although Rathenau believed it permissible for the government to make a stringent investigation into the origins of an applicant for an official position, he held that

principled exclusion, with no exceptions, must cease. If there were only a handful of Jewish officials and officers—and should there not be as many righteous men among half a million people as in Sodom and Gemorrah—then the Jewish population would feel that the state does not make the Jewish question a matter of [religious] belief, but of education. They would not turn to professional opposition [to the government] because of political hopelessness. . . . Rather the masses would measure themselves according to the few exceptions and would glimpse in them a goal attainable through self-education.[125]

Further, if the state would act with wisdom and discretion, it could prevent the "best" of the Jews from becoming alienated and disaffected. A policy which allowed for selective employment of the talented, qualified, and highly Germanized Jews would be not only just but prudent.[126]

This was Rathenau's solution to the Jewish question: a combination of Jewish self-reform and judicious, but not indiscriminate, tolerance by German society and state. Nowhere did Rathenau take issue with the charges brought against the Jews by anti-Semites and, in fact, he echoed and endorsed a number of those accusations. Rathenau accepted the negative image of Jewry with only one important reservation: the claim that there was a small, aristocratic elite among the Jews which had succeeded in freeing itself from pernicious Jewish traits and thus was entitled to enjoy freedom from the restrictions which fell upon other Jews. Granted that the Jews were decadent, corrupt, and outrageously un-German, none of these attributes was indelible or absolutely fixed into the nature of German Jewish life. "The traces of two thousand years of suffering have been burned in too deeply to be washed away with eau de Cologne," he said, but with the Germanized elite leading the way, the Jewish masses could be brought fully into German life and society. Clearly Rathenau saw himself as a prime example of that leadership group.[127]

In some of his later essays and letters Rathenau again returned to touch on some of the themes first dealt with in *"Höre Israel."* In light of some of these later expressions, that first essay and Rathenau's own Jewish dilemma become more lucid. In one of his aphorisms, for example, Rathenau wrote:

The epitome of the history of the world, of the history of mankind, is the tragedy of the Aryan race. A blond and marvelous people arises in the North. In overflowing fertility it sends wave upon wave into the southern world. Each migration becomes a conquest, each conquest a source of character and civilization. But with the increasing population of the world the waves of the dark peoples flow ever nearer, the circle of mankind grows narrower. At last a triumph for the South: an oriental religion takes possession of the northern lands. They defend themselves by preserving the ancient ethic of courage. And finally the worst danger of all: industrial civilization gains control of the world, and with it arises the power of fear, of brains, of cunning, embodied in democracy and capital.[128]

Rathenau identified strongly with these beleaguered "blond and marvelous" Aryans. He admired Junker ideals and wished to make them his own, even to the point of buying and restoring an old Prussian castle at Freienwalde. He longed with what his biographer called "such passionate pathos" to become a part of that Ayran race which was his ideal, and he tried to carry out in his own life the program of conscious adaptation he had urged in *"Höre Israel."*[129]

Yet he failed to become a complete Aryan because he was, and could not cease being, a Jew. Almost twenty years after *"Höre Israel"* had been published, he wrote:

I have and recognize no other blood than German, no other *Stamm*, no other *Volk* than German. Were I to be driven from my German soil, still I would remain German and nothing would be changed.

You speak of my blood and *Stamm*, even once of my *Volk*, meaning the Jews. The only things that bind me to them are those which bind every German to them: the Bible, the memory and the figures of the Old and New Testaments.

My ancestors and I have been nourished by German soil and German *Geist*. . . . My father and I have no ideas which were not for Germany and were not German; as far [back] as I can follow my family tree it was the same.

I have remained in the Jewish religious community because I do not wish to evade any reproach or hardship, and I have experienced both down to the present day. Never has an insult of this sort made me indignant. Never have I repaid my *Volk,* the German *Volk,* with a word or a thought of that sort. My *Volk* and each of my friends has the right and the duty to reprimand me wherever he finds me inadequate.[130]

Rathenau remained a Jew, a fact that he never forgot nor allowed others to forget. He continued to be haunted by the awareness that he was destined to be one of a dark, timid race living amidst the fair and courageous Aryans. "In the youth of every German Jew there comes a moment which he remembers with pain as long as he lives: when he becomes for the first time fully conscious of the fact that he has entered the world as a citizen of the second class, and that no amount of ability or merit can rid him of this status."[131] That moment had seared Rathenau's consciousness and left him for life a torn and divided soul. Having accepted the values and prejudices of German culture, including the dominant German aversion to Jews and Jewishness, Rathenau remained a Jew, always hating that part of himself which Germany had taught him to hate. Hating it, but unable to excise it from his being.

Although both Weisler and Rathenau urged a solution to the Jewish question on the basis of total Germanization, their concepts of what that would entail were quite different. Weisler, expressing the position of non-Jewish German liberalism, advocated conversion as an instrument of acculturation, a proposal from pre-emancipation times which, as we have seen, had long been prominent in discussions of Jewish integration. But Rathenau had accepted the ideas and images of contemporary völkisch thought, a pattern of thinking which had become fashionable after the emancipation.[132] Reflecting the secularization of the Jewish question which had proceeded apace through the past century, Rathenau cast his discussion in a thoroughly modern form, one in which the question of religious belief or disbelief had become largely irrelevant. Hence he dismissed conversion as an unworkable tactic and demanded that Germanization be accomplished through deliberate, self-conscious Jewish adaptation to the ideal standards of Ayran culture. Germanization was to be effected only by means of the laborious work of re-education needed to strip an alien people of all vestiges of its "south-eastern" ways. Rathenau's vision of the ideal Germany was not, like Weisler's, a restatement of the liberal *Einheitskultur* but the modern dream of a völkisch community in which Jews could qualify for participation only by sacrificing their offensive Jewishness and being transfigured into new beings.

Moreover, it is significant that both Weisler and Rathenau, the Jewish spokesmen for German liberalism and the völkisch ideology, defined their solutions to the Jewish question in terms which made it impossible for them to carry out in their own lives what they demanded of others. Weisler (by refusing to be converted) and Rathenau (by asserting himself to be one of the elite which, through self-sacrifice, postpones salvation of self in order to save others) preserved that very Jewish identity which they believed had to be abandoned in order to become fully German. Out of their own *Zerrissenheit*, their inner confusion and self-hate, they had created visions of a future in which others of Jewish descent might be spared the conflict they had known and be at home in their beloved Germany in a way that would never be granted to them.

Jewish liberals who supported the Centralverein came largely from the same highly acculturated groups in the Jewish community who were addressed by Weisler and Rathenau. Their acceptance of the anti-Semitic evaluation of Jewish behavioral traits and their concession that these characteristics provoked an aversion to Jews among the general population reveal the degree to which German cultural images had been incorporated into their thinking as well. They agreed with the radical critics of Jewish life that there was a need for further Germanization of Jewry, but their call for more acculturation, expressed in the slogans "inner mission" and "elevation" of Jewish behavior, was bound up with their commitment to the emancipation ideology and its fundamental assumption that adoption of German identity did not require extinction of *all* Jewishness. Thus, although the Centralverein was intensely integratory, it was never "assimilationist" in the sense in which that term can justly be used to describe Weisler and Rathenau; it defended the possibility of continued Jewish existence in Germany and rejected the claim that acculturation had to eventuate in Jewish self-obliteration. To sustain this argument, adherents of the emancipation ideology had already developed a critique of the concept of Germany as an *Einheitskultur* (see p. 76), but Rathenau's call for Germanization had been based on an appeal to the völkisch ideology, a more recent doctrine which demanded and received a special response from the Jewish liberals.

The dominant Jewish attitude toward völkisch and racial thought was negative. Jewish leaders generally recognized the danger to the Jewish position in such doctrines, and they denied the claims that the Jews were a race and that racial or völkisch criteria were the basis for German identity.[133] Thus arguing against the alleged Aryan character of Germanness, Eugen Fuchs maintained that "to be a German, the form of the skull, the color of the hair, the line of the nose and the size of the body are not decisive, but the energetically active will."[134] Special emphasis was placed on the mixed racial makeup of both Jews and Germans, from which it was concluded that racial essence could not possibly be a basis for national identity.[135] As the *Jüdische Presse* asserted, concisely summarizing the position of the adherents of the emancipation ideology, "The Jews are not a race, [and] moreover, one in general really does not know what a race is."[136] And it also observed, in another context, "The concept of *race* belongs to the most dangerous slogans of our time."[137]

Yet precisely this "dangerous" concept was used occasionally by Jewish liberals in their discussions of the nature of Jewishness, with, however, one important proviso: they never drew the conclusion that the racial character of the Jews doomed them to be outsiders in Germany, and on occasion it was even argued that the Jewish racial nature facilitated Jewish integration. Noting the prevalence of "Germanic" characteristics among German Jews (blonde hair, blue eyes), one writer in the *Allgemeine Zeitung des Judenthums* argued that as a result of intermarriage with the Aryan Hittites in antiquity the Jews had become a mixed race with strong Indo-Germanic blood features. Since the Jews already had a substantial component of Aryan blood, it followed "that also according to descent the Jews in no way stand so far from the Germanic tribe as it appeared earlier, that also a drop of Indo-Germanic blood flows in their arteries, just as they have long become *one* in heart and feeling with the great German *Volk*."[138] Similarly, another writer argued that Aaron and Moses were to be identified with Aryan national gods, and that therefore the Jews should not be considered by the European world as a foreign element but as the *"unmixed continuation of the ethnic elements"* united in the European nations.[139] Rather deftly turning the racial argument against the anti-Semites, these liberal Jews implied that the Jewish racial nature, partially rooted as it was in the Aryan race, made the emancipation "scientific" and "natural," an expression of the fundamental racial affinity of Jews and Germans.

Such Jewish racialism was, however, the exception rather than the rule in liberal circles, where there was a clear awareness that völkisch and racial concepts were among the most important and most ominous weapons in the arsenal of modern anti-Semitism. The appearance of such ideas among defenders of the emancipation ideology is testimony to the pervasive influence and appeal of the völkisch ideology in Germany at that time, although it is interesting to see that even when used by Jewish liberals, these concepts were subordinated to and made to serve their basic commitment to integration. That commitment was most often expressed in a rather different definition of Jewish identity than that of racialism, the definition set down in the name of the

Centralverein deutscher Staatsbürger jüdischen Glaubens—
Jewishness as a matter of religious faith.

The emancipation law of July 3, 1869, had declared: "All existing
limitations on civil rights and the rights of citizens which derive from
differences of religious confession are hereby abolished."[140] By emphasizing "Jewish faith" as the basis of Jewish identity, the Centralverein was expressing itself in accordance with the category by
which established German law understood and defined the Jews,[141]
and the leadership of the organization frequently emphasized the
exclusively religious nature of being a Jew. Hence, in an 1897 attack on
Zionism and its claim that the Jews were a nation, Eugen Fuchs
summarized the basic position of the Centralverein vis-à-vis Jewish
nationalism and Jewish identity:

A strengthening of Jewish *Volk*-feeling and *Volk*-consciousness is incom-
prehensible to me, for I do not know of a Jewish *Volk* and a Jewish national
principle since the destruction of the Jewish kingdom.

I know only a Jewish community of faith [*Glaubensgemeinschaft*] and want only
that the *loyalty to the community of faith* will be strengthened without detriment
to the loyalty to the fatherland.

According to nationality, that is, according to speech, education, upbringing,
manner of thinking, sensitivity, hatred and love; according to birth; in short,
according to my physical and spiritual individuality I am German. Only the
community of faith to which I belong is Jewish.[142]

Yet this emphasis on exclusively religious identity was not readily
reconcilable with the undeniable fact that for centuries, and even in the
late nineteenth century, Jewishness had meant something more than
religious faith and cultic practices. Many who were Jews professed
religious principles, if they did so at all, which were indistinguishable
from those of many non-Jews; moreover, there was a sense of
relatedness and cohesiveness among Jews which seemed to extend
beyond the lines drawn by religious factions, uniting Orthodox and
Reform. Recognizing these factors, spokesmen for the Centralverein
and other liberal Jews occasionally articulated the view that Jewish
identity in Germany was not exclusively a matter of adherence to
Judaism, but also was defined by a consciousness of common descent
(*Abstammung*). Being Jewish was thus conceded to be more than a
question of membership in a religious community, but also less than
participation in a *Volk*.

In his classic lecture on the nature of German national identity, "*Was
heisst National?*", Moritz Lazarus had argued that as a result of

acculturation the Jews had become subjectively *Deutsche*. But, he added, "Only our *Abstammung* is not *deutsch;* we are not *Germanen;* we are Jews, therefore Semites. . . . Only through *Abstammung* are we distinguished from the other [*Deutsche*]."[143] The same view was expressed by the Centralverein in the last of a series of ten theses against anti-Semitism which it published in 1902: "No one will be rejected who has staked life and property, spiritual and moral possessions for the fatherland, be he Jew or Christian, of Aryan or Semitic *Abstammung*. Higher than everything stands the fatherland; the well-being of the fatherland, however, rests upon justice."[144] And this sense of common *Abstammung* among Jews, along with membership in a community of faith, it was agreed, created a bond with other Jews in foreign lands.[145]

Such were the nuances of Jewish identity defined by Jewish liberals to counterpose the formulations of Jewishness advanced by those at the farthest margins of the community (Zionists, radical assimilationists like Weisler and Rathenau) or those standing against it (anti-Semites). Yet never was Jewish identity defined by the Centralverein and those close to it in any way that would prevent the Jews from also being Germans. Whatever being a Jew meant, it did not mean membership in a peculiar nation or *Volk* or utterly alien race. The emancipation decree had declared that Jewish religious faith was compatible with German citizenship, and even when the liberals acknowledged that Jewishness went beyond religion and was a matter of *Abstammung* or of race, it was always within the context of the basic drive for permanent integration—without disappearance—into Germany.

The development of the defense campaign under the direction of the Centralverein had considerable impact on the emotions which came to infuse this framework of Jewish identity. Some Jews who supported the defense work, like the followers of Hirsch Hildesheimer, were already rather close to Jewish communal life and tradition, but many others experienced a return to the community through defense activities and found a way of overcoming at least some of their estrangement and alienation. Although critics caustically noted this suddenly rediscovered Jewishness and labelled it *Trutzjudenthum* (defiance Judaism), the establishment of the Centralverein created a vehicle through which many who were formerly distant from the Jewish community might rejoin Jewry and express in a positive manner, consistent with their deep German patriotism and their commitment to Enlightenment values, that sense of Jewish identity which had been provoked in them by the anti-Semitic attacks.[146] In a 1917 memorial speech for Maximilian Horwitz, chairman of the Centralverein, Eugen

Fuchs reflected on the way in which Jewry had become healthy through defense:

And so the Centralverein developed from purely negative defense activity to a positive revivification of Judaism. . . . To be proud of [one's] individuality, not to disavow the fathers because it is a higher nobility of the soul gladly to remember the fathers; not to disappear totally in the surrounding world; not to shut out the new, but [also] not to abandon the old; not to break with the hallowed customs of one's childhood home. Not assimilation but a renaissance of Judaism![147]

Fuchs noted that his own Jewishness was first brought to full consciousness by the anti-Semitic movement, and he, like the many others who came to the Centralverein from highly acculturated backgrounds, experienced through defense activity a greatly strengthened sense of group cohesiveness and self-assertiveness as a Jew.[148]

An important factor in building this positive sense of Jewish identity was the emphasis placed by the Centralverein on *Öffentlichkeit* (public self-defense), as opposed to quiet work behind the scenes like that carried on by the Committee. *Öffentlichkeit* had been designed principally as the tactic most appropriate for undermining the effect of public anti-Semitic agitation by creating a widely disseminated Jewish counter-argument to the previously unanswered and unchallenged propaganda. But *Öffentlichkeit* also had great impact on Jewish self-awareness in that it called upon those who supported or engaged in it to be willing to come forward publicly as Jews, speaking in behalf of Jewish and German interests. Moreover, because this public defense was explicitly Jewish and not conducted under the banner of general liberal politics or of non-denominational organizations, awareness of Jewish identity was further strengthened among the adherents of the Centralverein. In supporting the Centralverein, one made an act of self-avowal as a Jew, and there was a powerful surge of new-found Jewish pride among those who returned to their beleaguered Jewish community in its time of difficulty.[149]

It was believed that this sense of pride would now become the motive power for correcting those deficiencies in Jewish behavior which contributed to anti-Semitism. Moved by pride, not by the self-hatred so evident in Weisler and Rathenau, Jews would devotedly discipline themselves and elevate their behavior and that of their fellows. As one leader of the Centralverein declared in exhorting his listeners to support Jewish defense activities: "Every battle is resolved through a legion of individual battles. Let us be careful, each one for himself, that in these individual battles the individual soldier proves himself to be without blemish. In a kind of inner mission test carefully every intended action so that you will be mindful of the responsibility which arises from the unfortunate prejudice which burdens the defects of the individual on the shoulders of the group."[150] So Jews were called upon to be better than average morally,[151] and through their exemplary behavior enthusiastically to enter in the "competition for the crown of honor as the best citizens of the fatherland."[152] "More than others," Martin Mendelsohn wrote, the Jews "should avoid all that can in the remotest be interpreted as arrogant and unseemly."[153]

Thus, through unifying Jewry in self-defense, the leaders of the Centralverein sought not only to combat anti-Semitism but also to resolve the brooding ambivalence over Jewish identity which afflicted so many in that age. Acculturated Jews were enabled to rediscover their Jewishness positively, through self-affirmation, and to take a course quite different from that of Weisler and Rathenau and the hundreds who sought out conversion or other forms of Jewish self-denial. Yet even the Centralverein's resolution of the identity conflict brought something less than a sense of relaxed harmony and serenity with oneself. Instilled with pride as a Jew and German, one was required to be ever watchful and take great care to avoid all provocative behavior.[154] The "crown of honor" as best citizen of the fatherland was not granted to those unwilling to engage in strenuous effort.

THE FAILURE TO DRAW ORTHODOXY INTO A UNIFIED ORGANIZATION

At its inception the Centralverein had declared that one of its primary aims was the creation of an organization which would unify all German Jews in the struggle against anti-Semitism. In its first public proclamation, issued in the fall of 1893, the Centralverein had announced: "We summon all German citizens of Jewish faith to join our endeavors."[155] This declaration was more than a rhetorical flourish, for the program of establishing a public organ of Jewish self-defense to be a counterweight to anti-Semitism required broad support from the Jewish community. The Centralverein was designed as an interest group, like the Bund der Landwirte or one of the other similar organizations which proliferated in Germany in the late nineteenth century; and like these other bodies it proposed to unite, represent, and defend all who shared a common concern, namely, defense against anti-Semitism, the movement which had attacked indiscriminately the position of all Jews in the Reich.[156] Thus the Centralverein hoped to bring into being a unified structure in which all Jews, regardless of their political or religious commitments, might unite in self-defense. As Curt Pariser declared: "In the battle for our rights, we Jews must first of all form the central phalanx; we must organize ourselves around a firm central point, such as the Centralverein forms, for only in solidarity is there a chance of success."[157] The Centralverein was to be, Eugen Fuchs hoped, "a corporative union of all Jews," including "not a small number of notables but *the whole of Jewry*."[158]

Yet the Jewry to which this appeal for unity was addressed had long been divided into several distinct factions. Since the earliest period of the struggle for emancipation, disunity had been the established pattern of Jewish communal life. Notwithstanding the general agreement among German Jewry that their future was indissolubly linked to the *Rechtstaat* and German Kultur, the community was severely divided between those whose interest in Jewish affairs was nominal or almost non-existent, and those who identified more closely with Judaism. Among the latter, moreover, there were deep schisms between Reform, Conservative and Orthodox elements. In addition, and mirroring conditions in Germany as a whole, which had only recently achieved political unification, there were persisting regional divisions and local loyalties which sustained in some areas a suspicion of efforts at centralization.[159] Amidst such highly diversified and often antagonistic factions and interests, the Centralverein faced formidable obstacles in trying to realize its goal of establishing a unified organization. Only the powerful threat of anti-Semitism, the Centralverein hoped, might provide an impetus that would bring these disparate components together for the first time.[160]

As we have seen, a good deal of the appeal of the Centralverein's call for self-defense was directed to those highly acculturated Jews who, under the impact of anti-Semitism, had experienced an awakening of Jewish self-consciousness. Despite its claims to non-partisanship in religious matters, the Centralverein was clearly recognized as an expression of the least traditional elements within German Jewry, a coloration which enhanced its prospects for enlisting support among that broad mass of Jews who had felt, and in many cases continued to feel, little impulse to engage in Jewish self-defense. Many of the arguments advanced by the Centralverein in justification of defense and in condemnation of passivity were addressed to those who had the most highly attenuated sense of Jewish identity. They were, in effect, appeals from one wing of acculturated Jewry to another even more acculturated faction. The Centralverein did have a good measure of success in these efforts and ultimately the major part of liberal Jewry gave it full support.[161]

But a truly unified Jewish front for self-defense would also have had to include not only those standing to the left of the Centralverein, but also those to its right, and in particular the ranks of German *Sonderorthodoxie* (separatist Orthodoxy). German *Sonderorthodoxie* (also referred to as *Austrittsorthodoxie,* secessionist Orthodoxy) was a religious movement founded by Rabbi Samson Raphael Hirsch (1808-1888). In 1851 Hirsch had agreed to be the rabbinical leader of a group of Orthodox Jews in Frankfurt-am-Main who were struggling to break away from the Reform-dominated Jewish community and achieve sufficient independence to determine their own religious policies without the interference of the non-Orthodox. Later, with the help of Rabbi Azriel Hildesheimer (1820-1899), Hirsch convinced the liberal parliamentarian Eduard Lasker to introduce legislation permitting the Orthodox to establish separate institutions beyond the authority of the established communities with their Reform leadership. Although opposed vigorously by the Reformers who wished to preserve communal unity, the legislation was passed in 1876, and subsequently separatist congregations were established in four cities, including Frankfurt, where Hirsch served, and Berlin, where Hildesheimer led the *Adass Jisroel* community and established a rabbinical seminary.

In formulating the ideology of the movement, Hirsch made it clear that he was not advocating a return to the ghetto. Under the slogan *"Torah im derech eretz"* (loosely translated, tradition together with secular culture), Hirsch attempted to create the ideological and institutional basis on which one could be a "Torah-true" Jew, faithfully observing all the commandments of the traditional system and, at the same time, a full citizen of the state and a participant in its culture. [162] A gifted writer and apologist, Hirsch led the Orthodox response to the Reformers by helping to create and rationalize a life-style that was cultured, modern, German, and also highly traditional with regard to Judaism. That life-style became the model of German Jewish identity for thousands of Orthodox Jews in the Reich, especially in South Germany. It was preached and defended in the pages of *Der Israelit,* a weekly founded by Hirsch at Mainz in 1860.

At his Berlin seminary, Azriel Hildesheimer carried the program of *Sonderorthodoxie* into the training of those who were to become rabbis for the separatist communities. A thorough education in traditional rabbinic studies was combined with modern academic disciplines. Defining the philosophy of the seminary, Hildesheimer advocated "unconditional agreement with the culture of the present day; harmony between Judaism and science; but also unconditional steadfastness in the faith and traditions of Judaism. . . ."[163] Unlike Hirsch, however, Hildesheimer did not carry the principle of separation to the point of breaking off all relations with the larger Jewish community, and he insisted on continuing active participation in its affairs. Hence his son and deputy, Rabbi Hirsch Hildesheimer (1855-1910) served as a member of the Committee and was active with non-Orthodox Jews in Ezra, an organization which promoted Jewish colonization in Palestine. Moreover, general Jewish affairs were discussed regularly in the pages of the weekly journal *Die Jüdische Presse,* co-edited by father and son.[164]

With the resurgence of anti-Semitic agitation in the early 1890s, Orthodox spokesmen at first joined in the growing chorus calling for active Jewish self-defense. In words and tones similar to those of other Jewish publications, *Der Israelit* called for "Germans of Jewish faith" to take the initiative in founding organizations to spread *"aufklärende Schriften."* Such writings, it said, must be distributed free of charge in hundreds of thousands of copies throughout the German masses. Funds must be collected for this purpose, and orators sent out to conduct counter-agitation against the anti-Semitic rabble-rousers. "Every attack against our people and our parentage must be refuted in a serious, scientific manner," *Der Israelit* urged. *"Sich wehren, bringt Ehren"* ("defending oneself brings honor") it reminded its readers, and declared: "Arise, Israel, to battle."[165] And in March 1893, *Der Israelit* used a Purim discourse to issue a warning against Jewish passivity in the face of the rapidly growing threat. Asserting that "the word is a power" for enlightenment, it urged Jews to spread the truth about Judaism, even as Esther had centuries before.[166] When the anti-Semitic parties had surged to victory in the elections of the early summer of 1893, *Der Israelit* castigated the Jews for relying too heavily on the activity of their Christian friends in defense work. Such outside help was always welcome, it said, but "in the essential matter we must rely upon our own strength."[167]

In the early 1890s, therefore, the Orthodox appeared ready to join with other groups in the Jewish community in carrying out concerted, organized self-defense. At that time cooperation with the non-Orthodox in such a matter of common interest seemed possible, and the proposals for action offered by *Der Israelit* were identical to those being urged by liberal Jews. These possibilities, however, were effectively destroyed by the publication of Raphael Löwenfeld's *Schutzjuden oder Staatsbürger,* with its call for liberal Jewry to disassociate itself publicly from the Orthodox. Löwenfeld's attack evoked some enthusiasm among his liberal readers, such as one in Dessau who praised the pamphlet for preparing the way for a separation of the "thinking German Jews from ossified Orthodox, international Judaism which no longer has a right to exist."[168] Its reception in Orthodox circles, of course, was radically different.

Rahel Straus, a niece of Löwenfeld, was a young girl at the time living with her Orthodox parents. She recalls that when the pamphlet by her uncle arrived, "Mother locked [it] away so that it might not fall into the hands of the children. She found it to be so un-Jewish and so totally opposed to that which she wanted and hoped for the Jewish people."[169] The response in her home was moderate compared to the outraged reaction of the Orthodox press. In a scathing lead article, the *Jüdische Presse* charged Löwenfeld with betraying the growing sense of Jewish solidarity evoked by the anti-Semitic movement. The extent of his betrayal was demonstrated by comparing citations from Löwenfeld's pamphlet with passages from a speech by Stöcker and pointing out the close similarity between the two. It charged that Löwenfeld's call for an end to all association by liberals with the Orthodox who, in Löwenfeld's words, "have understood neither the spirit of the time nor our position in the state," was tantamount to unleashing the full force of the anti-Semitic mob on the Jewish traditionalists.[170]

When the Centralverein was organized a few months after Löwenfeld's pamphlet appeared and declared its goal of becoming a united organization in which all Jews, regardless of religious belief, might join, it faced the difficult task of winning to its ranks those Orthodox who had been so deeply wounded by *Schutzjuden oder Staatsbürger*. On the one hand, the Centralverein openly recognized that the publication of that work had been the initial impulse for its formation as a Jewish defense organization, but on the other hand, the Centralverein could not possibly hope to become the voice of a united German Jewry so long as it was identified so clearly with Löwenfeld's stringent anti-Orthodoxy. To resolve the dilemma, the Centralverein tried to disassociate itself from the remarks critical of Orthodoxy in the body of the pamphlet and to claim that the six theses with which Löwenfeld concluded his work were an effective basis on which all Jews could agree. Martin Mendelsohn attempted precisely this strategy in his report as presiding officer at the first annual meeting of the Centralverein in Berlin in 1894, and a year later Eugen Fuchs took up the same theme, declaring that "though the contents of [Löwenfeld's] writing divided, the theses united." He argued that since religious and political matters are questions to be decided by individuals alone, it was irrelevant to the Centralverein what one's position might be with regard to Orthodoxy or Reform. The Centralverein, he said, embraced all Jews, no matter what religious leanings they might have. Just as in defending a fatherland against a foreign enemy there should be no differences between political parties, so too all Jews, whether Orthodox or Reform, must stand together against the anti-Semites.[171]

Going beyond these declarations, the Centralverein attempted to demonstrate its rejection of Löwenfeld's anti-Orthodoxy more concretely by identifying with the traditionalists on those issues which were of greatest concern to their faction, namely, the anti-Semitic attacks on the Talmud and the campaign against ritual slaughter (*shechita*). The Talmud had long been a favorite target of the anti-Semites, and from among its great wealth of diverse teachings, enemies of the Jews since the middle ages had extracted citations to show the alleged perniciousness of rabbinic teachings. The campaign to outlaw ritual slaughter, however, was of more recent origin, as anti-Semites, first in the 1880s and then with greater intensity in the 1890s, pressed efforts to convince legislators and the public that *shechita* was inhumane and an example of inveterate Jewish cruelty to the weak.[172]

Jews who did not accept Talmudic teachings or laws as authoritative and who did not observe the dietary laws had no personal stake in either of these issues, and the Centralverein could probably have followed Löwenfeld's demand for a clear declaration of non-concern without alienating its liberal membership. Yet the Centralverein actively supported the Orthodox in these matters and thereby gave what it hoped would be convincing proof that it was genuinely nonpartisan on religious questions and prepared to defend all Jews from attack. Hence, in his first report on the work of the *Rechtsschutzkommission* in 1894, Eugen Fuchs stated: "Whether the individual Jew is Orthodox or *freireligiös*, whether he is a Caftan-Jew or a Reform Jew—a common danger threatens all. One must not believe that when the Jews are threatened in their civil status because of the Talmud only those who believe in the Talmud are called upon for defense and that one only needs to abandon the Talmud in order to be recognized as a member of civil society with equal rights. . . ."[173] In response to the attack on *shechita*, the Centralverein instigated the publication of a collection of scientific opinions from physicians and veterinarians defending the sanitary and humane basis of Jewish ritual slaughter.[174] It called for Jewish solidarity in resisting anti-Semitism which masqueraded as a concern with the protection of animals. Free-thinking Jews were warned that by cooperating with the *Tierschutzvereine* (Animal Protection Leagues) and supporting so-called "humane" slaughter legislation, they would be allowing themselves to be used by the enemies of the Jews in their attack on the religious liberty of the Orthodox.[175]

The Centralverein's repudiation of Löwenfeld's separatism and its activity in issues of greatest immediate concern to the Orthodox were effective in winning the cooperation of some of the traditionalists, and the Hildesheimers did give support to the new organization. Hirsch Hildesheimer, in particular, collaborated with the Centralverein on the *shechita* issue,[176] and the *Jüdische Presse* occasionally reprinted statements or speeches by Centralverein leaders, thus giving a clear measure of endorsement to the opinions and activity of the group.[177] Moreover, in major features, the approach of the *Jüdische Presse* to anti-Semitism and *Abwehr* was essentially the same as that advocated by the Centralverein, and a specifically Orthodox analysis, built upon traditional religious principles, was never offered. The importance of defending the Jewish position in the *Rechtsstaat* through open, courageous defense; confidence in the ultimate triumph of right and justice; fervent devotion to the German fatherland and to the Kaiser; rejection of all radical solutions to the Jewish question, whether through mass emigration, Social Democracy, or political Zionism—in advocating all these positions the *Jüdische Presse* demonstrated its endorsement of the emancipation ideology as articulated by the Centralverein.[178]

Yet in winning the cooperation of the Hildesheimers, the Centralverein had hardly achieved a major victory in the struggle to create a unified organization. The Hildesheimers had long evinced their willingness to participate in general communal affairs with non-Orthodox Jews. Their support of the Centralverein despite the affront of the Löwenfeld pamphlet was an expression of their pre-established readiness to join in ventures of common interest with other groups within Jewry. The less moderate Orthodox, who expressed their views through *Der Israelit*, however, remained hostile and, like the Hildesheimers, continued to maintain a position who had long been held by them. The hope of the Centralverein that the threat of anti-Semitism had so altered conditions in the Jewish community that universal cooperation would be possible for the first time proved false.[179] From the point of view of the ultra-Orthodox, modern anti-Semitism had changed nothing with regard to the circumstances within Jewry. And just as the new anti-Semitism had evoked from the Centralverein no new ideological positions but only a restatement of the emancipation ideology, so too did the group gathered around *Der Israelit* now enunciate once again their long-established ideas and interpret the latest developments in terms of their traditional views.

For *Der Israelit*, the Centralverein was indelibly tainted by virtue of its association with the Löwenfeld publication. Shortly after the founding of the Centralverein, for example, Dr. Eduard Biberfeld, a rabbi in Karlsruhe, greeted the new organization with a lead article sarcastically entitled: "The Organization with the Long Name." Alluding to *Schutzjuden oder Staatsbürger*, he argued that those who were interested in gathering together all forces for defense against anti-Semitism should have assiduously avoided any connection with a work which expressed such a hatred of traditional Judaism. The Centralverein, however, had not disavowed the pamphlet, and for this reason, Biberfeld argued, no Orthodox Jew could support its activity. Noting that the new organization had established a *Rechtsschutzbüro* (Legal Protection Bureau) to assist Jews who had been injured because of their Judaism, he reprinted the text of a letter he had sent to the bureau asking their assistance in defense against Löwenfeld's pamphlet. "I consider myself, as a Jew—and my Judaism—injured by [this] writing," Biberfeld declared in his letter, quoting as proof several offensive passages from the pamphlet. The bureau did not answer, and for Biberfeld this silence was sufficiently eloquent. "Let us not," he concluded, "disturb their circle in the future."[180]

During the years that followed, *Der Israelit* repeatedly attacked the Centralverein and its publications. It charged the Centralverein with following an "assimilationist" policy and declared that when people "who, factually, in their entire lives, stand outside of Judaism" found a Jewish organization, very little useful but "much that is perverted and dangerous" will result.[181] Although the leaders of the Centralverein pleaded for Jewish unity under their auspices, *Der Israelit* found them so far removed from "true and genuine Judaism" that they had no notion of the enormous abyss between them and the traditionalists.[182] As one writer put it, "One could repair a leaky ship with sticking plaster more easily than one could heal this rupture with theses."[183]

The tactical operations of the Centralverein in defense work came under close scrutiny, and *Der Israelit* charged them with harming Jewish public relations through tactless defense. When an official of the Centralverein pilfered a songbook from an inn and then became involved in a losing law suit with the innkeeper, *Der Israelit* took the Centralverein to task for devoting all its energies to petty insults while great monstrosities went unchallenged. And on another occasion in which the Centralverein had published remarks contrasting Jewish theology with Christian, *Der Israelit* commented that such tactics, like those of the anti-Semites, were provocations creating friction between religions.[184]

The very best that *Der Israelit* could say about the Centralverein's tactics was that, when they were not destructive, they were useless and without any effect whatsoever. "Does [the Centralverein] believe that with its weapons—law suits and literature—even one anti-Semite has been converted or that even *one* anti-Semite has been influenced toward enlightenment? No matter how great its faith in itself, [the Centralverein] does not believe this."[185] Moreover, the Centralverein's claim that it was able to increase Jewish self-respect and positive self-consciousness through its propaganda activities was dismissed as purely rhetorical. From a tactical point of view, the operation of the entire organization was "completely mistaken."[186]

Der Israelit criticized the underlying philosophy of the Centralverein as well as its tactics. Whereas the Centralverein claimed that circumstances in Germany demanded an active Jewish self-defense organization working in full public view, the Orthodox argued that accepting such a platform was bound to bring about increased isolation between Jews and Christians and, ironically, would lead to geographical concentrations of Jews and ultimately the reinstitution of the ghetto.[187] Similarly the ideology of the Centralverein necessarily implied a narrowness of political vision; rather than having a "grand national point of view," the Centralverein demanded that things be seen from the highly limited vantage point of a "tiny bundle of Jews [who] become the middlepoint and fulcrum of public influence." The Orthodox, who had been accused by Jewish liberals of resisting assimilation to German life, now leveled the same charge at the Centralverein:

Instead of battling shoulder to shoulder with all champions of the great liberal idea of the equality of all before the law, and thus giving practical proof of national assimilation in political affairs . . . through the [Centralverein's] action the participation of Jewish fellow-citizens in political processes and the judging of these from a general point of view is paralyzed and hindered. Moreover, at the same time, a manner of thinking is cultivated which applies a selfish criterion to all questions of public life: Is it helpful to our Jewish fellow-citizens? Or, put more mildly: Does it injure our opponents, the anti-Semites? But the only correct point of view is that which measures political processes with the criterion of the *salus publica* and not with that of the *salus judaica*.[188]

Hence, *Der Israelit* concluded, anyone who is animated by a "modern spirit" will avoid all affiliation with that *"Sonderbündelei* [little separatist pack]."

In contrast to this consistently hostile attitude toward the Centralverein, the Orthodox spokesmen welcomed the activities of the Christian defense organization, the Verein zur Abwehr des Antisemitismus. While *Der Israelit* generally ignored the Centralverein's activities, except to attack them, it reported favorably and at length on the proceedings and publications of the Verein.[189] The Centralverein was depicted as a *Denunziantenverein*, rashly and thoughtlessly thrashing about against the anti-Semites, but the Christian leadership of the Verein judged affairs, *Der Israelit* reported, with "wider vision and greater tact" and was not committed to the foolish policy of acting in the public view. Therefore the Verein constituted the "only proper and effective organization" for fighting anti-Semitism. Through its very

existence the Centralverein hampered the activities of these "unpreju-
diced Christian fellow-citizens [who fight] devotedly for the equality of
all citizens of the state."[190]

Although hostile to the Centralverein, the ultra-Orthodox did not
reject the emancipation ideology. Like their less traditionalist
coreligionists, they affirmed, without serious qualification, the importance of German citizenship and patriotism and the possibility of
retaining Jewish identity within German state and society. Orthodox
Jews, however, had a special understanding of what Jewish identity
entailed. For them, as for their ancestors in pre-emancipation times, to
be a Jew meant to live under the yoke of the covenant. To be a Jew
meant to observe faithfully all the *mitzvot* implied in that covenant,
both ritual and ethical, as defined authoritatively in the developed
rabbinic tradition. To be a Jew meant loyalty to the commandments of
the God of Israel no matter what the concrete circumstances of daily
life.

The Orthodox believed that Israel's loyalty to the covenant would
not be unrewarded. The all-powerful Master of the Universe faithfully
repays goodness and relentlessly punishes laxity and sinfulness. He
moves men and nations through history, guiding them and their
actions for His divine purposes. No disaster or misfortune is fortui-
tous. Although He sometimes seems to work in strange and terrible
ways that are difficult for men to comprehend, everything is designed
to fulfill His plan for mankind. Moreover, since the Jewish people has a
special role to play in realizing that plan, God is particularly watchful of
Israel and highly sensitive to every act of disobedience or faithlessness
on her part. Whenever a calamity befalls Israel, therefore, it is not a
sign that God has abandoned His chosen people or that the forces of
evil have conquered. It is rather one more proof that God loves His
people and, like a father chastening his beloved child, is punishing
Israel in order to bring the Jews back to their special responsibilities for
fulfilling the Torah.

Although all Jewish traditionalists shared these religious presuppositions, only the group gathered about *Der Israelit* developed the
premises of Orthodox Judaism into a pattern of response to anti-
Semitism distinct from that offered by the liberal Jewish community.
While the Hildesheimers' high degree of involvement with the broad
Jewish community allowed them little latitude for expressing a specifically Orthodox approach to anti-Semitism, the ultra-Orthodox
were under no such organizational or ideological constraints. As a
result they could articulate an analysis of the meaning of anti-Semitism
and offer a tactic for combatting it which diverged widely from those of
liberal Jewry. Using the concepts of traditional Judaism as their

intellectual weapons, they forged a unique reaction to anti-Semitism, one that enriched the spectrum of German Jewish responses.

For a number of decades *Sonderorthodoxie* had devoted much of its energy to a running battle with Reform Judaism, a movement which it believed responsible for the growing laxity in religious observance. During this period of intense polemics, the Orthodox identified the Reformers as their chief enemy; whatever the external enemeies of Israel might do, the Reformers bore a special guilt for undermining the traditions of Judaism from within. When anti-Semitism emerged as a factor in German-Jewish affairs, therefore, the new movement was interpreted in terms of what had now become a long-established anti-Reform stance within Orthodoxy.

In 1894, for example, *Der Israelit* carried a lead article entitled "Antisemitism; a Beneficial Necessity for Judaism." The article asserted that the leaders of the anti-Semitic movement from Stöcker through Ahlwardt were all actually "tools in the hand of the Creator," implements used by God to bring Israel back to the Torah. The great unbelief and religious indifference among Jews was the true cause of anti-Semitism, and anti-Semitism was actually *"ein göttliches Erziehungsmittel"* [an instrument of divine education] and an admonition from God to all Jews, showing them the need for returning to the synagogue and the Jewish school. When this return had taken place, anti-Semitism will have served its purpose and would wither away and disappear.[191]

Those most responsible for the betrayal of Israel's covenant with God were the Reformers. For a full half-century the Reformers had abandoned one tradition of Judaism after another, arguing that this was necessary in order to achieve full civil equality. The Reformers had reasoned that if the religious walls separating Jews from Germans were removed, then the Christians would hasten to tear down the political barriers that isolate Jews. But, *Der Israelit* observed, now that "everything has been so radically reformed that scarcely anything of the old Judaism is left intact, the anti-Semites cry out: 'Our struggle is against the Reform Jews, not the Orthodox.' " What clearer proof could there be that it was not the seclusiveness of the Orthodox but the importunity and obtrusiveness of the Reform Jew which the Christian resented? These efforts at acculturation through religious reform were thus now shown to have been erroneous.[192]

When the *Allgemeine Zeitung des Judenthums* issued a plea for Jewish unity and an end to the feuding between religious factions within Jewry until the common, external foe had been dealt with, *Der Israelit* responded angrily:

We are of the firm, unshakable opinion that all the Stöckers and *Kreuzzeitungen* in the world are not as great a misfortune for us as our own covenant-betraying Jewish brethren, who publicly trample the statutes of Judaism and call themselves Reform Jews. . . . *The existence of Reform Judaism in itself is a greater calamity for our holy Jewish cause than all the truths and lies taken together which anti-Semites serve up in their small local newspapers with their tiny circles of readers. . . .*[193]

If the Reformers now pleaded for Jewish unity in confronting anti-Semitism, it was only because they felt too weak to deal with the current crisis. As *Der Israelit* put it, "Reform Judaism is, at present, a toothless lion which cannot help but lose every battle, and which therefore preaches peace only until, he hopes, he will become strong again. But, as is well known, old lions cannot grow new teeth."[194]

Furthermore, *Der Israelit* argued, this was hypocritical. The Reformers alone bore responsibility for any schism in the Jewish community today. They, not the Orthodox, were the ones who had conducted a campaign against the holy law, who had preached lies from the pulpits and seized the leadership of communities in order to strip the *gesetzestreuen* Jews (those faithful to traditional Jewish law) of the possibility of fulfilling the commandments. The goal of the Reformers was the annihilation of Judaism. Therefore, in any area where specifically Jewish religious matters were touched upon, even to the slightest degree, there could be absolutely no cooperation with them.[195]

Some Orthodox spokesmen developed the interesting, but not fully convincing thesis that there was a special relationship between the abandonment of traditional Judaism and the rise of racial, nonreligious anti-Semitism. The old *Judenhass* was directed at the Jew because of his Judaism. To be hated because of one's religious convictions and then to suffer as a result of faithful adherence to ancestral traditions was to wear the glorious martyr's crown. Bearing such hatred was a highly honorable vocation, one whose honor was heightened because a way to escape was always open to the persecuted. With a few drops of baptismal water, the object of the hatred, Judaism, could be washed away and *Judenhass* ended.

Martyrdom on behalf of religion was one thing. "But to be hated because one has darker eyes and a nose formed in a somewhat different way from that of the normal Aryan nose—that is flatly intolerable." There was not enough baptismal water in existence to obliterate the fact of Jewish descent. This strange new type of Jew-hatred, the Orthodox argued, was the direct result of the efforts by Jews to reform traditional faith. Acting in the naive hope of disarming

Judenhass and turning enmity into friendship by abandoning their Jewish mission, the Reformers had made one concession after another to Christianity. So that the Christian visitor might not be offended by what he saw and heard in the old synagogue, the Reformers had created temples with organs, German prayers, insipid sermons, and even a catechism on the Christian model. And what had been achieved? "One can no longer take offense at our religion; so they fall back upon race and proclaim racial hatred." Hence it is clear that the Reform movement has "harmed us more than all the external enemies of the Jews taken together." By abandoning traditional Judaism and all its unique features, they have created the conditions under which *Rassenhass* could emerge as the successor to *Judenhass*. [196]

Granted their unique perspective about the origins and meaning of the anti-Semitic movement, what did the ultra-Orthodox suggest as a tactic of response? How did they propose to cope with the growing hostility which seemed to threaten the security and well-being of German Jewry? True to its traditionalism, *Der Israelit* was quite unconcerned about the social anti-Semitism which was the bane of less observant Jews. When *the Allgemeine Zeitung des Judenthums* published a lead article commenting on the sad phenomenon of anti-Semitism penetrating the summer resorts and cautioning its readers to exercise circumspection, a writer in *Der Israelit* responded with an editorial noting that he had never encountered anti-Semitic insults in some fifteen to twenty years of summer vacations. *"This is due,"* he argued, *"to the fact that I keep kosher. The only ones who will be insulted are those who do not keep kosher and who push their way to a Christian table d'hôte where they are not wanted."* Every Christian has the feeling that the Jew does not belong at his table, and he does not know what to do with a Jew who eats pork. What should be done in order to avoid the possibility of being insulted? *"Stay away* [from the non-kosher tables]. This will promote understanding . . . this is required by our God and His Law."[197]

Taking up the same theme, another commentator noted that the Orthodox are not the ones who are offended when *Frau Geheimer Registrator* or *Frau Geheime Commerzienräthin* announces that Jews are no longer welcome at her coffee parties, "because we have never forced our way into this society. We are not the ones who slink away, humiliated and indignant, from the *table d'hôte* of the Christian hotels when people move away from us. Because we have never sat ourselves down at such [a table]. . . ."[198] Hence the traditional life-style of the Orthodox made certain manifestations of anti-Semitism irrelevant to them, and the consternation of the non-kosher Jews at being rejected from Christian resorts and social circles only served to vindicate the

Orthodox. The Jew who forced his way into such places received what he deserved. The only sound defense against such discrimination was a return to observance of the traditional food laws.[199]

This attitude was expanded by some Orthodox spokesmen into an overall posture toward the whole anti-Semitic movement. They argued that since hatred of the Jews was a rod of chastisement called into being by God to punish His people for deviating from the Torah, then the only effective means of combatting anti-Semitism was to return to the Torah. Anti-Semitism revealed God's paradoxical way of working in the world. Through this instrumentality God tried to bring Israel back to an awareness of its true and proper vocation—the faithful observance of the Torah. "In the cultivation of the Torah and the fulfillment of its duties we find ample compensation for all that which an entire world so narrow-mindedly denies [us]." Hence, one observer concluded, anti-Semitism may have highly desirable effects: "Perhaps anti-Semitism constitutes a turning point for the better in the religious perceptions of our time."[200]

In the last analysis, the Orthodox argued, the Jew had no other means of self-preservation and salvation than "the loyal fulfillment of God's commandments and the formation of our entire life according to the norms which constitute the content of Judaism." The highest and only successful form of defense was a "complete and faithful return to our duties." Those who sought the sources of anti-Semitism in external circumstances, such as the complicated social and political conditions of the day, were self-deceived. The true source lay within the Jew who had been unfaithful to the law, and for this reason all the conventional defense activities—declarations, pamphlets, protests —were totally ineffective and without value. Once the disastrous results of Jewish apostasy from the Torah were recognized, the only effective responses to anti-Semitism were to become Jews once again in the traditional sense and to fight those Reformers within Jewry who lead the community away from its true vocation.[201]

Since a return to Torah-true Judaism was the only appropriate response to anti-Semitism, the ultra-Orthodox spokesmen argued that any frontal counterattack on the anti-Semites was a futile and misguided use of Jewish energies. "Whoever wishes to serve Judaism today," *Der Israelit* said, "must commit himself to it without reservation. [Judaism] is not served through protests and declarations. The significance of the printed word is exaggerated. . . ."[202] The copious self-defense literature was "without any value."[203] On the eve of the year 1893, the very year in which the anti-Semitic movement reached its apex, one writer expressing the official opinion of the editorial staff of *Der Israelit* asked: "Do we believe that our fathers and mothers in

Egypt could have alleviated their miserable fate in the slightest through protests, denials, asservations and similar means? Hatred of the Jew can be written out of existence by means of brochures, newspapers, and printed matter . . . about as effectively as [can] cholera."[204] Continuing in that mood of resignation mixed with ultimate optimism that characterized many of the Orthodox responses, he pointed out that God, and God alone, had the power to bring the Jews relief and liberation. "It is God Himself who has brought the suffering to us, and it is God Himself who has brought us healing and salvation at every time, and will bring it [this time]."[205] And Isaac Hirsch, writing of "Israel's Only Salvation," noted that the faithfully religious Jew need not fear the anti-Semitism of the day. Like his ancestors who experienced far more severe trials and punishments, he knows that God will rescue His chosen ones, even as He did at the time of Pharaoh, Sennacherib, Nebuchadnezzar, and Titus. Hence, Hirsch concluded, "we can look calmly at the attacks and threatening dangers."[206] When he is loyal to the Torah, the Jew is a creature of eternity, tied to a divine, unchangeable realm, and blessed, as a result, with a certain equanimity in the face of temporal hatred.[207]

CONCLUSION

Although *Sonderorthodoxie* went its own way in developing a response to anti-Semitism, the leadership of the Centralverein effectively articulated and organized the reaction of the major part of the liberally minded Jewish community. Under their guidance a vigorous restatement of the concepts which had long underwritten the course of Jewish integration into Germany was developed, and the emancipation ideology reached its most consummate form of expression. With energy and determination the leaders of the Centralverein used the ideas of the Enlightenment and of political liberalism to defend Jewry and Germany from the threat of anti-Semitism. Although fealty to the emancipation ideology set rather severe limits to their thinking and tactics, within these boundaries the beleaguered Jewish leadership did virtually all that could have been expected of them. With passion and rigor they defended the liberal values upon which they believed their fate and that of Germany depended; they carried out a defense program which, within the framework of the *Rechtsstaat*, effectively exploited the possibilities of legal and propagandistic self-defense; and they made valiant efforts to forge a united community in resistance to anti-Semitism.

Yet in those same decades when the emancipation ideology was so zealously defended by the organized Jewish community, another, very different form of response to anti-Semitism was offered by some elements within German Jewry who were convinced that Jewish nationalism offered the only adequate answer to the Jewish question. These early German Zionists were numerically insignificant, and during the period encompassed by this study they never amounted to more than a few handfuls of intellectuals, professionals, and university students. Nonetheless, the emergence of Zionism in Germany had great importance because it unleashed a radical challenge to the emancipation ideology from *within* German Jewry. Hence the Zionists' interpretations of anti-Semitism and their proposals for dealing with it demand special attention and rather extensive analysis, and we turn now to an examination of the structure of ideas by means of which they transmuted and eventually abandoned the emancipation ideology.

CHAPTER FOUR

First-Generation Zionists

Within the scope of this study it is neither necessary nor possible to present a full history of the Zionist movement in Germany.[1] Rather, our interest is limited to a consideration of Zionism as one of the most important ways in which German Jewry reacted to anti-Semitism. Zionism was not, of course, a purely reactive phenomenon, although Zionist leaders were confronted with this charge and sensitive to it.[2] And by concentrating on those aspects of Zionism which illuminate the response of Western Jewry to anti-Semitism, we in no way deny the importance of other factors in the emergence and articulation of modern Zionism, especially in Eastern Europe where the Jewish population was largely unintegrated into general society.

Accordingly, our discussion of German Zionism concentrates on three primary questions: (1) What was the attitude of the Zionist movement toward anti-Semitism, and what did it regard as the nature and cause of anti-Semitism? (2) How did Zionists define Jewish identity, and to what extent did that definition constitute a rejection of the emancipation ideology? (3) In light of its understanding of anti-Semitism and its definition of Jewish identity, what was the attitude of the Zionist movement toward defense activities in Western Europe, and what tactics did it consider most appropriate as a response to anti-Semitism?

These questions can best be answered by first considering the thought of several major Zionist figures and journals. In doing so, it will be seen that before World War I the challenge to the emancipation ideology initiated by the first-generation Zionists (Herzl and his closest associates, largely men born before 1870) grew to radical proportions among the second-generation Zionists (those largely born after 1870).

104

The lines between these two "generations" were by no means rigid or perfectly defined, and in many ways (e.g., exposure to university anti-Semitism) older and younger Zionists were shaped by similar experiences. However, once Herzl and those of his generation had broken with the liberal consensus, the way was clear for those of the next generation—mostly university youths who had grown to maturity under the impact of fully developed anti-Semitism—to move beyond the formulations of the older Zionists to extreme anti-liberal ideological positions. Finally, we shall analyze the nature of this anti-liberalism to see to what extent it constituted a disavowal of the long-established tradition of German Jewish liberalism.

In this analysis special attention is paid to the way in which German Zionists responded to the anti-Semitic assertion that the Jews were defined by a völkisch or racial essence which set them apart from "authentic" Germans. These völkisch and racial ideas constituted the quintessence of anti-liberalism, and by examining the attitude of Zionist thinkers to these concepts we will be able to gauge the extent to which the emancipation ideology was modified or deserted by Jewish nationalists in Germany. In doing so we will have occasion to note the confusion of terminology which reigned in these discussions as several important terms—*Volk, Rasse, Stamm*—were used interchangeably by some writers. This lack of clarity is hardly surprising, however, in light of the way in which these ideas were frequently used with imprecision not only by Zionists, but by German publicists, anti-Semites and, as we have seen, Jewish liberals.

As discussed earlier, the patterns of thought that had shaped the aspirations of the German Jewish community during the long struggle for emancipation in the nineteenth century had a tenacious hold on that community. The belief in human progress and man's essential rationality, the emphasis on universal truths and values, the abiding confidence in the power of law to effect peaceful change, and the dedication to the *Rechtsstaat*—all these tenets were still staunchly defended at the end of the century by the leading spokesmen for German Jewry. Nothing illustrates the grip of the emancipation ideology on German Jewry better than the way in which it continued to shape the thinking even of those who conducted the first thorough critique of the consensus ideology, namely the first generation of Zionist leaders in the West, exemplified by Theodor Herzl and several of his associates—Max Bodenheimer, Franz Oppenheimer and Nathan Birnbaum.

These men represent an identifiable type. All born before 1870, they received their early schooling before the emergence of modern, political anti-Semitism. They were a product of the hey-day of liberalism and came from the same social and cultural background as the leadership of the Centralverein. They were all bourgeois, steeped in German *Kultur*, trained to respectable professions, and prior to their Zionist activities, rather uninvolved in Jewish religious or communal affairs.[3] They all, however, rejected the dominant Jewish response to anti-Semitism and offered instead an analysis of anti-Semitism, a definition of Jewish identity, and a tactic for defense that were profoundly different from those of the established community. Nonetheless, the proposals of Herzl and his early co-workers perpetuated in a new configuration some of the most important elements of the very emancipation ideology that, in other essentials, they were rejecting.

THEODOR HERZL

In retrospect, the most remarkable feature of Theodor Herzl's childhood and education is that they were so unremarkable. Born into a middle-class household in Budapest in 1860, duly confirmed in a modernized temple at the age of thirteen, raised with all the accepted expectations and cultured habits of the Jewish bourgeoisie of the time—in all of this there is nothing unusual. His father was a successful merchant, and his mother, a dominant and persistent influence throughout his life, was a devotee of the German classics who consciously sought to instill the German cultural heritage in her children. She was especially ambitious for her son. She wanted him to be a model of German culture. In her dreams, as Ludwig Lewisohn has put it, "he was to transcend the Jewish street; he was to be a great man among the men of German speech and deed."[4] When young Theodor entered the university in Vienna to study law in 1878, he was following a pattern that marked the lives of thousands of his contemporaries as the talented offspring of the Jewish middle class flocked to the universities and then on to respectable professional careers.[5]

During these student years Herzl dealt with the Jewish problem for the first time. In February 1882 he read an account of the persecution of the Jews in the Middle Ages and was moved to write in his diary his first recorded thoughts on anti-Semitism. The enforced isolation of the Jews, he wrote, had "prevented the physiological improvement of their race through crossbreeding with others." And, he continued, "Basically the Jews have a different physical and mental physiognomy . . . because they interbred rarely with members of other nations. . . . Crossbreeding of the Occidental races with the so-called Oriental one on the basis of a common state religion—this is the desirable great solution."[6] This racial analysis and solution for the Jewish question was never developed in Herzl's later statements; it represents an early formulation in his understanding, one which he would reject completely in his mature thought. But the assumption that the Jewish problem would be solved by total disappearance of Jewish distinctiveness (here defined as racial in character) through assimilation (here achieved through intermarriage or "cross-breeding") was to remain an element in Herzl's plans for the future of the diaspora after the establishment of the Jewish state. Like the assimilationists Weisler and Rathenau, Herzl had already envisioned an end to Jewry in the West as the ultimate solution to the Jewish problem.

The day after he had made these notes Herzl read Eugen Dühring's *The Jewish Problem as a Problem of Race, Morals and Culture* (1881), the first attempt to establish a "scientific" basis for anti-Semitism. Dühring had argued for the reversal of the emancipation and the re-establishment of the ghetto, and as one biographer of Herzl notes: "The reading of this book must have had upon him the effect—approximately—of a blow between the eyes." Writing angrily in his diary, Herzl defended the Jews from Dühring's charges, and then concluded, "The centuries have brought no change into this Christian morality . . . but even these nursery tales of the Jewish people will disappear, and a new age will follow, in which a passionless and clear-headed humanity will look back upon our errors even as the enlightened men of our time will look back upon the middle ages."[7] In these terms, what Lewisohn calls "echo[ing] the babble of the enlightenment,"[8] Herzl confidently asserted the same position of many Jewish liberals at that time: modern anti-Semitism was only a reprehensible anachronism, a stunted throwback to an earlier and more ignorant age, and it would certainly be eliminated in the relentless march of humanity toward full enlightenment. For Herzl then, as for the bulk of German Jewry, anti-Semitism was only *"ein verschlepptes Stück Mittelalter"* (a misplaced piece of the Middle Ages) which would inevitably be repudiated by a mankind growing toward enlightenment.[9]

These early expressions by Herzl on the Jewish problem indicate clearly the high degree to which he accepted those attitudes which had wide currency among highly acculturated German Jews. In later years he recalled of this period: "At first, the Jewish Question grieved me bitterly. There might have been a time when I would have liked to get away from it—into the Christian fold, anywhere." Although he also asserted that "I have never seriously thought of becoming baptized or changing my name,"[10] Herzl's consideration of such steps as possible solutions for his personal Jewish problem testifies to an involvement with patterns of response which characterized the most highly assimilated sections of Jewry. He was then, Alex Bein has written, "so far from Judaism that only pride and a decent respect for the feelings of his parents stood between him and baptism."[11]

In the decade or so that followed the completion of his university studies Herzl practiced law for a time and then began to build a reputation as a playwright and journalist. Now and again he encountered personal anti-Semitic insults, and occasionally his reports as a correspondent for the *Neue Freie Presse* touched on some of the more dramatic anti-Semitic incidents and court trials of the time.[12] The emergence of the anti-Semitic political parties and their successes at the polls in France, Germany, and Austria moved him to renewed and deeper interest in the Jewish question. In the early 1890s, before Austrian political anti-Semitism and the Dreyfus case had sharpened his perceptions into the program outlined in *Der Judenstaat*, Herzl considered two possible courses of action which, he then believed, might be effective in checking or ending anti-Semitism: sophisticated defense and mass baptism of the Jews.[13]

In January of 1893 Herzl was approached by Regina Friedländer, the widow of the founder of the *Neue Freie Presse*, who asked him to cooperate with the Austrian *Verein zur Abwehr des Antisemitismus*. Herzl responded to her request by writing a critique of the organization and its program. He recommended duels to combat social anti-Semitism and suggested that only the complete disappearance of the Jews through baptism and inter-marriage could end the problem. Baron Friedrich Leitenberger, an industrialist and leader of the Verein, then wrote back to Herzl taking issue with his conclusions.[14]

Herzl's letter of January 26, 1893, responding to the Baron has been preserved and provides illuminating material on his thinking at that time. He argued that social anti-Semitism was not of major importance, and that it could be resolved in one of two ways: "(1) The fight with brutal force against the symptoms. Half a dozen duels would considerably elevate the social position of the Jews. (2) The curative process of the evil. The Jews must rid themselves of characteristics for which they are justly rebuked." Herzl then discussed the possibilities of efficacious defense against anti-Semitism. While bowing to the good intentions of the Baron and his co-workers, and conceding that, in principle, a social and economic elite could often influence public opinion in Austria, he argued that the efforts of the Verein zur Abwehr des Antisemitismus were too late and hence doomed to failure. The force of the anti-Semitic movement had grown far too strong for it to be stopped successfully by publishing appeals to reason and refuting slurs directed against the Jews. A decade earlier these activities might have had a profound impact in stemming the rise of the anti-Semitic movement, "but the time has long passed when it was possible to accomplish anything by polite and moderate means." Herzl concluded: "I am only certain that today it is too late for the type of fight against anti-Semitism which you conduct."[15]

Herzl did not categorically reject the possibility of any effective defense activities. Conceding reluctantly that a journalistic battle against anti-Semitism might be possible, Herzl sketched the outlines of the kind of newspaper that would be required: one with a large and established circulation which would then slowly and subtly be adapted to the purposes of defense and which would have absolutely no Jews on its editorial staff. Only such a journal would be capable of achieving results far beyond the capacities of the Baron's *Freie Blatt,* an ineffectual publication which "convinces only its subscribers, that is, people who were already convinced." He called the *Freie Blatt* "no newspaper, but a circular which does not circulate" and which accordingly hasn't "the slightest practical value."[16] Although Herzl had not yet formulated his Zionist program, his later attitude toward *Abwehr* was already fully articulated in this letter to Baron Leitenberger. His skepticism about futile public posturing which does not influence those it is supposed to reach hardened later in the decade and led Herzl to his consistent refusal to divert the energies of the Zionist movement into the defense activities favored by the consensus.[17]

In the same letter to Baron Leitenberger, Herzl suggested that only mass conversion to Christianity would put an end to anti-Semitism. In defending that suggestion he wrote:

My statement that the Jews should resort to conversion is half banter, half earnest. I can make such a statement because I will not become converted. But my son Hans? When I think about him, I do believe that the burden of Judaism will teach him the laws of humaneness. But I ask myself whether I have the right to make life unnecessarily difficult for him, as it was and will continue to be for me.

When he grows up, I hope he will be too proud to adjure his faith, although he will obviously have as little of it as I have.

Therefore Jewish boys should be converted at a very early age so that they can neither be for or against it. Submergence among the people.[18]

This thought later (1896) crystallized into a rather dramatic fantasy:

About two years ago I wanted to solve the Jewish Question, at least in Austria, with the help of the Catholic Church. I wished to gain access to the Pope . . . and say to him: Help us against the anti-Semites and I will start a great movement for the free and honorable conversion of Jews to Christianity.

Free and honorable by virtue of the fact that the leaders of this movement—myself in particular—would remain Jews and as such would propagate conversion to the faith of the majority. The conversion was to take place in broad daylight, Sundays at noon, in Saint Stephen's Cathedral, with festive processions and amidst the pealing of bells. Not in shame, as individuals have converted up to now, but with proud gestures. And because the Jewish leaders would remain Jews, escorting the people only to the threshold of the church and themselves staying outside, the whole performance was to be elevated by a touch of great candor.

We, the steadfast men, would have constituted the last generation. We would still have adhered to the faith of our fathers. But we would have made Christians of our young sons before they reached the age of independent decision, after which conversion looks like an act of cowardice or careerism. As is my custom, I had thought out the entire plan down to all its minute details. I could see myself dealing with the Archbishop of Vienna; in imagination I stood before the Pope—both of them were very sorry that I wished to do no more than remain part of the last generation of Jews—and send this slogan of mingling of the races flying across the world. [19]

Of course, this plan remained unfulfilled, and Herzl gave up the idea after discussing it with Moritz Benedikt, his chief at the *Neue Freie Presse*. [20]

By the mid-1890s then, Herzl had considered and rejected the major options available to German Jewry as responses to anti-Semitism. Neither a defense program nor the disappearance of the Jews through total assimilation by conversion were accepted by him as workable solutions to the Jewish question, although the fact that he even entertained the possibility of mass baptism shows that before becoming a Jewish nationalist Herzl did consider radical programs not sanctioned by the established Jewish community. The stringent defense he had grudgingly conceded to Baron Leitenberger as potentially workable was within the boundaries of consensus liberalism. Mass baptism, however, was not, and in rejecting that as a possibility Herzl groped toward some sort of plan that might bring a practical solution to the Jewish question. He offered that plan in *Der Judenstaat*, which was published on February 14, 1896.

In *Der Judenstaat* Herzl presented an analysis of the Jewish problem which was profoundly different from that accepted by the defenders of the emancipation ideology, and also from those ideas he had considered earlier. The essential feature of Herzl's argument was that anti-Semitism could not be understood simply as the product of agitators, as the result of religious prejudice, or as a vestigial holdover from medieval times. However much the Jewish liberals might defend them, none of these explanations was tenable. Modern anti-Semitism, he claimed, was a product of the emancipation. It was not an ephemeral phenomenon but a powerful social movement created by those very forces which had temporarily brought the Jews from the ghetto and moved them in the direction of integration into European society. "Modern anti-Semitism," he said, "is not to be confused with the persecution of the Jews in former times, though it does still have a religious aspect in some countries. The main current of Jew-hatred is today a different one. In the principal centers of anti-Semitism, it is an out-growth of the emancipation of the Jews."[21] Modern anti-Semitism, hence, was not a pre- but a post-emancipation force, due not to the failure of the emancipation to be consummated but rather to its great success.[22]

The emancipation of the Jews from the ghetto had brought not only civil liberation but also a new and dangerous involvement of Jews in the economic and political structure of Christian society. Having been shaped into a bourgeois people in the ghetto, the emancipation brought the Jews into direct competition and conflict with the gentile middle classes. Increased prosperity for the Jews had led to accelerated assimilation into general society and also to a growth in Christian envy and, ultimately, to hatred of the successful, assimilated Jew. When educated Jews reacted to anti-Semitism by turning to socialism, anti-Semitism was only increased; likewise, well-intentioned attempts to transform economically marginal Jews into agriculturalists only brought the Jew into friction with the peasantry. Even emigration, as then carried out, merely served to spread anti-Semitism by creating the conditions for Christian-Jewish conflict in new areas of the world. Herzl concluded: "Anti-Semitism increases day by day and hour by hour among the nations; indeed, it is bound to increase, because the causes of its growth continue to exist and are ineradicable."[23]

The causes of anti-Semitism were ineradicable in the sense that they were inherent in the structure of post-emancipation life. The emancipation had brought two *nations* into destructive tension, with the inescapable result that the weaker of the nations, the Jewish, was continually the prey and victim of the host people. To Herzl the Jewish question was thus a national question, and its solution demanded a national solution: the establishment of a Jewish state.[24] Thus Herzl denied the major premise upon which the emancipation ideology was built, namely, that a harmonious resolution of Christian-Jewish tension could be achieved within European society.

Herzl defended his conclusions by using a form of structural analysis rarely considered by consensus spokesmen in their discussions of anti-Semitism. He buttressed his arguments with a lucid description of the economic, political, and social realities which shaped the Jewish condition. Consider, for example, his description of the Jewish involvement in finance and of the drift of Jews into the socialist movement:

We are what the ghetto made us. We have without a doubt attained pre-eminence in finance because medieval conditions drove us to it. The same process is now being repeated. We are again being forced into money-lending—now named stock exchange—by being kept out of other occupations. But once on the stock exchange, we are again objects of contempt. At the same time we continue to produce an abundance of mediocre intellectuals who find no outlet, and this endangers our social position as much as does our increasing wealth. Educated Jews without means are rapidly becoming socialists. Hence we are certain to suffer acutely in the struggle between the classes, because we stand in the most exposed position in both the capitalist and the socialist camps.[25]

This realism and attention to structural factors as sources of anti-Semitism was quite different from the mode of thinking which dominated the established Jewish community. As we have seen, the Jewish leadership assumed that the basic structural change implicit in the civil and economic emancipation of the Jews had been salutary. Since the structure of German-Jewish life, like the capitalist system in which it was imbedded, was sound, there was no need for examining it closely. Some reform might be needed, but the Jewish liberals maintained (largely by their failure to raise any questions about them) that the economic and political foundations of the emancipation were stable.

Yet that is precisely what Herzl denied, partly by his conclusions, but also most cogently by his willingness to give attention to the underlying bases of the emancipation. The existence of anti-Semitism was, he maintained, a sign of profound structural distress, and that distress could be alleviated only by a bold structural solution: the establishment of a Jewish state. Anything less would simply not work.[26]

Herzl's analysis of the Jewish question entailed both profound pessimism and optimism. Unlike the spokesmen for the Jewish community who acted on the assumption that anti-Semitism could be defeated or controlled, Herzl asserted that there was no hope for a favorable resolution under current circumstances:

Can we hope for better days, can we possess our souls in patience, can we wait in pious resignation till the princes and peoples of this earth are more mercifully disposed towards us? I say that we cannot hope for the current to shift. And why not? Even if we are as near to the hearts of the princes as are their other subjects, they could not protect us. They would only incur popular hatred by showing us too much favor. . . . The nations in whose midst the Jews live are all covertly or openly anti-Semitic.[27]

And again: "A dream, an illusion it was for us to believe that anti-Semitism would disappear. It grew; it is growing."[28] But Herzl also argued that once the Jewish state was established and the organized, orderly emigration of the Jews was under way, anti-

Semitism would begin to decline and, ultimately, disappear completely.

Once we begin to execute the plan, anti-Semitism will cease at once and everywhere. For it is the conclusion of peace. When the Jewish company has been formed, the news will be carried to the utmost ends of the globe by the lightening speed of our telegraph wires.

And immediate relief will ensue. The intellectuals whom we produce so superabundantly in our middle classes will find an immediate outlet in our organizations. . . . And so it will continue, swiftly but smoothly.

Prayers will be offered up in the temples for the success of the project. And in the churches as well! It is the relief from an old burden, under which all have suffered. [29]

Elaborating on this theme in his address to the First Zionist Congress, Herzl argued that "Zionism is, simply, a peacemaker." He conceded that one can never speak of a complete exodus of Jews from their present lands to the Jewish state, and in refuting the charge that Zionism fostered dual political loyalties, he said:

Those who can or want to be assimilated will remain behind and will be absorbed. When, after a suitable agreement with the interested political factors, the Jewish migration begins fully, it will continue for each country only as long as each wants to give up Jews. How will the discharge cease? Simply through the gradual decrease and final cessation of anti-Semitism. Thus we understand and thus we expect the solution of the Jewish question. [30]

As some Jews leave and the remainder are assimilated, anti-Semitism withers away. Without Jews, there can obviously be no anti-Semitism.

So long as anti-Semitism exists, however, it is not to be lamented or denounced but used as the motor force driving toward a solution of the Jewish question.

The decisive factor is our propelling force. And what is that force? The plight of the Jews. . . .

Now everyone knows how steam is generated by boiling water in a kettle, only rattling the lid. The current Zionist projects and other associations to check anti-Semitism are tea-kettle phenomena of this kind. But I say that this force, if properly harnessed, is powerful enough to propel a large engine and to move passengers and goods. . . . [31]

By declaring the emancipation unworkable and calling for a separation of the Jews from the nations in which they live, Herzl was open to the charge that his program was fostering anti-Semitism. Indeed, when *Der Judenstaat* first appeared it was reviewed favorably by only one publication, an anti-Semitic paper in Hungary. [32] Both Jews and non-Jews who were committed to the emancipation attacked Herzl for aiding the anti-Semites. For example, Dr. D. Leimdorfer, a preacher in

Hamburg, charged that "the enemies of the Jews use this [Zionist] movement to our disfavor, [and] see in it 'renewed proof' of their 'correct' judgment of the *homeless Jewish nation which lacks a fatherland*."[33] In Austria Joseph Bloch claimed that by seeing the emancipation as a tragedy Herzl had aligned himself with the most extreme German nationalists, and Emperor Franz Josef himself declared: "Herzl's collaboration with the German nationalists, the mortal enemies of the monarchy, gives me constant concern."[34] Chlomecki, President of the Austrian parliament, met with Herzl in an attempt to persuade him to limit Zionism to a program of philanthropic activity on behalf of the settlement of Jews in Palestine, and on that occasion he said to Herzl: "If your intention and the objective of your propaganda is to foster anti-Semitism, you may reach this objective. I am absolutely convinced that by such propaganda anti-Semitism will grow and that you will bring a bloodbath upon Jewry."[35]

In *Der Judenstaat* Herzl had already anticipated these charges and argued against them. Zionism, he wrote, does not harm those who claim they are only "Israelitic Frenchmen" and not part of the Jewish nation; it simply does not concern them. It is a "private affair for Jews alone," and those who wish to assimilate will not be harmed by it. "It would, rather," he wrote, "be distinctly to their advantage. For they would no longer be disturbed . . . but would be able to assimilate in peace, because present-day anti-Semitism would have been stopped for all time. . . ."[36] Arguing later in the pages of *Die Welt* against the *Protestrabbiner* who reacted to the call for a Zionist congress by calling upon all Jews to boycott the proceedings, Herzl wrote:

Whose position do we make worse? Is there a single reproach which has not already been directed against us? The inflammatory and provocative speeches which have been aimed at us ninety-nine times will be delivered against us for the one hundredth time. But we do not believe even that. We have clear signs for the fact that our loyalty and our acting in open view is not disagreeable, even to our opponents before whom we tread quietly. Finally, great suffering speaks out of our movement, and with the human one always finds the path to the hearts of men.[37]

Nonetheless, the public-relations-conscious German Jewish leadership continued to find Herzl's program and organizational activities embarrassing, for despite Herzl's claim that Zionism constituted the only effective answer to anti-Semitism, the presence of Jews who agreed with the anti-Semites that the emancipation was unworkable was, to say the least, a cause for concern.

The foregoing discussion of Herzl's program has emphasized those aspects of his thinking in which he broke clearly with accepted positions. This is only proper because, as we shall see, within a decade

Herzl's writing and organizational work helped to crystallize a program of Jewish nationalism that was drastically set against consensus liberalism. Despite the real radicalism of Herzl's Zionism and the several significant areas in which his proposals did constitute a sharp departure from the practice and philosophy of the established Jewish community, Herzl's Zionism can also be seen, in part, as a restatement rather than a total rejection of the Enlightenment tradition. Notwithstanding his redefinition of Jewish identity in terms of nationalism, his rejection of defense, and his description of anti-Semitism as a structural phenomenon, Herzl also reasserted the validity of values central to the emancipation ideology.[38]

The entire thrust of Herzl's program was a conscious attempt to realize Enlightenment ideals through the Zionist program. Consider, for example, his constant insistence that Zionism achieve its goals through legally sanctioned and orderly procedures (a charter and planned emigration); and consider, too *Altneuland*, his utopian novel which depicted the realized Jewish state as a kind of perfected bourgeois paradise, a Vienna without communal tension caused by anti-Semitism. As he declared in his opening address at the First Zionist Congress in 1897: "Zionism is a civilized, lawful, *menschenfreundliche* movement."[39]

Even when Herzl criticized the Enlightenment in *Der Judenstaat*, he pointed out that it was not the Enlightenment per se which was inadequate as an answer to the Jewish problem, but rather its slowness in realization: "I believe that man is steadily advancing to a higher ethical level; but I see this ascent to be fearfully slow. Should we wait for the average man to become generously minded as was Lessing when he wrote *Nathan the Wise*, we would have to wait beyond our own lifetime, beyond the lifetimes of our children, of our grandchildren, and of our great-grandchildren. . . ."[40] He believed that the Enlightenment program would work in principle, but that the Jews could not wait for it to be accomplished. Hence Zionism was necessary as an accelerated means of achieving precisely what the Enlightenment had proposed: a rational, orderly end to the Jewish problem brought about in order to bring benefit to all mankind and to advance the perfection of humanity. As Herzl wrote:

The road to universal humanity is still a long one, even though it is not without hope of attainment. We too want to march along it, but in a different way than the magnanimous Mendelssohn did it. We do not want to give up our own nationality; on the contrary, we want to cherish it, and that, not by any means aggressively but only defensively. Moreover, we want to cultivate a friendly feeling toward other peoples and also to help lessen the antagonisms that exist between them. For such a task the Jewish people is perhaps peculiarly fitted, because its members were for so long scattered among the various peoples.[41]

Or as he wrote in response to an attack by Pastor Naumann:

The Zionist ideal does not exclude 'human', generally humanitarian ideas; it includes them. . . .
   And in the future one of the most beautiful and greatest tasks of Zionism will be to demonstrate through deed and behavior that nothing human is foreign to us. . . .[42]

And again, he declared in his address to the Third Zionist Congress:

We want to raise ourselves to a higher standard of life, to spread well-being, to build new highways of communication among peoples, and to find new expressions for social justice. And just as our beloved poet [Heine] created new poetry out of his very pains, so we are preparing, out of our suffering, to create progress for mankind, which we serve. . . .[43]

   Herzl's commitment to Enlightenment values is especially clear in his attitude toward the supposed racial characteristics of the Jews. A racial definition of Jewishness constituted the essence of anti-Enlightenment, for to assume that the nature of Jewish existence was determined by inherited characteristics was equivalent to a full rejections of the belief that the Jewish problem could be solved through rational self-help, legislation, or education. Yet on this issue, Herzl is clearly a non-racist. He had moved beyond the vague racial musings of his youth and asserted: "We are an historical unit, a nation with anthropological diversities. . . . No nation has uniformity of race."[44] After meeting Israel Zangwill for the first time, Herzl noted in his diary: "He accepts the racial point of view. I have only to look at myself and at him in order to reject it. What I mean is: we are a historic unity with anthropological variations. . . ."[45] Occasionally, as we shall see, Die Welt carried articles exploring Jewish racial identity sympathetically, and völkisch attitudes were often expressed there. Herzl, however, never accepted these concepts of racism and Volkism that were so important in the vocabulary of many younger Zionists.[46]
   Nothing reveals more clearly Herzl's commitment to the Enlightenment than his abiding confidence in the rationality of the gentiles. He knew the West European heads of state were disturbed by the Jewish problem, especially since growing anti-Semitism forced large numbers of young Jews into the ranks of the socialists; yet even in discussing socialism, Herzl showed his reliance on an appeal to rational responses among the gentiles.[47] He was convinced that when it was properly explained to them, these Christian leaders would realize Zionism was a rational and orderly way to dissolve the appeal of revolutionary parties to the Jews. Hence Herzl stressed the anti-socialist attitude of Zionism in his contacts with gentile statesmen, and he repeatedly reminded

them that by supporting his movement they would be striking at one of the sources of the strength of the radical left. He believed that these statesmen would accept Zionism, out of their own self-interest, as a rational policy.[48] As he had written in *Der Judenstaat*: "Nor will their [the Jews'] exodus in any way be a flight, but it will be a well-regulated movement under the constant check of public opinion. The movement will not only be inaugurated in absolute accordance with the law, but it can nowise be carried out without the friendly cooperation of the interested governments, who will derive substantial benefits."[49] That cooperation, he believed, would certainly be forthcoming.

MAX BODENHEIMER AND THE FORMATION OF THE ZIONIST MOVEMENT.

Some six years before Herzl's *Der Judenstaat*, Max Bodenheimer (1865-1940) had come independently to the idea that mass Jewish settlement in Palestine was the solution for the suffering of the East European Jews.[50] When Herzl appeared, Bodenheimer was one of the first German Jews to rally to his cause as a supporter and lieutenant.

Bodenheimer's background was strikingly similar to that of Herzl (religiously non-Orthodox; educated to German *Kultur*; bourgeois), and he may be taken as paradigmatic of those few, but intensely committed German Jews who organized and sustained the German Zionist movement in its first stages of development. His thinking is significant because it illustrates the way in which the Zionist idea was expressed in Germany by those who were actively involved in the struggle to propagate the Herzlian theses and win adherents. In Bodenheimer's own statements, and in those expressed in the literature of the organization he helped forge and lead, the idea of Jewish nationalism was first broached to hundreds of German Jews who had never read *Der Judenstaat*.[51]

In his youth Bodenheimer accepted the patriotic and "enlightened" attitudes which characterized his generation, the last to be born before the emergence of the anti-Semitic movement. He was conscious of close ties to the German nation and of a "vigorous patriotic feeling."[52] He later recalled that when he entered the Gymnasium, "I saw the surrounding world through the eyes of an elevated cosmopolitanism; I believed in the progress of *Kultur* and in the brotherhood of peoples in the spirit of humanism." Even when he encountered anti-Semitism during lessons on the New Testament which stressed the role of the Jews in the crucifixion and in incidents involving his fellow students, he remained bound to *Deutschtum* and firm in his belief in human progress, although some doubts about the curability of the *"eingewur-zelter Judenhass"* ("inveterate hatred of Jews") in Germany had begun to plague him.[53]

His first response to anti-Semitism in his days as a university student was to consider forming a Jewish student fraternity, not for the purpose of fostering Jewish nationalism, but to demonstrate the basic Germanism of the Jewish student population. Like many other eman-cipated Jews, he then thought that the causes of anti-Semitism were rooted in the occupations followed by Jews and in their lack of tact. A cultured German Jewish fraternity would improve the image of the Jew and refute the claims of the anti-Semites.[54]

Bodenheimer came to Jewish nationalism rather suddenly in 1889, He recalled that the awakening came upon him as he was considering intentional assimilation as his personal solution to the Jewish problem: "While shortly before I had still struggled with the decision to cast off Judaism and seek an asylum from *Judenhass* in new surroundings where no one would know my ancestry, I was now filled with a holy enthusiasm to serve the cause of my people." He then followed with intense interest the ritual murder trials at Konitz and Tísza-Eszlár, the pogroms in Russia, and especially the anti-Semitic movement led by Stöcker and Ahlwardt in Germany. His observation of these events confirmed him in his newly accepted Jewish nationalism. "These incidents awakened me out of a beautiful dream," he wrote. "It seemed to me as if until then I had been blind to the condition of the Jewish people." He was now convinced that the root of the Jewish problem lay in the homelessness of the Jews, and that only two courses of action were open: disappearance through total assimilation or Jewish nationalism.[55]

In his first published essay, *Wohin mit den russischen Juden? (Whither the Russian Jews?)* (1891), however, Bodenheimer addressed himself not to the problems of German Jewry but to the *Judennot* (Jewish misery) of the East European community. In it he argued for the establishment of Jewish agricultural colonies in Palestine and Syria in order to alleviate the suffering of the Jewish masses in Russia. The pamphlet was suffused with the same rationalism and optimism that Herzl later expressed in his proposals, attitudes that were characteris-tic of the first generation of Zionist leaders who had been schooled in the liberal values of the Enlightenment. Hence Bodenheimer argued that the establishment of the Jews in agriculture would refute the anti-Semitic claim that the Jews have an innate disinclination to working the land and are traders by nature. His faith in the goodness of man was intact, and he believed that a scheme such as the one he offered could be a contribution to human progress. "Our faith in the magnanimity of the nations," he said, "has not yet been so severely shaken by the hate-filled spirit of anti-Semitism that we do [not] confidently hope that the peoples of the entire world will decide to obliterate this barbarism. . . ."[56] For Bodenheimer the settlement of the Jews in Palestine was a means of implementing and accomplishing the goals of the Enlightenment, not of betraying them.

Bodenheimer's proposal awakened little interest among the German Jews to whom it was addressed. The affluent and enlightened were striving for dissolution within the German nation, he noted, and the religiously Orthodox were too absorbed in the obscurity of their religious concerns to be capable of a political act.[57] Nonetheless he pressed ahead with David Wolffsohn, a Lithuanian Jew settled in Germany, as his collaborator; and in 1892, they founded a group in Cologne to propagate the idea of a political solution for the Jewish question.[58]

These earliest pre-Herzlian efforts at building a Jewish nationalist organization in Germany were undertaken with considerable circumspection and moderation. In the early 1890s, Bodenheimer recalls, students inclined to Jewish nationalism carefully concealed their goals under the name *Humanitätsverein* (Humanitarian Organization) in order to avoid the break with their parental homes which open espousal of their ideas would have brought. Bodenheimer's own work in its earliest phase, including his essay *Wohin mit den russischen Juden?*, expressed the sort of philanthropic activity which was accepted and respectable in the German Jewish community, and Bodenheimer also continued to serve as a member of the board of directors of the local Cologne branch of the Verein zur Abwehr des Antisemitismus.[59]

When Herzl began his public activities on behalf of the Jewish state, Bodenheimer was among the first in Germany to join with him. With Wolffsohn and Moritz Levy, Jr., he founded a *Nationaljüdische Vereinigung* in Cologne and engaged in active propaganda on behalf of the Herzlian program. In 1897 they published their own formulation of that program as a series of theses.[60]

As we have seen, Herzl believed that those Jews who would be unable or unwilling to settle in the Jewish state when it was established would simply assimilate totally into the nations where they resided. Herzl thus had accepted without reservation the claim of the anti-Semites that a Jew was obligated to declare himself exclusively and unequivocally for one nationality or another. Bodenheimer and his colleagues, however, confronted the problem of organizing German Jewish support for Zionism in the midst of a clearly unsympathetic community which was sure to ask how one might support Jewish nationalism and still preserve a position as a citizen of Germany. The issue was complicated by the probability that the establishment of the Jewish state and the resulting decrease in anti-Semitic tensions were not imminent, and also by an awareness in Bodenheimer's group, not shared by Herzl, that for some Jews preservation of Jewish identity was not merely a reflex reaction to discrimination but a matter of positive religious or historical affirmation. Hence the theses published by the Cologne group show a sensitivity to issues which Herzl had ignored.[61]

The tone was set in the careful phrasing of the first of the three theses: "Bound together by common descent and history, the Jews of all countries constitute a national community. This conviction in no way infringes the active patriotic sentiments and fulfillment of the duties of citizenship on the part of the Jews, and in particular of the German Jews toward their German fatherland."[62] Having defined the existence of a harmonious balance between membership in the Jewish national community and citizenship in the German state, the theses went on to describe the failure of the emancipation to secure "the social and cultural future of the Jewish *Stamm*" and the need for the establishment of a Jewish state in Palestine as the only solution to the Jewish problem. Finally, a program of practical activity was offered: support of Jewish colonies in Syria and Palestine, cultivation of Jewish literature, history, and the Hebrew language, and improvement of the social and cultural position of the Jews. Conspicuously absent were any references to religion as a component in the definition of Jewishness and any mention of defense as a means of safe-guarding Jewish rights within the lands where they were presently living.[63]

The subtle change in emphasis these German Zionists wrought in Herzl's program did not allay the fears of some that the Jewish community might be polarized by active propagation of Zionism. Professor Herman Schapira, an old *Hovevei*-Zionist, was convinced that the enthusiasm of the young political Zionists would create "modern party warfare" by provoking an ideological confrontation with their opponents. Bodenheimer had written to Schapira denigrating "the German Jews . . . who fear nothing in the world more than a shadow on their pure and exclusively German nationality." Schapira had a more charitable view of the motivations of the German Jews and replied that the central task of the Jewish national movement should be "to find points of unity," not to precipitate inner Jewish factionalism.[64]

The first broadsheet issued by the German Zionist organization in 1897 could hardly have reassured Schapira.[65] It was permeated with the very doctrinaire self-assertiveness against which he had warned. The Jewish national movement, it asserted, is "the only living [movement] in modern Judaism." After noting that the importance of a movement is not determined by the number of its adherents, the leaflet declared Jewish nationalism gains its power from the fact that it alone understands the meaning of modern anti-Semitism and offers a reasonable solution to it. The "comfortable Philistines" underestimate the depth of anti-Semitism, and every time there is a momentary pause in the cries of the anti-Semites, "our big children imagine in their naiveté that anti-Semitism is dead." The Zionists alone know how to decipher the true pattern of events, and therefore they constitute "the only tendency in whose veins pulsing life flows; it is therefore the most important Jewish current of the present."

While some Jews speculate whether the anti-Semitic movement is culturally and morally justified, the Zionists answer:

No, a thousand times no. It is not justified. It is an insult to all culture. It is the ruin of all ethics. It is the archenemy of the idea of mankind. But, it is there. It lives. That is a sad, bitter fact with which we must once and for all come to account. . . .

Hatred of the Jews appears to be indissolubly blended [*unlösbar verschmolzen*] with the emotional life of the Aryan peoples. The misery is not diminished by all the pretty words about the progress of humanity.

Going beyond Herzl's structural explanation of anti-Semitism, the German Zionists declared that hatred of the Jew is rooted in the psychic makeup of the German people. Like Herzl, they declared that the educational and propagandistic efforts of the German Jewish community would never be effective in eradicating anti-Semitism. Only implementation of the Zionist program could do that.

Moreover, total assimilation as a solution was impossible:

We have been told with pathos: "assimilate yourselves, and then it will be better." We have done it. We have assimilated ourselves up to our noses. We have mimicked all the customs and practices of the nations without testing them for value. We have neglected our own culture and scoffed at our own customs. And what has it availed? We have remained Jews in the eyes of the nations, i.e., not confessors of the Jewish faith but sons of another *Stamm*.

Rather than lamenting this turn of affairs, the Zionists accepted it as proof of the failure of both the emancipation and of assimilation. They accepted, too, the anti-Semite's designation of the Jews as a foreign entity: "The Zionists consider all the sons of Israel as brothers, all the daughters of Judah as sisters, who have a common parentage, a common history, and a common future. The place of birth is accidental; the borders of a land are displaced by external political relations, [but] the community lies in the blood [*die Gemeinsamkeit liegt im Blute*]. We are members of one great family. . . ." The German Zionists also continued to insist that their program represented a fulfillment, not a betrayal of the methods and goals of the Enlightenment: "The Zionists are not bad Jews and not enemies of civilization. They are animated by a burning love for the Jewish *Volk,* and they seek to unify the historic Jewish *Geist* with the teachings of modern political economy. They seek a rational solution for the Jewish question by means of reason and experience." Instructed by the anti-Semites in the realities of European life, and accepting without embarrassment these deep ties of kinship as a basis, the Zionists alone, it was claimed, offered an honorable and rational solution to the Jewish problem.

Although Bodenheimer and his collaborators had abandoned the concept that the Jews were a community of faith or confession and with regularity used the term *Stamm* as a designation for Jewry, they did not speak of a Jewish *Rasse* or *Volk.* [66] Like some of the spokesmen for the Centralverein, they were conscious of those ties of heredity and heritage which bound Jews together, but this consciousness of Jewish *Abstammung* did not lead to adoption of the terminology and concepts of the fashionable anti-liberal ideologies of Volk and race. Despite their open espousal of Zionism, Bodenheimer and his associates remained dedicated to much of the Enlightenment tradition.

FRANZ OPPENHEIMER

From 1902 on, Theodor Herzl was in frequent contact with Franz Oppenheimer (1864-1943), a distinguished sociologist and advocate of agricultural cooperatives. Oppenheimer cooperated extensively with Herzl in the years before his death and joined actively in the work of the Zionist movement, addressing the stormy Congress of 1903 in which he argued for the establishment of peasant cooperatives in Palestine as a precondition for mass immigration. [67] While accepting Jewish nationalism, however, Oppenheimer remained an outspoken German patriot and a defender of the classical values of the Enlightenment within the young Zionist movement.

The son of a Berlin Reform rabbi, in his youth Oppenheimer had been educated in the fashion of the assimilated German-Jewish middle class. [68] He remembered his school experiences as having been free of anti-Semitic overtones; he had been fully integrated into the academic and sport life of his Christian classmates and demonstrated considerable prowess as a duelist. [69] Reform Judaism soon lost whatever appeal it may once have had for him, and he early declared himself "fully assimilated" and "confessionally completely neutral," although he resisted the temptation to undertake a conversion of convenience to Christianity on the grounds that such a step would be dishonorable. [70]

His family's deep attachment to German society and nationhood had an abiding impact on the young Oppenheimer. He later recalled his father's dictum: "I am a German, and as such I am loyal, sincere and without falsehood." Oppenheimer considered himself *"Deutscher aus Herzensgrund."*[71] He prided himself on his *"märkisches Heimat-bewusstsein"* and declared that this sense of German rootedness was in no way in conflict with his Jewish identiy.[72] As a university student he once offered to defend his honor as a German and a Jew by challenging an entire anti-Semitic fraternity to a hundred duels.[73]

Oppenheimer's attachment to Zionism came largely out of his feelings of compassion for the sufferings of East European Jewry, and Zionism was not for him a means of redefining his personal identity as a Jew. That question he had settled, and as a self-conscious German patriot, he became a defender within the Zionist movement of those liberal values which had shaped his consciousness since his youth.

Oppenheimer's continuing commitment to those values was revealed most clearly in his criticism of racial definitions of Jewishness which had been propounded by the anti-Semites and which, to his dismay, he saw being accepted by some of the younger Zionists. He proudly recalled that his own family roots were compounded of both Sephardic and Ashkenazic elements, and added: "I expressly do not say: blood, because the Jews, like all other peoples, are compounded out of the most variegated blood currents or, if one positively insists, races." His participation in the Sixth Zionist Congress at Basel in 1903 had great impact on him; as he recalled later: "What struck me most was the fact that my co-religionists in Western Europe had approximated the type of their host peoples to a degree which I had never previously thought possible." He observed the melange of people—an English military officer, a leading Dutch banker, a Danish physician, large numbers of East European Jews—and concluded: "Now I experienced directly the exceedingly strong race mixture from which this psychically united conglomeration had arisen: from purely Nordic, tall, blonde and blue-eyed type to yellow-skinned, slant-eyed Mongoloids; from purely Arabic to nearly Negroid type—all gradations were represented." Explaining this immense variety, Oppenheimer argued that from the fifteenth century B.C. the population of Palestine had been racially mixed, and that subsequent invasions and settlements had increased the degree of racial mixture there as peoples of various origins mingled and merged. In the diaspora untold numbers of individuals of assorted ancestry were added to this *"Rassenchaos"* until, as the culminating step in this process of amalgamation, the Khan of the Chazars brought his entire people into Judaism. Oppenheimer concluded: "Scientifically, it is absurd to speak of a Jewish race."[74]

Oppenheimer conceded that rationalistic attempts to refute the notion that Jews are a race would not be successful so long as this myth was politically useful to the anti-Semites.[75] He was outraged, however, to find that same myth propounded and defended by other Zionists. He had hoped that the Jewish state in Palestine would be another Switzerland, offering equality of rights to all religious and linguistic groups.

Then, of late, that evil spirit of the time won the upper hand a bit in German Zionism. A racial pride swaggered which was nothing other than the photographic negative of anti-Semitism, according to that law of social psychology discovered by Gabriel Tarde, which he has designated "imitation par opposition." (No more mental power is required to do always exactly the opposite of the opponent, always placing a positive value where he places the negative, and vice versa, as to imitate him completely. . . .)[76]

In opposition to this Jewish racial chauvinism, he defended his personal "assimilationist" definition of Jewish identity:

Even in Zionist circles, I have never concealed in the slightest that I am completely "assimilated." When I examined my inner feelings, I found ninety-nine percent Kant and Goethe and only one percent Old Testament, and even that really only by way of Spinoza and Luther's Bible as intermediaries. I feel myself completely German, but I have never been able to understand why my Jewish tribal consciousness [Stammesbewusstsein] should not be compatible with my German folk and culture consciousness [Volks- und Kulturbewusstsein], and I was therefore never an assimilationist.[77]

Oppenheimer's sense of Jewish identity did not conflict with his deep attachment to the German nation, in the liberal sense in which he understood the latter. Opposed to romantic definitions of nationalism, whether offered by German or Jewish Volkists, and true to the canons of liberal nationalism, he saw no contradiction between his Jewish consciousness—expressed as Stammesbewusstsein—and loyalty to Germany. Though a Zionist, he remained close to those consensus spokesmen who believed Jewish religious identity and German citizenship were fully compatible.[78]

NATHAN BIRNBAUM

Nathan Birnbaum (1864-1937) was one of the most unusual of Herzl's early co-workers. Birnbaum came from a family only recently moved from Galicia into the sphere of Western Jewish life. His father was descended from a west Galician Chassidic family, and his mother was of an old rabbinic family in north Hungary that traced its roots back to the medieval scholar Rashi.[79] Nathan was born in Vienna and received a secular education; in later years he was to describe himself as both a *Westjude* (Western Jew) and an *Ostjudenstämmling* (offspring of Eastern Jews).[80] Hence, as Robert Weltsch has observed, Birnbaum represented that special type of Jewish intellectual with roots in Eastern Europe and in Western culture. Although educated in German culture, he labored at extending his ties with the folk life of the Eastern Jewish masses—to the point of learning Yiddish in his maturity. Eventually Birnbaum accomplished a rather remarkable spiritual pilgrimage by leaving Zionism, returning to Orthodoxy, and becoming a champion of Jewish autonomism in the Diaspora.[81]

He began, however, as a Jewish nationalist long before Herzl and is credited with having coined the very term "Zionism."[82] He was one of the founders of the first Jewish nationalist student fraternity, Kadimah, in Vienna in 1883, and from 1885 to 1887 and again from 1890 to 1893 he served as editor of the Zionist publication *Selbst-Emancipation*. In 1896 he joined with Herzl, participated in the First Zionist Congress the next year, and for a time served in the Zionist executive. In 1898 he broke with Herzl and political Zionism. During his period of involvement with the Zionist movement, however, he wrote numerous articles and reviews in which he dealt with most of the major issues with which this study is concerned.[83]

Several years after he had broken with Herzl, Birnbaum published an article entitled "A Few Thoughts About Anti-Semitism" under his pseudonym, Mathias Acher. There he recalled his earlier reactions to anti-Semitism and made a confession about his feelings:

There was a time when I confronted *Judenhass* with a certain good will. I witnessed its activity with a kind of enjoyment. I was almost happy with its successes and progress. If I did not always express these feelings frankly, this was due to a kind of tactical restraint which I believed I had to lay upon myself in order not to offend too much those whom I wanted to win for Jewish national endeavors. How gladly I would rather have scandalized them with the full truth by calling to them: The wicked knaves [i.e., the anti-Semites] are indeed right. Their insults may not be pleasant to listen to and are certainly not valid in their absolute form, but they are nonetheless only the stammering expressions of the very correct perception that an unbridgeable gap yawns between the Jews and the non-Jews, that both have opposite ideals of beauty and morality. They are right, and we are right. And it is good that they storm so. We know now at least where we are. As long as their aversion was quiet and furtive, we did not know that, and we were also not aware of ourselves.[84]

Birnbaum had been an advocate of Jewish nationalism before political anti-Semitism had reached its full power; when the anti-Semitic movement emerged, he welcomed it because, as a committed Jewish nationalist, he saw in it a force which articulated with clarity the fundamental realities of Jewish life in Europe. Anti-Semitism was an inescapable, and not entirely regrettable, feature of Jewish life.

Birnbaum regarded anti-Semitism as an "ineradicable, folk-historical phenomenon" which would not be uprooted by propaganda, reform, or even revolution. Notwithstanding the obvious social and economic components in contemporary anti-Semitism, Birnbaum maintained that "hatred of the Jews is first of all not an economic but a national phenomenon." The Jewish problem will be solved, he claimed, only when it is seen clearly for what it actually is: an instance of friction between nations, aggravated in this case by the fact that the Jews are scattered in many places and nowhere constitute a majority:

Everywhere they are found—too many to be lost in the multitude and also too few to impress their neighbors—they offer the most dangerous pretext for being persecuted: powerlessness. This powerlessness is the reason for the unavoidability of national friction between Jews and non-Jews and lends the hatred of Jews that potency which makes it impossible to compare it to any other national hatred . . . [such] unavoidability and intensity joined with one another . . . justify the weighty apprehension that hatred of the Jews could portend a serious danger for the peace of the community.[85]

These special circumstances of the Jewish nation in the Diaspora insure the continuance of virulent anti-Semitism, which is a "pure racial antipathy."[86]

Birnbaum regarded the energetic defense activities of the consensus as farcical.[87] The Jewish "social conservatives" (his term for the established community's leaders) foolishly consume their energies in the impossible task of changing the emotional biases of the masses. Their attempt to get at "an old inherited need to hate" with doctrinaire counterproofs is laughable.[88]

Abwehr is a still-born idea. Abwehr could emerge only in rationalistic brains, only among people who want to explain history armed only with logic, and who take no notice of the fullness of influences from instinctual and emotional life. What is not "rational" is not "moral" to them, and what is not "moral" is decayed and can easily be destroyed through "reason." A movement which is based on such pre-instinctual philosophical foundations cannot succeed, and hence it is understandable that Abwehr has suffered defeat after defeat although it has labored for years with a great expenditure of capital, knowledge, and, in part, character. It cannot prevent the growth of anti-Semitism—despite its "irrationality" and "immorality"—among men of thoroughly noble and pure nature, as well as among the most shabby and impure elements.[89]

Birnbaum's denigration of defense was similar to that of the other Zionist spokesmen of his generation. But even before he left the Zionist movement, his conception of Zionism was significantly different from that of Herzl. Herzl believed that the creation of the Jewish state would lead to the disappearance of the Jewish problem because through the twin processes of emigration and assimilation the Jews would disappear from Europe. We have noted how Max Bodenheimer accepted the main lines of Herzl's formulation but, moved by tactical and organizational necessity, was sensitive to the possibility that some Jews would remain in exile after the establishment of the Jewish state. Birnbaum went one step further than Bodenheimer, and foreshadowing the exile autonomism which he later championed, he argued as a matter of principle that not all Jews would leave the lands of their birth for the ancient homeland:

Although the individual Jew may have a fatherland, the Jewish people has none and that is its calamity. The Jewish people must once again feel its own piece of earth under foot and draw new material and moral strength out of the homeland. Yet this should not be understood as if it is being demanded that all Jews leave the states where they presently live in order to populate their chosen *Volksheimat.* That is not meant. *The idea of Jewish nationality aims not at uniting all Jews in one land but at creating a national center for Jewry.*[90]

Yet, Birnbaum argued, even such limited emigration would solve the Jewish problem in Europe and end the pressures of anti-Semitism on those remaining, unassimilated Jews. With the beginning of the migration to the homeland, the percentage of the Jewish population would sink below that saturation point at which intolerance becomes manifest. "Anti-Semitic tension would decline perceptibly and naturally as the decrease in Jewish population caused a moderation of the struggle for existence." Moreover, another important factor besides the demographic transformation would emerge from the establishment of the homeland and have a powerful effect in reducing the impact of anti-Semitism: "The consciousness of belonging to a living people which has its own home—a state for joyous creativity for the sons at home, a state of refuge for the sons away—will also enoble and civilize, strengthen and harden the Jews of the Diaspora. The curse of ridiculousness which makes misfortune doubly difficult will give way; [the Jews'] entire position among the peoples will become normal and healthy." Finally, the very existence of a homeland would make possible a new tactic against anti-Semitism: by mounting protests on behalf of persecuted Jewry, the Jews of Palestine would be able to carry on a kind of international defense of far greater effectiveness than the feeble work being done in Germany. When it became clear that the Jews too had a defender and advocate in international affairs, the civilized world would be liberated from the illusion that the Jews are *vogelfrei,* people outside the law who could be mishandled at will.[91]

Like the other major Zionist figures of his decade, Birnbaum was sensitive to the charge of the Jewish liberals that Zionism betrayed the universalistic heritage of the Enlightenment. His response, like that of Herzl, was to defend Jewish nationalism as the true repository of that tradition. The success of Zionism, he argued, will not mean a retreat from humanity and its concerns, but rather the creation of a foundation upon which the Jews can once again make major contributions to all civilization. The Jews, after all, are Oriental in their inherited spiritual and mental characteristics, and Occidental by virtue of their long centuries of residence in the West. Once re-established in Palestine they will work not merely for their own glory and safety but will prove to be the only suitable intermediaries in the great task of reconciling the peoples of the East and the West.[92]

Jewish nationalists, he continued, do not regard the idea of humanity as the opposite of the idea of nationalism, but believe that "nationality is the necessary medium for contributing something to the totality." They see in it "love and not hate, order and not dissolution." That the actions of many nations contradict this view indicates only that these peoples are not yet ready for the *true* national idea and are still in the grip of the old aggressive spirit which pervaded pre-nationalistic forms of human association. Hence the Zionists are making a unique contribution to mankind: by accepting the national idea free of all the dross of previous European epochs, and by offering the only effective way to end anti-Semitism, the Zionists can rightly claim to be "good and devoted fighters in the front ranks for a unified mankind." "The achivement of this goal [a Jewish national home]," he continued, "means giving rise to a new era in which anti-Semitism will have finally lost completely all *raison d'être,* and the civilized world will be spared from a movement which brutalizes national feeling and stops the ennoblement of mankind." Hence the Zionists are the most effective workers for the welfare of humanity and not the Jewish liberals who cling to the old slogans of cosmopolitanism. Birnbaum concluded that "the solution of the Jewish question in a Jewish nationalist sense would be synonymous with an acceleration of the social development processes of mankind."[93]

Anti-Zionists also err in charging Zionism with undermining Jewish patriotism in Germany and other lands. Birnbaum responded that both in its present form as a movement struggling for its goal and in the future when that goal will have been achieved, Zionism was "a guarantee for a true patriotic consciousness by the Jews toward the individual states in which they live, and for the most intimate adherence to the individual peoples in whose midst they live." Since the victory of Zionism means the end of anti-Semitism, the Jews outside the national center would no longer have cause to be hesitant in their patriotism toward the lands of their residence. Once the nations saw their Jewish citizens as brothers from the Jewish nation, they would witness how great will be the real and genuine Jewish enthusiasm and readiness to sacrifice for fatherland and brother nation.[94]

Thus far we have seen that Birnbaum dealt with the same basic issues which absorbed other leading Zionists of his decade in largely the same fashion as they did, albeit with an occasional variation in nuance. In addition, Birnbaum also dealt seriously with the challenge of Social Democracy and the alternative interpretation of the Jewish problem which it offered. Herzl and most of the bourgeois German Zionists were largely concerned with winning support for their movement in the public consciousness and among affluent and acculturated Western Jews, and they rarely considered socialism except to condemn it. Birnbaum, however, was deeply aware of the appeal of Social Democracy for Jewish youth who might otherwise be won for Zionism; he felt constrained to deal with the socialist analysis of anti-Semitism and to refute it.[95] In doing so he used Völkisch terminology and conceptions that were almost never employed by the other Zionist spokesmen around Herzl. Although clearly linked with Herzl, Bodenheimer, and Oppenheimer, Nathan Birnbaum had special significance as a forerunner of a type of Zionist thinker which was even then emerging among the next generation of Jewish nationalists.

The Social Democrats had argued that anti-Semitism was purely a product of the crises and frictions in the capitalistic system, and that with the destruction of that system, hatred of the Jews, along with all other forms of social tension rooted in the old economic order, would disappear. They concluded that only by working for the socialist revolution could one act toward ending anti-Semitism. Zionism was a wasteful diversion of energies from the focus of the struggle: the destruction of capitalism.

Birnbaum addressed himself to this argument in a lecture, "Die jüdische Moderne," ("Jewish Modernism") which he delivered to the Zionist student fraternity Kadimah in Vienna in 1896. He argued that even if it were conceded that a revolution might end anti-Semitism ultimately, the aftereffects of the old order would live on, perhaps for generations. The new socialist world would not emerge overnight, and the old anti-Semitic attitudes would certainly persist. "It could be a thousand years until humanity has arrived at the last, positively the last Jewish persecution."[96] Clearly the Jews could not wait in continuing suffering for the promised but postponed amelioration.

Aside from the slowness of realization, socialism offered no real solution to the Jewish problem because of a fundamental error in its basic conceptions. By emphasizing economic factors and elevating them to determinative status in human affairs, the historical materialists neglected the "history of man as a *Rassenwesen*" (racial being). Because they ignore the fundamental differences among men, the socialists fail to perceive that changing the social structure of a society without dealing with national or racial tensions that do not have economic roots is fruitless.[97] Both nationality and race are realities of social organization that can be neither ignored nor wished away.

What is the source of nationality? If nationality were defined in terms of political allegiance or language, then those who claimed that by accepting German citizenship and adopting the German language the Jews had become fully part of the German nation would be right. Birnbaum could not define nationality as a matter of citizenship or linguistics without conceding valuable points to the German Jewish opponents of Zionism. He invoked, rather, the following argument: "The firm foundation of nationality is always and everywhere race, [whether] a pure or a mixed race. When a race becomes ennobled in the course of its development by going through [the stage of a] *Rassen-Kultur*, it becomes a nationality. Nationality in itself has nothing to do with the state or with language." Since nationality is linked to race, it is absurd to deny the nationality of the Jews because they lack both a state and unified national language, or to claim that the Jews have given up their own nationality by accepting another nation's state and language as their own. "Since state and language are not among the essential persistent features of nationality, there can be no doubt about the contemporary existence of the Jewish nationality. For no one can contest its racial quality."[98]

For Birnbaum the Jews were a nation rooted in racial unity, a fact demonstrated conclusively by the perception of the peoples among whom the Jews live. Even the assimilated Jew who had abandoned his religion preserved the features of the Jewish racial community—"a characteristic völkisch past which it is impossible to lay aside, a certain characteristic temperament, a characteristic mode of thinking. . . ." The Jews are not only a nation but perhaps one with "the strongest national feeling of all the peoples, which is entirely natural even from the materialistic point of view since it is racially the most strongly marked nationality [*da er die rassenmässig ausgeprägteste Nationalität ist*]."[99]

Though still tied to those familiar values of reason, progress, and humanity that characterized these early Zionist figures, Birnbaum pointed the way for the next group of younger thinkers who would break even further from the consensus and its axioms. In enunciating a racial definition of nationality, he had accepted the concepts of the völkisch movement and hence helped give currency within Zionism to principles which constituted a radical denial of the emancipation ideology.

CHAPTER FIVE

Second-Generation Zionists

The positions of Herzl and his associates were, as we have seen, still quite close to the emancipation ideology. Although breaking radically with the liberal Jewish community on the crucial question of Jewish nationalism, these first-generation Zionists continued to affirm and defend a number of the most important values of the Enlightenment, and with the exception of Birnbaum, they remained aloof from the blatant anti-liberalism of völkisch and racial thought. Seen as a response to anti-Semitism, their Jewish nationalism was still closely linked to the modes of thought which had long been dominant among German Jews and testifies to the continuing power of the emancipation ideology.

Herzl, Bodenheimer, Oppenheimer, and Birnbaum had all endured the shock of the newly emerged anti-Semitic movement as young adults. The young men who formed the second generation of Zionist advocates in Germany, however, had all grown up in the wake of the widespread agitation of the late 1870s and 1880s, and many of them entered their maturity and began their university studies in the 1890s when political anti-Semitism reached its zenith. As we shall see, many of those who came into the Jewish nationalist clubs and student fraternities in that decade of acute political crisis for German Jewry proved receptive to ideological positions which broke even more radically from those sanctioned in the organized community, and from their ranks came the most fully developed rejection of the emancipation ideology.

To understand this development we must consider the major factors which shaped the attitudes of Jewish youth in Germany at the turn of the century, both the general intellectual climate in Germany and the

132

specific influences which impinged upon young Jews. Then we shall deal with the responses of the Zionist youth and analyze the nature of their reactions to the challenge of anti-Semitism and their advocacy of ideas that scandalized both the established Jewish community and their older colleagues in the Zionist movement.

THE GENERAL SITUATION

At the end of his great work *Die deutsche Volkswirtschaft im 19. Jahrhundert,* Werner Sombart described the general mood in German politics as the twentieth century began:

The great ideals which still filled our fathers and grandfathers with enthusiasm have turned pale. The national idea is worn out, after the German Reich was established in mightily blazing enthusiasm. What is offered to us today as nationalism is an insipid secondary infusion which is no longer able to excite anyone greatly. Hollow phrases must conceal the inner desolation. The same is true of the great political ideals for which our ancestors went to their deaths. In part they have been realized, and in part their lack of importance has been recognized. The young generation smiles with condescension when it reads about the struggle for political freedom, and the commemorative celebrations of the great times of enthusiasm have become ridiculous farces. New political ideals, however, have not arisen. . . . Thus the nineteenth century ends with an enormous deficit in inspirational ideals in which the times just past were so overly rich. [1]

With the ideals that had animated the previous generation now bankrupt, Sombart saw the masses turning to the pursuit of their immediate material interests. Bereft of noble guiding principles to restrain them, he believed men would give themselves over to "unprincipled, desolate opportunism" and a "dull attitude of business as usual."

The alienation of German youth from the aspirations of their fathers was not restricted to politics. [2] A pervasive sense of dissatisfaction appears to have settled onto the younger generation at the end of the century as many of the children of the affluent middle class turned in disgust from the patterns of life and thought which their parents embodied. As one scholar, Howard Becker, has characterized them: "They thought that parental religion was largely sham; politics boastful and trivial; economics unscrupulous; education stereotyped and lifeless; art trashy and sentimental." [3] They claimed to have seen through the hypocrisy that dominated their elders and openly rejected the conventions of the sterile bourgeois city life into which they were born and of the university culture in which they were maturing. They felt a "deep disgust" about Wilhelminian society, and they longed for something less artificial and more natural, something richer in emotional warmth than the stuffy, insincere life-style of their parents' generation. They were especially distressed by the transformations that rapid industrialization was inflicting on German society and landscape and by the alienation of men from their fellows and from nature which increasingly characterized the life of the urban classes.[4]

Two major modes of expression were available through which youth could express their deeply felt dissatisfactions.[5] Some found their way into German Social Democracy, which offered them a developing, dynamic political movement with a growing mass base and a carefully worked out ideology. According to that ideology the evils that distressed them had their roots in industrial capitalism. In order to deal effectively with the malaise capitalism brought upon both the working class and their oppressors, capitalism itself would have to be destroyed. Marx and Engels had already indicated the important role which middle-class intellectuals might play in the struggle to liberate the working class and all society, and more than a few German youth from university backgrounds gave their energies to the international struggle for socialism.

But many others took a quite different and essentially apolitical path by associating with the Youth Movement and the distinctive völkisch ideology which animated it.[6] Unlike the Social Democrats, the Youth Movement did not aim at any systematic or radical transformation of society as a whole, but rather at helping its members achieve immediately a style of life which was free of the defects they saw in bourgeois society. The artificiality and coldness of urban life were replaced by a return to the simplicity of nature and the close comradeship of the *Bund*. The return to nature meant renewed appreciation of the beauties of a countryside rich in the architecture and memories of pre-industrial decades, and also a rediscovery of the body, its beauty and its strength. The Wandervögel and Turner societies sought to bring their followers back to a more genuine mode of living in which primitive habits, hiking, gymnastics, campfires, and old folk songs replaced the softness and philistine conventions of the city. All the defects of urban *Gesellschaft* were immediately swept away in the *Gemeinschaft* of the youth group, where idealism was rekindled, instinct and intuition exalted, and a sense of vitality and organic wholeness recaptured. And all this was achieved without political involvement in the society they were opposing. By the act of withdrawal into a world of its own, the Youth Movement offered its participants at once a genuine, unalienated life—something promised by Social Democracy only at the end of a long and disciplined struggle.[7]

The longings of the young generation were articulated and

rationalized by a völkisch ideology. Romantic in inspiration, that ideology was an attempt to replace the rationalism and individualism of the Enlightenment and of political liberalism with an emphasis on the primacy of the Volk. By "Volk" the spokesmen for this ideology meant much more than "folk" or "people":

> Ever since the birth of German romanticism in the late eighteenth century Volk signified the union of a group of people with a transcendental "essence." This "essence" might be called "nature" or "cosmos" or "mythos," but in each instance it was fused to man's innermost nature, and represented the source of his creativity, his depth of feeling, his individuality, and his unity with other members of the Volk.[8]

Völkisch authors such as de Lagarde, Langbehn, and Gobineau were widely read, indeed almost obligatory reading in sections of the German middle class.[9] The ideas they propounded—particularly the primacy of instinct and feeling over reason, and the centrality of the Volk as a mystical entity binding its members into deep association with one another—became common currency in many German circles, especially among the youth and their leadership, who found in the völkisch ideology confirmation and exposition of the urges and frustrations they felt.

These concepts so pervaded the thinking of the young at the turn of the century that, as Mosse has suggested, there existed a "general völkisch urge" which penetrated even into the ranks of those most tied by tradition to the Enlightenment and liberalism: the Jews.[10] The völkisch ideology was, for its believers, "a new religion whose roots, like those of all religions and faiths, not only entered man's subconscious but penetrated deeper and became a whole new way of life."[11] Moreover, the völkisch ideology had the aura of being an avant-garde and future-oriented doctrine which promised to replace the stale slogans of the Enlightenment and liberalism with new heroic ideals of power and depth.

Much of the völkisch literature was openly anti-Semitic,[12] and it was clear to both German and Jew that the accepted image of the Jew as a bourgeois, urban liberal was diametrically opposed to the ideal man as described by the Youth Movement and völkisch thought.[13] Once membership in the Volk was defined in mystical or racial terms, it was clearly difficult, if not impossible, for the Jew to claim membership in that Volk, as he did in state and society. Not all who read völkisch literature approvingly drew radical racial or anti-Semitic conclusions from it. Some, like Karl Fischer, the founder of the Wandervögel, thought of the Jews as a separate but equal Volk and respected them as such;[14] and although some sections of the movement sought to exclude

Jews from membership, others accepted them and defended their participation.[15] But the völkisch ideology did give strong reinforcement to the claim of anti-Semites that the Jews were not and could not be part of what mattered most in Germany. Political anti-Semitism did decline in the years after 1893 when it had reached its peak, but with the ideological rationale of völkisch thought providing impetus, the movement for the exclusion of the Jews found renewed support, especially in the younger generation.

Heinrich Class, for example, the leader of the Pan-Germanists, noted that the older Germans in his group rejected both anti-Semitism and racism, and that his own anti-Semitism brought him into conflict with his parents: "We younger ones were advanced; we were national without reservations; we did not want to hear anything about tolerance if it protected the enemies of society and state; we rejected humanitarianism of the liberal type because our own people had to pay for it."[16] Hence, when Berthold Feiwel surveyed the situation of Jewry at the end of the first year of the new century, he noted with concern not only the continued growth of anti-Semitism but especially that "the maturing generation is flatly saturated with *Judenhass*."[17]

In short, the Jewish youth who entered the universities after 1890 encountered a generation of young Germans who were more likely to be anti-Semitic, and more profoundly anti-Semitic, than those met by their fathers and uncles two or three decades earlier. Moreover, the quality of the anti-Semitism which confronted the Jewish youth in the universities of the 1890s was different from that which their elders had known in their own student years; anti-Semitism was now "modern," expressed in the avant-garde vocabulary of racial or völkisch theories.[18]

THE SITUATION OF JEWISH YOUTH

The young Jews who grew into maturity in the period after 1890 were exposed to all the general trends described above. Sharing as broadly as they did in the cultural and academic life of Germany, they were subject to the same tensions, frustrations, and longings that found expression in the Youth Movement. But their situation was sharply distinguished from that of their non-Jewish colleagues by the experience of anti-Semitism. Born after the Emancipation Edict of 1869, they (like Herzl's generation) had never witnessed the struggle for civil rights. Many of their fathers and grandfathers had participated in the long campaign for equality and had enthusiastically celebrated their acceptance as Germans by active patriotism and military service during the Franco-Prussian War of 1870. The older generation remembered a time when Jews did not have full civil equality; their offspring had been born as part of an emancipated Jewry. But they had also been born into a society in which anti-Semitism was on the rise, and those young Jews who entered the universities after the middle of the last decade of the century had never known a Germany without an active and aggressive anti-Semitic movement. Moreover, in the university they were part of that sector of German society where anti-Semitism was most virulent and, in the various student organizations, most solidly institutionalized.

We have already discussed the emergence of the first Jewish student fraternities in the 1880s,[19] and there is ample testimony that the experience of youth spent under the impact of anti-Semitism was what Alfred Apfel called a *"Generationserlebnis."*[20] Gustav Mayer recalled that social anti-Semitism had been "endemic" in his student days, and the Jewish press dealt frequently with the plight of the young Jews who were, as one account put it, "incessantly rejected and cast out by anti-Semitic Germany."[21] Another observer wrote in 1900:

The Jewish student who previously sang, caroused, and dueled harmlessly in the Burschenschaften and corps sees himself today excluded by almost all the student organizations, even by the scientific ones, and referred to the Jewish student associations which would have been an unheard of phenomenon twenty-five years ago. Many social, music, gymnastic, and cycling clubs of the middle class which previously never would have considered such a thing [now] strictly turn Jews away.[22]

Casual social exclusion, rigid restrictions on membership in sport clubs and fraternities, occasional slurs and insults—all these abrasive pressures weighed on the young German Jew as he began his university career, at least as heavily as they had on Herzl a decade before.[23]

Despite their experience of anti-Semitism, many thousands of Jewish students continued to accept fully the attitudes of the established community. One was Gustav Mayer (b. 1871), who recalled that as a student he foresaw no future for anti-Semitism because he was convinced that the German people would become progressively stronger in "true humanity" with each passing generation. The progress of civilization, he believed, would soon cast anti-Semitism on the rubbish heap of history. He was distressed by Jewish fellow students who seemed resigned to the barriers which anti-Semitism had raised up.[24]

My view then was that the disharmonies which still existed between German Jews and German Christians . . . would die away with time and that both, entirely by themselves, would grow together, gradually, without serious interruptions. . . . It never would have occurred to me to doubt that in the future not only would railroad trains travel ever more quickly and postal service would become increasingly less expensive, but also that men would ever more thoroughly give up their prejudices. This meant for me, first of all, that the prejudices against the Jews which still existed among my compatriots would gradually disappear, and that the German Jews would be completely absorbed into the German people, yet without having to give up their venerable religion for this.[25]

Mayer rejected the Zionist movement when it emerged, and he declared in a letter to his father in 1897 that against the cry "Hie Zion!" he set "Hie Weimar!" "I held fast to the conviction that the German Jews did not belong any longer to this 'people without a land,' and that those among them who nonetheless saw themselves as Zionists thereby put an end to the entire course which their fathers and ancestors had entered upon since they have striven to become a part of German culture." Although he rejected those German Jews who wished to become "Asiatics," he confessed to rather different feelings toward the Aryans: "Yet I also looked with an admiration that was not free from envy upon the tall, blond, north German men who went their way so confidently and with such self-assurance, and upon the light, slender female forms who strode by me so proudly and untroubled. I felt myself inferior—not to the spirit, understanding, or feeling of these people, but to the strength of their will, their animal strength, and the sureness of their instinct."[26] Though proud of three hundred years of rootedness in Germany, even young Mayer, defender of the emancipation ideology, was conscious of powerful and attractive völkisch realities in which he did not share.

Many other sensitive Jewish youth, however, were more deeply troubled by anti-Semitism and found little comfort in the liberal interpretation of its meaning. One of them wrote in 1901: "Our ancestors a hundred years ago were Jews—full, complete Jews with all the sufferings which they endured. But what are we? Our parents have not raised us as Jews. Our enemies have not allowed us to become Germans. We became unsteady mongrels, doubly unsteady because our physical power of resistance has also become broken by the continuing sufferings."[27] Another wrote that same year: "We youth, who have gone to the gymnasium alone for thirteen years, who have lived and suffered from *Judenhass* as a self-evident fact—we snatch up the proud ideas of Jewish self-help happily and without hesitation. Since the fatherlands have been torn away from us, it gives us a spiritual homeland."[28]

The impact of anti-Semitism upon these young people in their formative years had helped provoke an awareness that a new form of understanding beyond that offered by the emancipation ideology was needed by those who were now convinced that they lacked "legitimate attachment to the German world."[29] They looked for explanations of anti-Semitism and of Jewish identity which would interpret more adequately the experiences which were shaping their self-consciousness. And like their gentile counterparts in the Youth Movement, "they also wanted to go forward into the future . . . [and] many of them wanted to find a new point of departure."[30] They too looked for ideals to which they might give themselves.

The existing options were not very promising. The modernized version of Judaism which many of them had been exposed to in their youth was not likely to capture their enthusiasm.[31] Moreover, the two major secular ideological alternatives which had become popular among the non-Jewish students were not acceptable to young Jews for whom Jewish identity was important. Social Democracy had no room for a special concern with Jewishness or anti-Semitism, and the völkisch ideology was at best neutral on the Jewish question. Uninspired by the established Jewish ideology, unmoved by the dominant expression of Jewish religiosity, and unable to embrace the avant-garde movements which their contemporaries found so appealing, many sensitive youth were in search.[32]

An additional factor in this situation was the growing presence at German universities of East European Jewish students, many of whom enjoyed the kind of ideological rootedness lacking among German Jews. After 1886 Russia had placed restrictions on the numbers of Jews who could be admitted to the university, and as a result hundreds went abroad to study, especially in Germany.[33] In the academic year of 1886/87 there were 129 foreign (East European) Jews enrolled in Prussian universities out of a total Jewish student body of 1,313 (9.8% were East European). But by 1905/06 the number had swelled to 483 out of 1,784 (27.1%).[34]

The Russian Jewish students had almost no relationship with the political life of Germany or with the German Jewish community. They participated in neither the structure of German Jewish life nor in the consensus ideology, but some of them were actively involved in fostering the ideas of Jewish nationalism among themselves.[35] In 1889 the *Russisch-Jüdische Wissenschaftliche Vereinigung* was founded in Berlin and became the first student organization in Germany to advocate Jewish nationalism.[36] Its only German member was Heinrich Loewe, who in 1892 founded a new group called *Jung Israel*, which included members of the earlier organization and of the colonization group Esra. Besides Loewe, a few other German Jews participated, and many of them later became active in the Zionist movement.[37]

For at least some German Jewish students the presence of these

Easterners was significant in that they were persistent advocates of a nationalist alternative which was not yet part of public awareness or discussion in the early 1890s. Even though few were involved directly, more were ultimately affected by those like Loewe who maintained intimate contact with the East Europeans and then were active later in working for Zionism among the students and in the general community.[38] The entrenched anti-Semitism of the university, the inability of the emancipation ideology to inspire universal enthusiasm, the limitations of the other ideological options, and the influence of the Russian Jewish nationalists—all these forces came to bear upon the young German Jews. As a result of these factors, from the 1890s on there were consistent signs of defections among the students from the established community's positions as a significant, and highly vocal, minority of young Jews accepted Jewish nationalist attitudes and ideas. This corrosion in unity of outlook among the students paralleled the crumbling of the liberal consensus among their elders which was wrought by the emergence of Herzl's political Zionism. The Zionism which emerged among the university youth, however, was not merely a restatement of the views of Herzl and his associates. The Jewish nationalism of the students was shaped by factors unique to their situation as *young* German Jews, and hence it often differed significantly in tone and content from the positions held by their elders in the movement.

Some of the youth who came to Zionism at this time were from highly traditional homes and had been reared as Orthodox Jews. For them Zionism was often a direct outgrowth of a strong consciousness established in childhood. In the words of one of them, "We were a *Volk* with our own tradition, own history, and own religion."[39] For these young religious Jews, as Max Jungmann recalled, Zionism gave "a new content" to an already accepted and deeply felt Judaism. Jungmann testified that "anti-Semitism played no role in my development toward Zionism," and that this was true of many others like him. Entrance into the Zionist movement was the result of emerging from "unconscious" to "conscious" Jewish nationalism.[40]

But Zionism also appealed strongly to another sort of young Jew, one whose roots in Judaism were more tenuous. Kurt Blumenfeld (b. 1884), for example, was the son of one of the few unbaptized Jews appointed to the Prussian judiciary. Until his conversion to Zionism, his knowledge of Jewish religious tradition had been meager.[41] For Blumenfeld Zionism was not simply a strategy for solving the Jewish problem or alleviating *Judennoth*; Zionism "gave us an answer to the problem of our individuality."[42] Blumenfeld and those who responded to him embraced Zionism out of a deeply felt personal need. He spoke of his discovery of Zionism as one would of a religious conversion: "When I offered reasons for my Zionism I always felt that I had not come to my views by way of a system or through thinking but through a revelation which again and again overpowered me."[43] He recalled that for him and his associates, "Zionism [was] the result of a difficult inner struggle . . . In our group we spoke about the conflict in which we were placed and which we could not evade. Zionism for us was a question of a serious choice. . . ."[44] To resolve this struggle by becoming a Zionist meant affirming their membership in the Jewish people and, simultaneously, openly accepting their rootlessness in Germany.

These young Zionists were "post-assimilatory" Jews, a term Blumenfeld coined to refer to a Jew "who belongs to the German culture and spiritual world by virtue of his education, but feels a lack of legitimate belonging to the German world."[45] Post-assimilatory Jews were those who had recognized that despite deep immersion in the German world they did not belong to this world and were without roots in it.[46] For them "the first sign of self-consciousness was a new feeling of distance vis-a-vis the German world."[47] With such an awareness one could live in Germany without conflict only so long as he affirmed his true Volk identity, "confronting the non-Jewish German world as a Jew, fearlessly." It followed that the fight against anti-Semitism was only a purposeless waste of energy. Blumenfeld declared that "we place no value on justifying ourselves to an anti-Semitic world," and even called for Jews to abandon voluntarily their efforts to occupy higher offices in the German state.[48]

Blumenfeld was active as a propagandist for Zionism among the youth, and those who responded to him did so enthusiastically. For the youth, he recalled, "my speeches were at the same time acknowledgement of their own situation and liberation from the spiritual servitude which the older generation had inflicted upon them."[49] He succeeded in awakening in his circle of young followers the consciousness of being part of "an elite which would conquer Jewish life through their moral power."[50] They felt "like a pioneer feels who risks taking a path over an abyss into a new world, one that is more real and true."[51]

Led by Blumenfeld, these young Zionists later scandalized their elders in the movement by insisting that emigration to Palestine be a part of the personal program of every German Zionist. Blumenfeld and his colleagues were conscious of a *Resonanzproblem* and sought a life in Palestine where a Jew might find that "natural resonance" which was not available to him in Germany. Only in the land of Israel, they argued, could this *Resonanzproblem* be solved, for only there could a Jew—not just a Russian Jew but every Jew—live his life in freedom, solving his life problems in an atmosphere where being a Jew was self-evident.[52] When the older Zionist leaders like Oppenheimer and Bodenheimer showed neither sympathy nor understanding for these longings, Blumenfeld became convinced that "these old Zionists, in [their] misjudgment of German life and of the political situation stood very close to the views of the Centralverein."[53]

THE STRUGGLE FOR STUDENT LOYALTIES

From the time that Zionism appeared as an organized movement in the 1890s it had a great appeal for some students, both those who were "post-assimilatory" and those from highly traditional backgrounds. Indeed, in the *Judenstaat* Herzl had anticipated this development: "The [Zionist] idea depends only on the number of its adherents. Perhaps our ambitious young men, to whom every road of advancement is now closed, and for whom the Jewish State throws open a bright prospect of freedom, happiness and honor—perhaps they will see to it that this idea is spread." And again: "I am well aware that reason alone will not suffice. Long-term prisoners do not willingly quit their cells. We shall see whether the youth, whom we must have, is ripe; the youth—which irresistibly draws along the aged, bears them up on powerful arms, and transforms rationality into enthusiasm."[54] As Herzl hoped, at least some of the youth were ripe, and those who responded did so with great enthusiasm. Hans Kohn recalled that Zionism at the turn of the century was essentially a movement of youth "full of the enthusiasm and joy of discovery of young men." Zionism offered these youth a worthwhile goal which captured their imagination and fostered their pride, and it also prepared a way for them back to a "new, unknown or forgotten world—Judaism."[55] These enthusiastic students filled the ranks of the Zionist movement in Germany and often constituted the majority of the audience in Zionist public meetings. "The bourgeoisie," Max Jungmann wrote, "on the whole kept its distance from the 'fanatical' Zionists. The youth created Zionism and drove it forward; they repeatedly sacrificed [for it]. . . ."[56]

Just as the Zionist movement had to struggle against the organized community in Germany as a whole, so too among the Jewish university youth, Zionist activists faced an array of established organizations in the *Kartell Convent* which were uninterested in Jewish nationalism or openly hostile to it.[57] Although the Jewish nationalist youth welcomed the growth of self-consciousness and Jewish pride which the *Kartell Convent* fostered, and saw in its activities a sort of proto-Zionistic movement away from assimilation, the *Kartell Convent* was firmly anti-Zionist. These liberal students maintained that anti-Semitism was a carry-over from darker days and was bound to disappear in time, albeit with a vigorous assist from alert and energetic Jews.[58] When anti-Semitism disappeared, so too would the Jewish fraternal organizations. Coming to Heidelberg in the early 1900s, Rahel Strauss found *Badenia*, the *Kartell Convent* affiliate, made up of young Jews who were distant from Judaism and who "wanted not only to know nothing about Zionism but also fought it energetically."[59] The *Kartell Convent* mentality was aptly symbolized in the *Viadrina* coat of arms, which bore no Jewish insignia but only a figure representing Germania and the colors of the old Burschenschaften, black, gold and red.[60]

Not all the Jewish students affiliated with the *Kartell Convent.* Many joined *paritätisch* organizations (those of mixed Christian and Jewish membership) like the *Freie Wissenschaftliche Vereinigung.* Such groups were devoted to the defense of liberal values, and in the course of time their already heavily Jewish membership increased until they were virtually all Jewish except in name.[61] In addition, many young students were unaffiliated with any movement, and the student Zionists founded new organizations specifically designed to win the uncommitted. The *Russisch-Jüdische Wissenschaftliche Vereinigung* and *Jung Israel* had already been founded as groups openly devoted to Jewish nationalism, and neither had been particularly successful in winning converts for Zionism.[62] In 1893 Bodenheimer and Oppenheimer established the *Jüdische Humanitätsgesellschaft,* and in 1895 a group including Max Jungmann and Martin Buber founded the *Vereinigung Jüdischer Studierenden*, both of which were intended to gain adherents for the idea of the Jewish state. Their leaders recognized that, as one of them noted, "Zionism was something strange and suspicious to the German Jews, and also to the youth whom we intended to recruit." In order to win students away from the *Kartell Convent* and the *paritätisch* (nondenominational) organizations, the *Vereinigung Jüdischer Studierenden* muted its Zionism and emphasized a "neutral *Tendenz.*" Its program emphasized the elevation of Jewish self-consciousness through the study of Jewish history and literature. Although dueling was looked down upon as assimilatory, fencing and other forms of athletics were pursued. On festive occasions the *Hatikvah* was sung, and the organizational colors were blue, white and yellow (the latter as a reminder of the medieval Jewish badge).[63]

An example of the way these Zionist groups worked to win support without openly proclaiming their Zionism is found in the role they soon began to play in the hotly contested elections for the directorate of the *Lesehalle.* Although the Burschenschaften and the Corps did not participate in these elections, the anti-Semitic *Verein Deutscher Studen-*

ten carried on an active campaign, opposed at first only by the *Freie Wissenschaftliche Vereinigung*. Dissatisfied with the tactic of opposing anti-Semitism under the banner of nonsectarian liberalism, in 1902 the *Vereinigung Jüdischer Studierenden* put up their own slate of candidates and mounted a dual campaign against both the anti-Semites and the liberal Jews. They appealed to the Jewish students:

Fellow students! We will be attacked most strenuously as *Jews*. As *Jews* we will be continually insulted. Should we then be prepared to leave the defense of our honor to other than Jews?

The *Freie Wissenschaftliche Vereinigung* consists entirely, or almost entirely of Jews, but it is the group which most energetically protests against being a Jewish organization as something to be condemned.[64]

Without once mentioning Jewish nationalism, the Vereinigung Jüdischer Studierenden argued that since only its candidates appeared openly as Jews, they alone deserved the votes of all self-respecting Jewish students.[65]

As the last year of the century began, *Die Welt* confidently claimed that the Zionist movement had been successful in gaining the loyalty of the youth: "All the youth, in so far as they are acquainted with our ideas and, in general, still feel Jewish stand behind us. For they feel instinctively that we can give them that great idea which they need in order not to degenerate into an enervating, stupefying life of pleasure. We have all that is healthy, full of the enjoyment of life, and certain of victory. . . . The youth are with us, and the new century toward which we are approaching belongs to them."[66] Such a claim was, in fact, somewhat premature. The bulk of the Jewish students continued to support, indifferently or actively, the liberal organizations, and only a small minority of the students actually affiliated with one of the various Zionist youth organizations which now proliferated.[67]

Yet the sudden growth of the Zionist student movement, and especially its zeal in propagating Jewish nationalism, was sufficient to provoke great anxiety among the leaders of the established community. The years at the turn of the century witnessed a campaign by the communal leadership to win the students for liberalism and blunt the thrust of the Zionist appeal.[68] The student sector became an arena in which young Zionists and liberals, represented largely by the Centralverein, fought an ideological struggle for the loyalty of the university youth.[69] After several years of active struggle against the anti-Semites, the Centralverein now recognized that it faced a serious challenge within the ranks of young Jewry. It responded with vigor, and with the talents of some of its leading spokesmen, for the loyalties of the next generation were at stake.[70]

In 1901, for example, the Centralverein arranged a meeting with Jewish students in Berlin to encourage their participation in its work. The speaker was sharply critical of the Jewish fraternal organizations which sought to redeem offended Jewish honor by challenging anti-Semites to duels. Such heroics, he noted, accomplish nothing in the struggle against anti-Semitism; moreover, in these exclusively Jewish associations there was no sign whatsoever of genuine and positive defense activity like that being carried out by the Centralverein. What did he recommend as an alternative course of action for the student who wished to fight anti-Semitism? Through close association with non-Jewish fellow students on neutral ground, he said, the Christians could come to know and understand their Jewish colleagues. Such fellowship among the *Finkenschaft* (those students who were not members of any organized students club) would undermine the ignorance and misconceptions which lead to anti-Semitism, and through such activities the students would be accomplishing, in their sphere of activity, what the Centralverein does throughout the nation.[71]

Although critical of the tactics of the Jewish dueling groups, the Centralverein had no quarrel with them on the grounds of ideology; none of the *Kartell Convent* affiliates questioned the principle that the Jew was German by nationality.[72] Yet the Zionist students denied that axiom, and at first the Centralverein responded by trying to induce them to work under the aegis of their organization. In June of 1901, Maximilian Horwitz, chairman of the Centralverein, delivered a comprehensive lecture to the academic youth on the relationship of students to his organization. He conceded that the power of anti-Semitism had been underrated at first, and that the Jewish community had relied too heavily on their Christian fellow citizens for defense against defamation. The idea of Jewish self-defense had then emerged and had found adequate realization in the Centralverein. Emphasizing the numerical strength of the Centralverein, which represented at least 100,000 Jews,[73] he claimed that it now constituted an effective pressure group because German officials knew that "the German Jews stand behind us." Horwitz then urged the students to accept their responsibility in the battle for right and justice; in particular he asserted that no organizational affiliation on their part could hinder them from working with the Centralverein:

They can be Zionists. They can condemn Zionism. They can meet together for scientific purposes or for the purpose of furthering student fellowship. They can take any standpoint which they wish—but the German student of Jewish faith today cannot evade his duty and obligation to join in the struggle to guarantee and to win civil rights for the German citizens of the Jewish faith.

That is the foremost duty of every Jew today . . . and the heightened duty of the German [Jewish] student because the future rests with him. . . .[74]

Horwitz' speech was significant as an example of the way in which the Centralverein attempted to play its self-chosen role as the unifying voice of German Jewry, even among the students where Zionism had gained a foothold.[75]

The Centralverein's hope of gaining the loyalties of the German Zionists was never fulfilled, and by the time another decade had passed it had abandoned the attempt.[76] The Zionists responded to the Centralverein's call for unity and cooperation in *Abwehr* with their consistent criticism of defense activites as trivial and wasteful. In place of the Centralverein's understanding of Jewish identity, the elder Zionists had already asserted a new definition of what being a Jew entailed and allowed, and the young Zionists went even further in their rejection of liberalism. "No man in the world will take contemporary liberalism seriously," one of them declared. "Assimilatory liberalism is dead, just like its step-brother, economic liberalism."[77] The whole era of the emancipation was dismissed as a "thoroughly unhistorical episode,"[78] and Adolf Friedmann (b. 1871) pointed out that although a kind of marriage of Judaism and liberalism had been consummated fifty years ago, one was entitled to ask: "Does one remain married to a corpse? Death divorces. What today still appears to indicate life in liberalism are at most reflex movements."[79] Zionism, the young Zionist argued, was post-liberal. Emancipated from the delusions bred by the emancipation, Jewish nationalism was the most progressive, idealistic and avant-garde movement in the Jewish community.[80]

What did these young Zionists propose to put in place of the emancipation ideology? To answer that question we must now examine in some detail the way in which the Zionist youth developed and expressed their understanding of Jewish nationalism by articulating a new Zionism based on the premises of the völkisch ideology.

VÖLKISCH ZIONISM

George Mosse has summarized the background to the emergence of anti-liberal thinking among the Jewish youth of Germany in these terms:

[The völkisch] ideology had special significance for young Jews growing to maturity within German culture. They also wanted to go forward into the future and . . . many of them wanted to find a new point of departure. The immediate past was the world of the ghetto, while the present symbolized the status quo within a society that had painted the Jews in unflattering stereotypes. . . . The stereotype of the Jew was presented as the antithesis of that genuineness which Germans longed for. Jews were described as intellectual, and therefore artificial. They lacked roots, and thus rejected nature. They were an urban people, possessed of special aptitudes for expanding even more the hated capitalist society. Many Jews felt this image of their own people to be appropriate, and many of the young, especially, thought they saw it exemplified by their parents.

Out of this complex of ideas, sensitive Jews formulated their own doctrine of revolt. . . .[81]

In fashioning that "doctrine of revolt," these young Jews adopted the conceptions and vocabulary of the völkisch ideology, and they spoke of the "new Jew" in almost precisely the same terms that their German counterparts used in describing the "new German."[82]

These conceptions were adopted by the Jews despite the fact that they had already been used by anti-Semites to justify doctrines of Jewish exclusion. For a Zionist, who accepted the separateness of the Jew, the use of the same thought models employed by the anti-Semitic movement was not scandalous or dangerous, as Jewish liberals might hold, but simply a recognition of an obvious truth: the Jews are a Volk and hence cannot be part of the German Volk. To be sure, Zionists and anti-Semites endowed such statements with fundamentally opposed emotional overtones, but neither would have doubted the axiomatic truth of their declarations.[83]

Indeed, the anti-Semites occasionally applauded the emergence of völkisch Zionism. One Dr. G. Stille wrote in the *Antisemitisches Jahrbuch* of 1901: "It is gratifying to observe that the importance of the racial question of blood is increasingly being recognized in the thinking circles of our Volk. In that connection unexpected help has arisen for us on the side of the opponent; the Zionists . . . have posted themselves on the racial standpoint and acknowledge that Judaism is something inborn and permanent which cannot be washed away with baptismal water."[84] Such acknowledgements supported the claim of the Jewish liberals that the Zionists were adding fuel to the fire of the anti-Semites, and as we have seen, the defenders of the emancipation ideology generally denied in the strongest terms that the Jews were either a Volk or a race.[85]

In earlier decades, only one major Jewish thinker, Moses Hess (1812-1875), had accepted a racial definition of Jewishness. In 1862 he wrote: "The Jewish race is a primary race which, despite climatic influences, accommodates itself to all conditions and retains its integrity. The Jewish type has always remained indelibly the same throughout the centuries." Hess used the notion of a Jewish race as the basis for a program of Jewish nationalism: "Judaism as a nationality has a natural basis which cannot, like a confession of faith, be supplanted by another. A Jew still continues to belong to Jewry by virtue of his racial origin even though his ancestors may have become apostates."[86] Anticipating the Zionist critique of defense by several decades, he had pointed out the futility of all efforts to end hatred of the Jews through the Enlightenment. "The reconciliation of the races proceeds of itself according to natural laws which we cannot create and alter arbitrarily," he had argued. "The masses will never be moved toward progress by rational abstractions."[87]

But Hess's suggestions had died stillborn, and there is no evidence that the new generation of younger Jewish thinkers at the turn of the century drew their conceptions from his work. Hess's ideas had never caught on because they came too early, at a time when the hold of the emancipation ideology on Jewish thinking had not yet been challenged by political and racial anti-Semitism and by the emergence of the Zionist movement. But now, decades later, in a far different intellectual climate, concepts like those he had suggested were rather more credible and, for the first time, found currency within some Jewish circles.[88]

In examining this development now a distinction must be made between the two different modes in which völkisch attitudes were expressed:

1. *Materialistic* völkisch thought was based on the sciences of biology, ethnography, and anthropology, and used the data and vocabulary of those disciplines. Terms like *"Blut"* and *"Rasse"* were used frequently in a literal, nonmetaphorical sense. Those who expressed themselves in this form did not deal with the existence of a realm transcending the immediate, material entities with which they were concerned.

2. *Transcendental* völkisch thought defined itself in nonbiological terms by using, most frequently, romantic concepts such as *"Volk,"* *"Seele,"* and *"Geist."* When more "scientific" terms (like *"Blut,"* and *"Rasse"*) were employed, their sense was often "softened" by their association with these concepts drawn from the vocabulary of romantic nationalism. Moreover, this version of the völkisch ideology was generally associated—in the hands of its Jewish advocates, at least— with some sort of link to that which transcended the Volk itself (e.g., humanity, mankind).

We turn now to consider some of the major expressions of both sorts of thinking.

Materialistic Völkisch Thought. "Are the Jews a Race?" was the head over an article by Leopold Laufer which appeared in *Die Welt* during its initial year (1897).[89] Laufer's essay was the first published effort of the recently launched Zionist movement to deal with this question, one that had already been answered negatively by the Jewish liberals and affirmatively by the anti-Semites. Laufer's answer is illuminating, for after discussing a number of assertions which had been made about Jewish racial identity, he concluded: "We do not consider the Jews to be an unmixed race but rather a Volk with many anthropological, racial characteristics." Thus in this first confrontation with the question of a Jewish race, the Zionists hedged somewhat, and without denying a racial component in Jewishness, refused to give race primary status.

Within a few years, however, discussions of the racial character of the Jews became less tentative and more assertive as one correspondent in *Die Welt* after another dealt with the subject sympathetically and, occasionally, in considerable detail.[90] For example, *Die Welt* reprinted the entire text of an article entitled "Ethos und Physis der jüdischen Rasse" by the young anthropologist Heinrich Driesmans. The article had first appeared elsewhere, and without endorsing or refuting its contents, the editors added a sparse note to the effect that since the question of a Jewish race is of such great importance, they considered it advisable to have authorities with various points of view express their opinions.[91] Driesmans had argued that the Jews should not be afraid of a discussion of the racial question, for all anthropologists accepted the Jewish race as a "model example." Dr. Paul Rieger, active in the Centralverein and preacher at the temple in Hamburg, had attacked Driesmans' contention by reasserting the liberal view that "Judaism is pure and simple a religious community" and that one can no more speak of a Jewish race or nationality than one can of a Catholic race or nationality. *Die Welt* carried the full text of Driesmans' letter of response to Rieger, in which he argued:

If you were even slightly acquainted with [the field of anthropology] then you would not defend yourself against the "typical characteristics" of your race and attempt to deny them, but rather would all the more emphasize them and make them more prominent. In a word, you would be proud in general of having typical characteristics and would find the pride of your race in them. For a Volk or tribe lifts itself out of the mass, out of the general *Völkerbrei*, precisely through its racial individuality, of which the characteristics offer external witness.[92]

On another occasion one Dr. M. Kretzmer wrote on the "Anthropological, Physiological and Pathological Characteristics of the Jews." Citing scientific studies of skulls exhumed from ancient Jewish cemeteries and the depictions of Jews on Egyptian and Assyrian monuments,[93] Kretzmer argued that the Jewish racial type was unique by virtue of its antiquity and continuity: "In ancient and modern times, the *Judenstamm* has cultivated and preserved characteristics throughout its exile from the homeland and during the dispersion through the rest of the world in a way known to us from no other *Menschenstamm*." Notwithstanding varying geographical, social and political forces, the Jews have preserved among themselves a "similar, characteristic form," marked by the following features:

The height is not great, on the average 162-165 cm. They have elongated bodies and short limbs. For the most part, the color of the hair and pupils is dark (brunette). Blondes and red-heads appear rarely among the Jews.

Although one or another of these marks may not always occur, like the color of the hair, the pupils, etc., this only confirms the phenomenon of the variability of individual appearances of race and type reported by Darwin and others. The relative proportion of the development of the body to that of the extremities and brachycephaly always remain characteristic of the *Judenstamm*.[94]

Kretzmer concluded that the Jews were not only a race with distinct inborn physical and spiritual features, but one that had preserved itself since the days of Abraham with remarkably little variation or change. For the last four thousand years, and in particular since the first Jewish settlement in Europe, "the *Judenstamm* has remained pure with respect to race."[95]

These discussions on the question of the Jewish race in *Die Welt* had potentially important implications for the developing ideology of Zionism. Although Herzl himself never accepted a racial definition of Jewishness, the argument in the pages of his journal that the Jews were a race gave powerful support to his conviction that the Jewish question was insoluble through assimilation. Seen as a racial question, hard, material, "scientific" evidence could be mustered to explain the existence of anti-Semitism and prove the impossibility of assimilation. Hence, Hugo Ganz argued that the Jews had learned from anti-Semitism that "assimilation is just as possible as conversion from the yellow to the red race." "Those who demand assimilation of us," he continued, "either do not yet know that a man cannot get out of his skin . . . or else they know this and then expect of us shameful, daily humiliation, which consists in feigning Aryanism, suppressing our instincts, and squeezing into the skin of the Aryan, which does not fit us at all. . . ."[96]

In a similar vein, Dr. Max Jungmann cited with approval various references by Gobineau to the purity of the Jewish race and especially his contention that "two civilizations which have come forth from totally alien races can touch one another only superficially; [they] can never interpenetrate each other, but rather always exclude each other." On the basis of Gobineau's theory, Jungmann concluded that "the Jewish *Geist* cannot strike any roots in the depth of the Aryan soul." Despite superficial adaptations in language, customs, and habits, the essence of the Jewish *Geist* remained unaltered; the *Geist* and all associated traits of the Jewish soul are carried by blood, and Jewish blood, as Gobineau had claimed, had remained remarkably pure and unmixed. From the racial standpoint, the only way the Jews might be able to be assimilated would be through full mixing of their blood with that of other, less pure peoples, and that would be a tragic error. "A genuine, inner union can only come about through complete mixing, by means of which in our case Judaism would go to ruin. The purer and hence more noble, more vital race must commit an unnatural suicide." Out of the union of two races, a better and higher mixed race results only rarely. "In most cases, it rather results in a deterioration of the human species and in a vague form of combined characteristics." Such a bastard nation, Jungmann concluded, is almost always degenerate.[97]

Yet such attempts to use racial concepts to underwrite the views of Herzlian Zionism were rather rare, and the potentiality of establishing the Zionist argument on a racial basis was largely unused. Official Zionism continued to be argued, as by Herzl himself, largely on the basis of political and economic analysis, and racial thinking was not invoked to support the major elements in the Zionist platform. *Die Welt* continued to explore racial ideas, however, especially with regard to the much discussed question of the physical degeneracy of the Jewish people.

The charge that the Jews were a degenerate race had been made frequently by the racial anti-Semites, and if this assertion embarrassed the Jewish liberals, it was especially challenging to those Zionists who accepted the general proposition that the Jews were a race. The outward signs of degeneracy to which the anti-Semites often referred were not denied by the Zionists, who agreed that the Jews—especially the suffering masses in East Europe—were physically debilitated. Yet to concede that the causes of this debility were found in the racial makeup of Jewry would be to deny the possibility that Jewish nationalism would be able to bring about a rebirth of the Jewish people. If the Jews were ineradicably degenerate by virtue of fixed racial traits, the realization of Zionist aims would be impossible.

Some young Zionists attacked this problem and found ways to maintain the notion of Jewish racial identity without conceding that the existing inadequacies in the present stock were permanent and beyond reform. Balduin Groller, for example, noted that the charge of Jewish physical inferiority was based largely on statistical averages according to which the Jews were shown to be weaker than other races. Groller claimed that the true character of a race and its capacities must be measured by the accomplishments of its finest exemplars, not by its masses. The fact that a number of Jews had distinguished themselves as acrobats and athletes (including the English boxing champion Sir Eduard Laurence Levy) was sufficient proof of the inherent physical strength of the race as a whole. If the majority of Jews did not match the achievements of these few, that was clearly because of the crippling effects of the massive poverty to which they were condemned, not because of any alleged racial inadequacies.[98] Emphasizing Groller's conclusion that the race as such was sound, another writer cited Tacitus on the physical health of the Jewish stock and called for the support of the Turnverein movement in order to effectuate the much needed and clearly achievable physical rehabilitation of Jewry.[99]

At the Second Zionist Congress in 1898 Max Nordau had declared: "We must aspire to create again a *Muskeljudenthum* [muscle Judaism]," and in the fall of that same year the first Jewish Turnverein, Bar Kochba, was formed in Berlin under the leadership of Wilhelm Levy, a student of philosophy.[100] Within two years a number of Jewish Turnvereine had sprung into existence (at least one of which had a women's division) and had begun publication of their own journal, *Jüdische Turnzeitung*.[101] By 1904 there were twelve Jewish Turnvereine in Germany, with the Berlin group alone claiming seven hundred members.[102]

The declaration of goals which appeared on the cover of the first issue of *Jüdische Turnzeitung* asserted that the primary aim of the new organization was a "healthy spirit in a healthy body." It attacked the "one-sided development of the spirit which has called forth our nervousness and spiritual exhaustion," and then set down the following principles:

We want to restore to the flabby Jewish body its lost tone, to make it vigorous and strong, nimble and powerful.

We want this, however, in a Jewish *Verein*, so that we strengthen in it at the same time the disappearing feeling of cohesiveness and elevate [our] sinking self-consciousness.

We want to restore value and honor to the old Jewish ideals for which our youth appear to have lost understanding almost completely.

Courageously and with energy we want to confront anti-Semitism, which indeed has today laid aside its uproarious form but has gained in intensity.

We want to foster a noble national feeling which is free from all vanity and by no means [do we] exclude work for mankind as a whole. Openly, before the whole world, we acknowledge our nationality, to which we preserve loyalty, as we conscientiously and faithfully fulfill our civil duties.

These are our goals![103]

Thus, from the beginning, the Jewish Turnvereine were openly and self-consciously nationalistic and saw group exercise in a Jewish organizational setting as a means of rebuilding both Jewish physique and national self-awareness.[104]

For the *Jüdische Turnverein* national self-consciousness entailed the recognition that the Jews were a community based on "common descent and history, and by no means on religious conviction."[105] Although frequent use of racial terminology was made, the gymnastic journal was rarely concerned, like *Die Welt*, with achieving a definition of Jewish racial identity. It assumed the Jews were a national community, and then devoted itself to the special role gymnastic activities might play in building the physical and spiritual strength of that community.

The Turner advocates had the task of achieving a rather delicate balance in their discussions. By pointing out symptoms of Jewish physical inadequacy, they had shown the clear need for physical education; yet their attempts to prove the weakness of the Jewish people could not be so overwhelming as to preclude the possibility of reform and rehabilitation. As a result the gymnastic spokesmen made frequent use of the terminology of race without committing themselves to a racial definition of Jewishness which might have implied, as the anti-Semites argued, that the Jews were incorrigibly degenerate.[106] Descriptions of the "extraordinary dissemination of nervous and mental illness" among Eastern and Western Jews due to "our inherited neurasthenic character," buttressed with statistics, were offset by articles denying the degeneracy of the Jewish race.[107] Emanuel Edelstein may have found the properly balanced formulation for the movement when he wrote: "Although it is also happily not true . . . that we *are* degenerate, unfortunately, symptoms of degeneracy have appeared. . . ."[108]

When the Turner spokesmen went on to argue for the efficacy of the Turnvereine in reversing these distressing signs, they offered justification that echoed an argument often used by the advocates of enlightenment earlier in the nineteenth century: the power of education as a means of reform. Hence one writer, after describing in some detail the alarming incidence of hereditary disease among Jews, castigated those who accepted with passive resignation the progressive deterioration of Jewry due to the effects of the laws of heredity. "In education a power is given," he wrote, "through which the nervous individuality can undergo beneficial or harmful transformation." Proper attention to the inherited nervous constitution of Jewish youth should dictate utilization of those specific educational techniques which can overcome hereditary limitations and defects, something which can never be accomplished with the current over-emphasis on the principle of intellectualism in Jewish education.[109] What sort of educational program would correct this imbalance?

Jewish youth of both sexes face with great urgency the duty of preparing a way for the better. . . . Therefore, my brothers, steel your youthful limbs with physical labor, in the garden and field, on the sawing-trestle and wherever it is possible to steel the muscles—in the gymnasium, in the fencing room and in the swimming school. Become nimble and supple, muscular and courageous as your ancestors were. Read Jewish history—the battles in which a Jeptha, a Saul, a David, a Samson show glory; read the battles of the Hasmoneans, the Maccabees [and of] Bar Kochba, which are not inferior to the heroic battles of all the nations. You will find therein a spur to become worthy of these distinguished figures.[110]

By engaging in these activities, a compound of group exercise and study of Jewish national history, the youth were offered a means of participating personally, through their own physical and intellectual activities, in the solution of the Jewish problem and the regeneration of the Jewish people. The Turnvereine offered its members, in short, a means of personal involvement in an effort of great historical significance, and a way of participating intimately in a cause which could appeal to their idealism.

Occasionally Turner activities were even related directly to the struggle against anti-Semitism, as in the reminder that pursuit of physical culture by Jewish youth would refute established anti-Jewish caricatures.[111] As one writer declared: "No one who has exercised a year in our ranks will any longer stand for an insult to his Judaism without raising an arm. And this defense of Judaism appears to be even more distinguished than [one made] with sword, pistol or even pen."[112] And the same theme of militancy was expressed in the songs created by the movement, as in one by R. Blum which declared, to the tune of "O Deutschland, hoch in Ehren": "Do not fear, do not waver, make yourselves ready for battle; let the courage of [your] ancestors glow within you, learn to take up weapons for the right."[113]

As might be expected, the established Jewish community did not react favorably to the emergence of the Jewish Turnvereine. In Hanover, for example, the community representatives adopted a resolution condemning both the name and the constitution of the local Jewish Turnverein. The name, they declared, was misleading because the Jüdische Turnverein did not represent the Jews of Hanover; moreover, the establishment of a separate Jewish gymnastic organization would only encourage confessionalism among the existing Turnvereine.[114] In defense of their movement, however, the Jewish Turner could cite the emergence of anti-Semitism in the German

Turnerschaft. At the fifteenth Kreisturntag held in Vienna in 1901, the German Turner organization decided by a vote of 120 to 15 that in the future only those groups who accepted Aryan members could affiliate. Rejecting the status of "second class gymnasts," The *Jüdische Turnzeitung* declared: *"Los von der deutschen Turnerschaft!"*[115]

Yet there was also an ideological justification for the separatism of the Jewish Turnvereine: gymnastic activities were not pursued merely for their own sake, but as part of a commitment to Jewish nationalism. The self-respecting Jewish nationalist, therefore, could not participate fully in the German Turnvereine which, even when not overtly anti-Semitic, were suffused with German *völkisch* consciousness. "Those Jews who are conscious of themselves know that they never belong to these truly self-conscious Germans," commented one writer, who then recommended conscious imitation of the established models of German gymnastic activity: "[There is] a necessity to awaken again among the Jews in Germany the sense of their special nationality through the powerful and proven means of *Turnerei* on the German model."[116] He wrote with great affection of the accomplishments of the German Turnvereine and emphasized that the development of Jewish national awareness did not entail enmity to Germany:

In the Turnvereine men and women will be educated who will partake of the cause of their Volk with heart and hand. Then a new generation will greet sunshine . . . with thirst for freedom and honor, with love for the German fatherland, but also for Judaism and the *Judenvolk*. . . .
Let no one believe that we national Jews are in any way enemies of *Deutschtum*. German sentiments are preserved among us to so great an extent that many more Ahlwardts and Count Pücklers must arise before our admiration of the German essence and our inclination to it is drained.[117]

The ambiguity expressed by this writer—that consciousness of Jewish nationality was still linked to abiding feeling for Germany—was characteristic of many in this generation, and his suggestion consciously to build the gymnastic movement on German models constituted a means of resolving the tension: the long tradition of German Turnerei would be appropriated by the young Jewish nationalists and put to the service of Zionism.

There is considerable irony in this development, for the founder of the German Turnvereine tradition which the Jewish gymnasts now embraced was Turnvater Jahn, who had written, some eighty years earlier, "Hatred of everything foreign is the German duty."[118] When Jahn established the first German gymnastic club, he barred Jews from membership and declared that "Poles, Frenchmen, priests, Junkers, and Jews are Germany's affliction."[119] Yet the anti-Jewish and xenophobic elements in Jahn's thinking were ignored by the Jewish youth, and they extolled his memory, citing with approval his "golden words" on the virtues of gymnastic activities.[120]

Yet, as George Mosse has pointed out, the Jewish Turner were plagued by the recurring problem of defining the uniquely Jewish component in their gymnastic activities, which were patterned so closely and so deliberately after German völkisch models.[121] For some the mood of aggressive self-development and the references to the Jewish heroic tradition were not enough. We turn now to examine the thought of those young Zionist writers who sought and found a deeper and more coherent rationale for Jewish nationalism.

Transcendental Völkisch Thought. Among some of the Zionist youth in Germany at the turn of the century a new term became current: *"Jüdische Renaissance."*[122] With this phrase they described their hopes for Zionism, aspirations that the political Zionism of Herzl did not satisfy. Influenced by Achad Ha-am's cultural nationalism, they saw Zionism as the rebirth of a Volk and its creativity even more than the creation of a political homeland. When the Fifth Zionist Congress failed to adopt the proposal that a Jewish publishing house be established to further the renaissance, a group of them, led by Martin Buber (1878-1965), struck out on their own and founded the Jüdischer Verlag. In the fall of 1902 their first volume, the *Jüdischer Almanach*, appeared with a foreword by Buber's associate, Berthold Feiwel.[123]

In Zionism, Feiwel wrote, the Jewish renaissance is accomplished, bringing about the creation of a new Jewish culture. Once before the Jewish Volk gave birth to an unforgettable culture, and although restricted in its creativity by long centuries of homelessness, "in the future [it] shall transpose its liberated racial powers into a new culture. Out of the marriage of the Volk with the motherland will grow the new *Geist,* which will be at one and the same time the unfettered, original *Geist* of the nation and the *Geist* of the new times." In this time of a "new Jewish *Volkstum,*" the *Almanach* intended to stimulate and interpret the already emerging "new, completely modern and completely national culture." This volume, and those to follow, had the additional purpose of showing those creative Jews who were alienated from Judaism and saw in it no possibilities for cultural expression a "living, creating, struggling, self-liberating Judaism." "Thus," it said, "on beautiful thoroughfares they shall find the way to their Volk and its future. The creators . . . [who] scattered their powers amidst foreign *Völker* without their being recognized and loved as Jewish, shall be gathered in one camp and united for one great purpose: for the preservation and development of the Jewish racial power and the Jewish Volk-personality." The distinctive "Jewish aesthetic ideal" would achieve full recognition, and out of the bounty of Jewish books,

Jewish paintings, and Jewish music a national pride would develop which would transform itself into "living Volks-energy."[124]

Although the full realization of the renaissance would have to wait the return to Zion, Feiwel claimed that signs of distinctive Jewish Volk-creativity were already evident. They had appeared most clearly in the work of the Eastern Jews who were still deeply rooted in their *Volkstum* and its tradition. But, Feiwel believed, they were also present, though hidden, in the creative work of those West European artists of Jewish descent "who, unconsciously, without pronounced national impulse, nonetheless give their works a specifically Jewish note through a *rassentümlichen Einschlag* [racial touch]."[125]

The völkisch motifs of Feiwel's introduction were delineated at greater length in the early work of Martin Buber, who was already the dominant figure in the effort to define and stimulate the Jewish renaissance as a völkisch phenomenon. Like his older contemporary Birnbaum, Buber was an "East-West Jew,"[126] a Jew with roots in East European life who was also part of the intellectual and cultural world of the West. In 1898 he had joined Herzl in the Zionist movement and for several years was active in Zionist organizational affairs, participating as a delegate to the Third Zionist Congress in Basel in 1899 and taking an active part in the direction of Herzl's weekly, *Die Welt*.

But Buber's interest in Zionism transcended the political aims set by Herzl.[127] Through Zionism Buber believed the Jews would not only bring an end to anti-Semitism and solve the Jewish problem but also might find a way to return to the original vitality of the ancient Hebrews.[128] In the *Jüdischer Almanach* he attempted to define those factors which created and preserved a Volk. Religious belief, he wrote, had only a secondary importance at best in defining a Volk; Volk-identity was constituted by other, far more powerful forces: "A Volk is held together by primary elements: blood, fate—insofar, as it rests upon the development of blood—and culturally creative power—insofar as it is conditioned by the individuality which arises from the blood."[129] For Buber, as for many German völkisch thinkers, racial factors were important in understanding the cultural capabilities and limitations of a people; they defined personality of the Volk and should be a source of pride. Counseling Jewish mothers to accept with pride the "Semitic" appearance of their children, he wrote: "They [Jewish mothers] will not be ashamed if their children look Jewish; on the contrary: they will be proud of it. Not merely because it is the *Typus* of their *Stamm*. They will also know that great masters of Holland and Italy regarded the Jewish *Typus* as an ideal of beauty. . . . They will try to develop this *Typus* of beauty, in so far as this is possible in a strange land."[130]

Yet Buber also held that racial factors themselves were subject to modification and alteration by other forces which act on the Volk and its blood: "In any case, one should not forget that these racial characteristics are not something final which cannot be traced back further, but are only the product of the soil and its climatic conditions, of the economic and social structure of the community, of the forms of life and of historical fate. . . . "[131] The Volk is not utterly bound by its racial heritage, and the rebirth of Jewish art, which Buber believed was taking place in his time, was "not an abrogation of the Jewish *Rassenwesen*" but only a new phase in its development.[132] It was true that racial factors explained why the Jews had failed to produce any significant visual art in antiquity, but these racial factors had been modified; the new Jewish art was being borne by Volk-characteristics which have developed so that "men who do not experience in their blood an artistic tradition" were now able to paint works of aesthetic merit. "The great historical wonder," Buber said, "is the fact that there are any Jewish artists at all, and also that in their vision and in their fashioning altogether quietly and secretly something of the Jewish mode of being [and] something of the original character of the pure blood which washes their optic nerves [and] the muscles of their hands becomes alive."[133] The full rebirth of Jewish artistic powers, however, would have to wait the return to Zion where the reunion of various elements of the Volk and the impact of those Palestinian climatic factors "under whose influence the race once arose" would have a salutary effect on the whole *Volksleben* (life of the Volk).[134]

Using these völkisch concepts, Buber attempted to evaluate Jewish authenticity as found in various cultural expressions. For example, he discussed at length the art of Lesser Ury and attempted to prove that it was *"echt jüdisch"* ("authentically Jewish") by finding in his work traces of the Jewish *Volksgeist*. [135] And when Herzl died, Buber wrote an unflattering obituary noting that the founder of political Zionism had been a Western Jew devoid of Jewish tradition and that it was "completely false to extol him as a *Jewish* personality." "Spinoza and Israel Baal Shem, even Heine and Lassalle were Jews," he contended. "Nothing fundamentally Jewish lived in Theodor Herzl. He was not a manifestation of the *Volkdämon*. In Golus the soul of our Volk has stammered only a few words which make known its innermost [being]; Herzl does not belong to these words."[136] "He was a whole man, but he was not a whole Jew," Buber concluded, and although willing to grant him admiration for his devoted work on behalf of Zionism, for Buber Herzl remained incomplete and deficient as a Jew.

Whereas young Buber had accepted the völkisch ideology and used it to define and give content to his Jewish nationalism, his closest friend, Gustav Landauer (1870-1919), accepted a völkisch understanding of Jewishness but rejected Zionism. Landauer was an anarchist, a follower of Kropotkin and Proudhon, and at one time editor of *Der Sozialist*, the organ of the independent socialists.[137] In his interest in Jewish identity Landauer was virtually unique among the Jews on the German left.[138] He believed that the Jews constituted a specific racial community and that the individual Jew was linked with all others through ancestral blood ties. "I sense my Judaism," he wrote, "in my gestures, my facial expressions, my bearing, my appearance, and these signs are to me proof that it lives in all that I am and undertake."[139] He saw the Jews as a Volk, a distinctive organic unit, equivalent to the German or Russian people, with unique linguistic and cultural traditions worthy of preservation.[140]

Yet, while considering himself a racial and national Jew, he refused to deny his Germanness. He saw no contradiction between being a Jew and a German:

I accept my fate and am what I am: my being German and being Jewish do no harm to each other and do much for each other's sake. As two brothers, a firstborn and a Benjamin, are loved by one mother—not in the same way but in the same measure—and as these two brothers live harmoniously with each other, both when their paths cross and when they go their separate ways, so I experience this strange and intimate dualistic unity as something precious. I fail to see a primary and a secondary in this relationship. I have never felt the need to simplify myself nor to unify myself through renunciation. I accept the complexity that I am and hope to be a unity of even more complexities than I am aware of.[141]

Moreover, Landauer believed the Jew could be himself and develop his Volk-consciousness even in Germany, and therefore he saw no need for a return to Zion. Indeed, arguing against Zionism, he claimed that the Jewish Volk is not linked to a territory, but through the very fact of being a nation while dispersed in the world, the Jews can most properly be a part of the future of humanity and its emerging unity, a unity which he believed would be a "Bund of multiplicity." In the diaspora the Jew can best fulfill the historic mission of his people in bringing about the redemption of mankind.[142]

Landauer's union of völkisch Jewishness with the needs and interests of humanity as a whole was evident in Buber as well, and in this they were clearly distinguished from many of their German counterparts. In the prospectus for *Der Jude*, Buber wrote with Chaim Weizmann of that young generation in whom the "living organism of the nation" was still powerful; in fostering that "living *Volkstum*," they noted "the development of the Jewish *Volk* represents only a partial phenomenon of the general development of mankind . . . and, above all, the Jewish Renaissance can be understood only in connection with those ideas which move modern society and modern *Völkerleben.*"[143] Buber saw his era as the *"Epoche der Kulturkeime,"* ("era of cultural germination") and Zionism was part of a great international movement marked by the *"Selbstbesinnung der Völkerseelen"* ("self-consciousness of folk-souls"). And speaking of the tasks facing the Jewish renaissance, he wrote: "We must remove much morbid matter and clear away many obstructions before we will be ripe for the rebirth of the Jewish Volk, which is only a subcurrent of the new renaissance of mankind."[144]

Although the Jewish völkisch thinkers rejected most of the presuppositions of the dominant German-Jewish ideology, they were still under the hold of Enlightenment universalism, as were Herzl and the other, older Zionists who did not accept völkisch thought. In Landauer and Buber we see most clearly the way in which the counterposed traditions of liberal humanism, long established in the Jewish community, and avant-garde romantic nationalism came together and mingled. Even in embracing the völkisch ideology, Landauer and Buber maintained a commitment to the universal which set them apart from the German Volkists, and in their thought one of the major emphases of the emancipation ideology was preserved.[145]

CONCLUSION

Over half a century has elapsed since the ideological struggles discussed in this study took place, and many have seen the judgment of history in the events of the years that followed. The emergence of Nazism out of the political and economic turmoil of the twenties, the implementation of Hitler's "Final Solution" for the Jewish problem during World War II, the establishment of the state of Israel in 1948—in all of this, it is often claimed, the naiveté of the emancipation ideology and the perspicacity of early Zionism are revealed. These tumultuous, tragic decades, it is said, settled once and for all the question of which view of the German-Jewish future was correct: that of the Jewish liberals or of the Jewish nationalists.

Yet one must question the fairness of such an assessment. No generation is ever granted that clarity of vision which would allow it to discern the shape of the future, and in the years before World War I not even the most dedicated Zionist spokesmen could imagine the depth of the horror which German anti-Semitism would one day create. Neither Jewish liberals nor Jewish nationalists were able to foresee the catastrophic events which later crashed in upon European Jewry, and although the destruction of Jewry ended the long career of the emancipation ideology in Germany, that system of ideas was not thereby proven "false."

Ideologies are perhaps best judged according to other categories. An ideology is a pattern of ideas which helps those who embrace it to organize their experience and account for the events of their existence. An ideology is always bound up with the perceptions, aspirations, and experiences of those to whom it appeals, and it is "true" or "false" to the extent to which it succeeds in interpreting reality for a particular group bound up in the concrete circumstances of a specific moment in time. Whenever a new fact or unexpected event occurs, an ideology is challenged to explain the novelty in a way that will be persuasive and intelligible. If, as events unfold, an established ideology is unable to interpret events in a way that is satisfactory to a significant number of its adherents, a new ideology offering an alternative analysis may emerge. But that new complex of ideas is not likely to be totally original, and while introducing innovations or radical departures from previously adopted positions, it is almost certain to perpetuate concepts and values from the old ideology.

161

Among German Jews at the turn of the century, a "true" ideology would have had to be one which could meaningfully interpret the existence of modern anti-Semitism to those emancipated Jews who perceived themselves as both Jewish and German. It would have had to show them how the fact of anti-Jewish hostility could be related coherently to their sense of identity. Seen from this perspective, the emancipation ideology was "true" in that it retained its position as the dominant mode of thought during the years under study and was able to explain and—through the vehicle of the Centralverein—deal with anti-Semitism in a way that was satisfactory to the vast majority of the Jewish community. The emergence of anti-Semitism did not evoke any dramatically new ideas from the leadership of emancipated Jewry because the traditional values of the Enlightenment and of political liberalism continued to offer what was perceived as an adequate interpretation of the critical tensions of the period. Although several new tactics of response were implemented (counter-propaganda, legal defense, the formation of a mass organization), all were forged within limits set by the emancipation ideology. The continued dominance of the emancipation ideology is proof of the powerful persuasiveness of those ideas which had so long justified the integration of the Jews into Germany, an integration which was, we must remember, challenged but by no means reversed in the years before 1914.

By the same measure, the emergence of Zionism in the 1890s demonstrates that the emancipation ideology could no longer command universal assent. Although most university youth continued to accept the views of their liberally-minded parents, a significant minority found their way into Zionism because it offered explanations of the Jewish problem, of Jewish identity, and of the hostility to which they were exposed personally which were, they believed, vastly more compelling than those presented by the established community. The rapid incorporation of völkisch and racial concepts into Zionist thinking by some of the young Jewish nationalists reveals dramatically the extent of the defection which was taking place. The ideological unity of German Jewry was shattered at this time, and by amalgamating the insights of Herzlian Zionism with the völkisch ideology, some of the most able young Zionists created a pattern of ideas which was to become of great importance in German-Jewish affairs. When liberalism entered its period of greatest crisis in the twenties and thirties, the German-Jewish community would confront that challenge with not one but two highly developed and disparate ideological traditions available to it.

Before World War I, however, the emancipation ideology continued to preserve its hold on the greater part of the German-Jewish community, and Ludwig Holländer, the *Syndikus* of the Centralverein, spoke authoritatively for most Jews when he addressed an assembly of the *Kartell Convent* in Frankfurt in the spring of 1914. With international tension mounting and the prospect of war looming large, he declared:

Loyalty is the root of our religion, as our religion is the root of our loyalty. Providence willed it that we were born as Jews. The commandment to every man of honor is: Rally round the flag! Round a flag which has been held aloft for 3,000 years, a flag which has remained immaculate. There is blood on it enough, but it is our own! That is the flag on which there stands inscribed: "The Lord is my banner!"

And Holländer concluded his impassioned speech: *"Deutschland, Deutschland über alles!"* [1]

ABBREVIATIONS

AZJ *Allgemeine Zeitung des Judenthums*
IDR *Im Deutschen Reich*
ISR *Der Israelit*
IWOS *Israelitische Wochenschrift*
JP *Die Jüdische Presse*
JS *Der Jüdische Student*
JT *Jüdische Turnzeitung*
OUW *Ost und West*
YBLBI *Yearbook of the Leo Baeck Institute*

NOTES

CHAPTER ONE

[1]G. Lichtheim, cited by Egmont Zechlin, *Die deutsche Politik und die Juden im Ersten Weltkrieg* (Göttingen, 1969), pp. 56-57. On the background to the emancipation, see Arthur Hertzberg, *The French Enlightenment and the Jews: The Origins of Modern Anti-Semitism* (New York, 1970); Jacob Katz, *Tradition and Crisis: Jewish Society at the End of the Middle Ages* (New York, 1961); *idem, Jews and Freemasons in Europe, 1723-1939* (Cambridge, 1970); *idem,* "The Term 'Jewish Emancipation': Its Origin and Historical Impact," *Studies in Nineteenth Century Jewish Intellectual History,* ed. by Alexander Altmann (Cambridge, 1964), pp. 1-26; Selma Stern-Täubler, "The German Jew in a Changing World," *YBLBI,* VII (1962), pp. 3-10; Ernest Hamburger, "One Hundred Years of Emancipation," *YBLBI,* XIV (1969), pp. 3-66; Reinhard Rürup, "Jewish Emancipation and Bourgeois Society," *YBLBI,* XIV (1969), pp. 67-91; Moshe Rinott, "Gabriel Riesser: Fighter for Jewish Emancipation," *YBLBI,* VII (1962), pp. 11-38; Azriel Shohet, *Im Hilufei T'kufot: Reshit Ha-haskalah B'yahadut Germania* ("Beginnings of Haskalah Among German Jewry") (Jerusalem, 1960). On the general German background, see: Franz Schnabel, *Deutsche Geschichte im neunzehnten Jahrhundert* (Freiburg, 1965); Koppel S. Pinson, *Modern Germany: Its History and Civilization* (New York, 1954); Theodore S. Hamerow, *Restoration, Revolution, Reaction: Economics and Politics in Germany, 1815-1871* (Princeton, New Jersey, 1958).

[2]Regarding the earliest treatment of Jewish emancipation in England, see Katz, "The Term 'Jewish Emancipation'," pp. 8-9. Katz discusses Toland and Locke, who were the first to apply the concept of the oneness of human nature to the Jews. On France, see Hertzberg, *French Enlightenment.*

[3]Katz, "The Term 'Jewish Emancipation'," p. 21. Consider the announced title in an essay contest sponsored by the Royal Society of Arts and Sciences in Metz, 1785: "Are There Means of Making the Jews Happy and More Useful in France," cited by Hertzberg, *French Enlightenment,* p. 328. On the impact of the new economic ideas on the discussion of the Jewish situation, see p. 76.

[4]Christian Wilhelm Dohm, "Concerning the Amelioration of the Civil Status of the Jews," trans. by Helen Lederer, mimeographed (Cincinnati: Hebrew Union College, 1957).

[5]*Ibid.,* p. 16. See also pp. 14, 18-19, 45, 48, 51, 59, 61-62, 80; Katz, "The Term 'Jewish Emancipation'," pp. 12ff.; Hertzberg, *French Enlightenment,* pp. 120, 185, 236, 292. For similar arguments used in France for granting the Jews rights in order to cure them of their ills, see the pamphlet written by the Jew Bernard de Valabrague in 1767 on behalf of the Jews of Avignon, discussed by Hertzberg, p. 62.

[6]On David Friedländer as embodying both points, see Michael A. Meyer, *The Origins of the Modern Jew: Jewish Identity and European Culture in Germany, 1749-1824* (Detroit, 1967), pp. 62-63, 68. On Friedländer's effort to substitute

the term "Israelite" for "Jew," see p. 197, n. 36. See also Hertzberg, *French Enlightenment*, for his discussions of the negative image of the Jew (p. 328), of the emerging image of the new Jew (pp. 266, 338), and of the prevailing assumption that emancipation was designed for the *new* Jew and was thus planned less for the Jew as he was than for the Jew as he promised to be after suitable reform (pp. 348, 364). Hertzberg points out that French thinkers had in mind a kind of "social compact" between the Jews and the state according to which emancipation and regeneration went hand in hand (p. 187). Note also that Napoleon's decrees of 1808 made the lifting of Jewish disabilities contingent on improvement by the Jews.

[7]Rürup, pp. 78-79.

[8]On the development of a neutral society between the traditional Christian and Jewish groups, see Katz, *Jewish Society*, pp. 245-259. See also Hanns Günther Reissner, *Eduard Gans: Ein Leben im Vormärz* (Tübingen, 1965), and Hugo Bieber, ed., *Heinrich Heine: A Biographical Anthology* (Philadelphia, 1956).

[9]Rinott, p. 17. See also Alexander Altmann, "The New Style of Preaching in Nineteenth Century German Jewry," *Studies in Nineteenth Century Jewish Intellectual History*, ed. by Alexander Altmann (Cambridge, 1964), p. 99. Altmann notes how Jewish sermons of the emancipation period stressed the need for occupational changes and pleaded with parents to give their children training in agriculture and the crafts. Consider also the statement by Isaac Marcus Jost in 1822: "Wenn die Juden ein Volk ausmachten, Grund und Boden besässen, in die Wagschale der Nationen ein Gewicht legten, also Gemeinschaft hätten, durch Vaterlandsliebe, Verfassung und Eigenthum, wie zum Beispiel die heutigen Griechen, so wäre es etwas anderes. Aber so wie die Umstände sind, bleiben unsre Bemühungen um Erhaltung der Eigenthümlichkeit fruchtlos, und vielleicht sind sie schädlich. Nur das dürfen wir wünschen, die durch leidenvolle Jahrhunderte entarteten Menschen wieder zur Menschheit zu führen, ihnen einen besseren Lebenswandel zu verschaffen, und ihrem Geiste eine andere Richtung ohne Rücksicht auf den Erfolg zu geben. Und das wollen wir aus allen Kräften zu leisten streben." Cited by Nahum N. Glatzer, ed., *Leopold and Adelheid Zunz: An Account in Letters (1815-1885)* (London, 1958), p. 35.

[10]Jacob Toury, *Die politischen Orientierungen der Juden in Deutschland* (Tübingen, 1966), pp. 29ff.

[11]*Ibid.*, p. 23.

[12]Cited in *ibid.*, p. 40.

[13]Cited by Rinott, p. 26. Similar sentiments expressed by Ludwig Börne are cited by Pinson, p. 67.

[14]Ben Halpern, *The Idea of the Jewish State* (Cambridge, 1961), pp. 78-79.

[15]Zechlin, p. 57; H. M. Graupe, "Steinheim und Kant: Eine Untersuchung zum Verhältnis von Theologie und Religionsphilosophie," *YBLBI*, V (1960), p. 141. On philosophical anti-Judaism, and particularly on Kant's attitude toward Judaism, see Nathan Rotenstreich, *The Recurring Pattern: Studies in Anti-Judaism in Modern Thought* (New York, 1964), ch. 2.

[16]See, for example, Max Wiener's classic *Jüdische Religion im Zeitalter der Emanzipation* (Berlin, 1933), which treats extensively the process of confessionalization among the neo-Orthodox as well as in Reform. See also Jacob J. Petuchowski, "Manuals and Catechisms of the Jewish Religion in the Early Period of Emancipation," *Studies in Nineteenth Century Jewish Intellectual History*, ed. by Alexander Altmann (Cambridge, 1964), p. 63; Altmann, p. 74,

on the change in the style of Jewish preaching to approximate, with few differences, the dominant Christian model; Nahum N. Glatzer, "The Beginnings of Modern Jewish Studies," *Studies in Nineteenth Century Jewish Intellectual History*, ed. by Alexander Altmann (Cambridge, 1964), pp. 34ff., on the way in which *Wissenschaft des Judentums* was used to integrate Judaism with world history and world religions, especially in the work of Gans, Zunz, Geiger, and Graetz; and Meyer, *Origins of the Modern Jew*, ch. 5. On ritual reforms, see David Philipson, *The Reform Movement in Judaism* (New York, 1907); W. Gunther Plaut, *The Rise of Reform Judaism: A Sourcebook of its European Origins* (New York, 1963); and Max Wiener, *Abraham Geiger and Liberal Judaism: The Challenge of the Nineteenth Century* (Philadelphia, 1962).

[17]Toury, *Die politischen Orientierungen*, p. 28.

[18]Cited in *ibid.*, p. 70. See also Riesser's statement: "Whoever disputes my claim to my German fatherland, disputes my right to my thoughts and feelings, to the language that I speak, to the air that I breathe, and therefore I must defend myself against him as I would against a murderer." Cited by Rinott, p. 25. Also consider Franz Oppenheimer's memory of his father: "Er war aber auch in seinem Bewusstsein ganz und gar ein Deutscher. Das erste was er mich lehrte, war der schöne Spruch: 'Ich bin ein deutscher Mann, treu und wahr und ohne Lüge'," in Franz Oppenheimer, *Erlebtes, Erstrebtes, Erreichtes, Erinnerungen* (Berlin, 1931), p. 26.

[19]Wiener, *Abraham Geiger*, p. 117.

[20]On Friedländer, see n. 6, *supra*. On the messianism of Reform Judaism, which constituted essentially an idealized version of German Kultur, see Eleonore O. Sterling, *Er ist wie Du, Aus der Frühgeschichte des Antisemitismus in Deutschland (1815-1850)* (Munich, 1956), p. 45.

[21]Katz, *Jews and Freemasons*, p. 96; Hamburger, pp. 10-11.

[22]On Freemasonry as one form through which emancipated Jews sought to express and realize their universal humanism, see Katz, *Jews and Freemasons*. In Masonic lodges Jews sought fellowship with Christians who had divested themselves of their traditional prejudices. Katz demonstrates that Masonic affiliation and leadership in religious reform were frequently combined, and that in Frankfurt, for example, the leadership of the Jewish community simultaneously introduced reform and enrolled in the local Masonic lodge (where their notions about religious reform found confirmation). See especially pp. 94, 118-119, 217-218.

[23]On Riesser, see Rinott, pp. 11ff., 17-18, 20, 26, 31, 33ff., and Fritz Friedländer, *Das Leben Gabriel Riessers* (Berlin, 1926).

[24]Toury, *Die politischen Orientierungen*, pp. 48, 68, 81-82, 90ff.

[25]*Ibid.*, pp. 98-99, 111, 115-116.

[26]*Ibid.*, pp. 120ff., 140.

[27]*Ibid.*, p. 148.

[28]Both quotations are cited in *ibid.*, p. 139 (Emphasis in original).

[29]Cited in *ibid.*, p. 137.

[30]*Ibid.*, p. 123; Robert Weltsch, "Introduction," *YBLBI*, XIV (1969), ix; Rürup, p. 85. See also Katz, *Jews and Freemasons*, p. 215, where he notes that for a time after 1871 the Masons liberalized their regulations regarding Jews. In 1872 one of the three Prussian mother lodges repealed its restrictive clause outright, and the other two made large concessions toward allowing Jews to participate in their activities.

[31]Weltsch, XIV, xvii; Hertzberg, *French Enlightenment*, pp. 307, 338; Katz,

Jews and Freemasons, p. 241. Katz also shows how dubious was Jewish acceptance even in such marginal groups as the Order of the Asiatics, and that the hardening of resistance to Jewish admission to the order began in the 1780s (pp. 47-48).

[32]Katz, *Jews and Freemasons*, pp. 150, 213-214.

[33]E.g., the thought of Görres (1776-1848), an ex-Jacobin, romantic Catholic influenced by de Maistre, Adam Müller (1779-1829), and F.J. Stahl (1802-1861). See H.S. Reiss, *The Political Thought of the German Romantics* (New York, 1955), pp. 1-43.

[34]See the letter written by Hermann Dachs, a Christian, to Moritz Lazarus on August 27, 1892: "Das Grundübel dieses ganz heillosen Unfugs [anti-Semitism] liegt jedoch m.E. in der ganz verkehrten Art unserer religiösen Erziehung. Wir Christen werden von Kindesbeinen an darauf hingewiesen, dass die Juden Christus ans Kreuz geschlagen haben, dass sie zur Strafe dafür aufgehört haben, ein Volk zu sein, dass sie ruhelos umherwandern müssen, usw." Cited by Toury, *Die politischen Orientierungen*, p. 338.

[35]Note, e.g., the tolerance shown by the Millenarists and Jansenists in eighteenth-century France; see Hertzberg, *French Enlightenment*, ch. VIII.

[36]Katz, *Jews and Freemasons*, pp. 77, 148.

[37]See, e.g., Jacob Katz's review of *Er ist wie Du*, by Eleonore O. Sterling, *Journal of Jewish Studies*, VIII (1957), p. 246. Katz notes that it is enough to read Zunz or Riesser to see that, although they were aware of anti-Jewish prejudice, they believed it was merely a holdover from the days of religious intolerance and was in decline.

[38]Sterling, *Er ist wie Du*, ch. III, especially pp. 75-76; Adolf Leschnitzer, *The Magic Background of Modern Anti-Semitism: An Analysis of the German-Jewish Relationship* (New York, 1956), p. 120.

[39]See Hertzberg, *French Enlightenment*, especially pp. 29, 59, 72, and ch. IX on Voltaire, Diderot, and D'Holbach. While adducing clear evidence for the emergence of secular, and in the case of D'Holbach, proto-racial anti-Jewishness, Hertzberg fails to demonstrate conclusively that the Enlightenment (and Voltaire in particular) was responsible for the ideological vocabulary and conceptualization of nineteenth-century anti-Semitism. Early nineteenth-century anti-Semitism owed more to völkisch and romantic nationalism than to the Enlightenment personalities discussed by Hertzberg. See H.R. Trevor-Roper, "Some of My Best Friends Are Philosophes," review of *The French Enlightenment and the Jews*, by Arthur Hertzberg, *New York Review of Books*, August 22, 1968, pp. 11ff.

[40]Rotenstreich, *Studies in Anti-Judaism*, chs. 1-3. On Kant, see also H.D. Schmidt, "Anti-Western and Anti-Jewish Tradition in German Historical Thought," *YBLBI*, I (1959), p. 41.

[41]Cited by Marvin Lowenthal, *The Jews of Germany* (Philadelphia, 1936), p. 229. See also Meyer, *Origins of the Modern Jew*, p. 70.

[42]E.g., Prof. Fries, a professor of philosophy at Heidelberg, declared that the Jews were a "state within a state" and demanded they be expelled because "Jewry is a social pest which owes its rapid spread to money and is accompanied by misery, tyranny, and taxes. . . . Ask any man whether every burgher and peasant does not hate and curse the Jews as robbers of their bread and as the plague of our nation." Cited by Lowenthal, *The Jews of Germany*, pp. 231-232. See also Meyer, *Origins of the Modern Jew*, pp. 139-140; Jacob R. Marcus, *The Rise and Destiny of the German Jew* (Cincinnati, 1934), p. 25; and Uriel Tal, "Ha-Anti-shemiut B'reich Ha-germani Ha-sheyni, 1870-1914"

"Anti-Semitism in the Second German Reich, 1870-1914" (unpublished Ph.D. diss., Hebrew University, Jerusalem, 1963), pp. 62-63. On the Hep-Hep riots of 1819, the only anti-Jewish violence of the period, see Eleonore O. Sterling, "Anti-Jewish Riots in Germany in 1819, A Displacement of Social Protest," *Historia Judaica*, XII: 1 (April, 1950).

[43]E.g., in the period 1840-1870, before the rise of racial anti-Semitism, the basic thrust of German governmental policies was aimed at achieving full assimilation through conversion and intermarriage. At this time some baptized Jews (e.g., Friedrich Julius Stahl and Eduard von Simson) were not only accepted in German public life but achieved prominence. See Arthur Prinz, "New Perspectives on Marx as a Jew," *YBLBI*, XV (1970), p. 117.

[44]E.g., H.E.G. Paulus, who wrote *Die jüdische Nationalabsonderung nach Ursprung, Folgen, und Besserungsmitteln* (1831), argued that the Jews were a nation but could end their separate nationality by conversion to Christianity. Rinott, p. 17.

[45]Sterling, *Er ist wie Du*, p. 126; Tal, "Ha-Anti-shemiut," pp. 63-64.

[46]Nathan Rotenstreich, "For and Against Emancipation—The Bruno Bauer Controversy," *YBLBI*, IV (1959), pp. 3-11, 33-35. In 1831, the same year Paulus published his essay (n. 44 *supra*), Eduard Meyer declared that the Jews were a race and questioned whether religious conversion could do away with Jewish distinctiveness. Rinott, p. 17. Note also the act of the National-Mutterloge in Prussia (one of the major Masonic organizations) which, in 1806, replied to its Magdeburg affiliate that no Jew could be accepted for membership even if he converted to Christianity. Katz, *Jews and Freemasons*, p. 74.

For evidence of proto-racism in the French Enlightenment, see Hertzberg, *French Enlightenment*, ch. IX, especially pp. 276, 286, 300, 307, 313. Hertzberg discusses D'Holbach's argument that the Jews had been shaped by their environment in such a way that there was no possibility of overcoming their alienation from European society (p. 276), and cites from Voltaire: "They [the Jews] are, all of them, born with raging fanaticism in their hearts, just as the Bretons and Germans are born with blond hair. I would not be in the least bit surprised if these people would not some day become deadly to the human race." (p. 300)

[47]Tal, "Ha-Anti-shemiut," p. 64.

[48]For details on the response to Bauer, see Rotenstreich, "For and Against Emancipation," pp. 11-18, and Eleonore O. Sterling, "Jewish Reaction to Jew-Hatred in the First Half of the Nineteenth Century," *YBLBI*, III (1958), pp. 103-121.

[49]See Sterling, *Er ist wie Du*, pp. 100 ff. Sterling notes how the Jews dismissed anti-Jewish sentiments before 1848 as not the true voice of the nation but of the *Pöbel* (rabble); Jews insisted that these sentiments were merely a carryover from earlier times. See also Toury, *Die politischen Orientierungen*, p. 72, on how the Jewish press, in order not to weaken the recently proclaimed union of Judaism and *Deutschtum*, underplayed the extent of the anti-Jewish violence during the Revolution of 1848. See also Sterling, "Anti-Jewish Riots," p. 141, on David Friedländer's reaction to the riots of 1819: "All this [hatred] has not disturbed a thoughtful Israelite for one single moment. We can depend with assurance on the forceful, wise governments as well as on the friendly German people who do not share this feeling [of hatred]."

[50]Eduard Bernstein, "Wie ich als Jude in der Diaspora aufwuchs," *Der Jude*, II (Berlin and Vienna, 1917-1918), p. 193.

[51]The literature on the rise of modern anti-Semitism is vast, but the most

important works include: Hannah Arendt, *The Origins of Totalitarianism* (New York, 1959); Paul W. Massing, *Rehearsal for Destruction* (New York, 1949); Peter G. J. Pulzer, *The Rise of Political Antisemitism in Germany and Austria* (New York, London and Sydney, 1964); Eva G. Reichmann, *Hostages of Civilization: A Study of the Social Causes of Antisemitism in Germany* (Boston, 1951); Tal, "Ha-Anti-shemiut"; U[riel] Tal, "Conservative Protestantism and the Status of the Jews in the 'Second Reich,' 1870-1914, "(Hebrew), *Zion*, XXVII: 1, 2 (1962), pp. 87-111; Uriel Tal, "Liberal Protestantism and the Status of the Jews in the Second Reich, 1870-1914," *Jewish Social Studies*, XXVI: 1 (1964), pp. 23-41; Kurt Wawrzinek, *Die Entstehung der deutschen Antisemitenparteien (1873-1890)* (Berlin, 1927). See also Leschnitzer, *Modern Anti-Semitism*, and Peter Viereck, *Meta-Politics: The Roots of the Nazi Mind* (New York, 1961).

On the general German background, see Pinson, *Modern Germany;* Golo Mann, *Deutsche Geschichte des 19. und 20. Jahrhunderts* (Frankfurt a.M., 1958); Arthur Rosenberg, *Imperial Germany: The Birth of the German Republic, 1871-1918* (Boston, 1964); and Thorstein Veblen, *Imperial Germany and the Industrial Revolution* (Ann Arbor, 1966).

[52]The crash of 1873 was followed by a depression lasting to the end of the decade. On the financial crisis of 1873 and the subsequent disclosure of corruption on the part of the political and economic liberals, see Mann, pp. 389ff., and Carlton J. H. Hayes, *A Generation of Materialism (1871-1900)* (New York, Evanston and London, 1941), p. 80.

On the relationship of social unrest attending industrialization and modern anti-Semitism, see Massing, E. Reichmann, and Tal's important criticism of their argument in "Ha-Anti-shemiut." Tal shows that the relationship between the two factors is not as simple and direct as Massing and Reichmann had assumed, and he properly emphasizes the importance of other phenomena in the emergence of anti-Semitism (e.g., propaganda and the Protestant ideologies). However, the fundamental importance of the profound structural changes taking place in Germany as essential components in the growth of anti-Semitism is obvious. See Tal, "Ha-Anti-shemiut," pp. 15-16, 18, 25, 27, 131-132. See also Hans Liebeschütz, "Problems of Diaspora History in XIXth Century Germany," *Journal of Jewish Studies*, VIII: 1, 2 (1957), pp. 103-111. On p. 108, Liebeschütz notes: "It is certainly no chance that anti-Semitism became a political force when the great economic crisis of the late 70s demonstrated that the enormous expansion which had created the space for the newcomers [the Jews] had, at least for the time being, reached its limits."

[53]Hans Martin Klinkenberg, "Zwischen Liberalismus und Nationalismus im zweiten Kaiserreich (1870-1918)," *Monumenta Judaica* (Cologne, 1963), pp. 311-312.

[54]Tal, "Conservative Protestantism," pp. 95-96, 99, 100ff., 111; Tal, "Ha-Anti-shemiut," p. 136. Among the groups associated with conservative Protestantism and its ideology of exclusion were the Deutsch-Konservative Partei, the Christlich Soziale Partei, the Freikonservative Reichspartei, the Bund der Landwirte (which appealed to the middle aristocracy for support), and the Evangelisch-Sozialer Kongress (in which some liberals participated). See Tal, "Conservative Protestantism," p. 90.

[55]Heinrich von Treitschke, "A Word About Our Jewry," trans. by Helen Lederer, mimeographed (Cincinnati, Hebrew Union College, 1958), p. 6. On Treitschke's rejection of racism, see Hans Liebeschütz, "Treitschke and Mommsen on Jewry and Judaism," *YBLBI*, VII (1962), p. 169.

[56]Treitschke's essay has been reprinted by Walter Boehlich, ed., *Der Berliner*

Antisemitismusstreit (Frankfurt a.M., 1965), along with the Jewish replies to Treitschke and his response to their criticisms. See also Liebeschütz, "Treitschke and Mommsen," and Michael A. Meyer, "Great Debate on Antisemitism: Jewish Reaction to New Hostility in Germany, 1879-1881," *YBLBI*, XI (1966), pp. 137-170.

[57]*Ibid.*, pp. 2, 5. Treitschke had special barbs reserved for the Jewish historian Graetz, who had spoken of Christianity in less than complimentary terms.

[58]*Ibid.*, pp. 33-34. Treitschke was responding to Moritz Lazarus' *Was heisst National?* See p. 29f. *infra*.

[59]Liebeschütz, "Treitschke and Mommsen," pp. 158 ff. Treitschke wrote: "The German Jewish problem will never be solved completely until our Israelitic fellow-citizens will be convinced by our attitude that we are a Christian nation and want to remain so." Treitschke, pp. 38-39.

[60]Treitschke, p. 7.

[61]*Ibid.*, p. 22; Liebeschütz, "Treitschke and Mommsen," p. 169.

[62]Treitschke, p. 3; Meyer, "Great Debate," p. 145.

[63]Tal, "Liberal Protestantism," *passim*; Tal, "Ha-Anti-shemiut," pp. 168ff, 196, 198-199, 202-203, 206-207, 211-212. Among the figures Tal discusses are Troeltsch, Ritschl, and von Zedlitz.

[64]Tal, "Ha-Anti-shemiut," pp. 168ff.

[65]*Ibid.*, pp. 175ff., 202, 205-206, 211. Among the liberals discussed by Tal are von Bennigsen, von Gneist, Rickert, Richter, and Barth, and the Verein zur Abwehr des Antisemitismus.

[66]Tal, "Liberal Protestantism," p. 41.

[67]Boehlich, p. 225; Liebeschütz, "Treitschke and Mommsen," p. 180.

[68]In "Conservative Protestantism," p. 91, Tal points out that since most Jews lived in areas with a predominantly Protestant population, the attitudes of the Protestant thinkers were of special significance. Although German Roman Catholics were also interested in a strengthened Christianity as the basis for political rule, education, society, and culture, they did not develop an ideological justification for anti-Semitism. Some Catholic publicists had also resorted to anti-Semitism in the heat of the Kulturkampf, but even they did not articulate a rationale for principled anti-Semitism. See Tal, "Ha-Anti-shemiut," p. 133; Massing, p. 81; Pulzer, pp. 273-274; and Ismar Elbogen and Eleonore Sterling, *Die Geschichte der Juden in Deutschland* (Frankfurt a.M., 1966), p. 264.

[69]Hays (p. 9) says that Darwinism was "the most captivating thought of the era." It had "ceased to be a tentative scientific theory and became a philosophy, almost a religion. . . . In conjunction with industrial materialism [Darwinism was] the chief philosophy of Europe in the 1870's." On Darwin and Darwinism, see William Irvine, *Apes, Angels and Victorians: Darwin, Huxley, and Evolution.* (New York, 1959).

[70]The classic expression of this movement was Arthur de Gobineau's "Essai sur l'Inégalité des Races," which had appeared in Paris between 1853 and 1855 but did not provoke great interest until considerably later when the intellectual climate, under the impact of Darwinism, had become more favorable. A German translation of Gobineau's work did not appear until 1898-1900. See Pulzer, p. 49.

[71]On the racial anti-Semites and their doctrines, see Massing, pt. 2; Fritz Stern, *The Politics of Cultural Despair: A Study in the Rise of the Germanic Ideology* (Berkeley and Los Angeles, 1961), ch. 1 (on Paul de Lagarde), and ch. 2 (on Julius Langbehn); Tal, "Ha-Anti-shemiut," pp. 47-49, 71; and A[lex] Bein,

"Modern Anti-Semitism and Its Effect on the Jewish Question," *Yad Vashem Studies*, III (Jerusalem, 1959), pp. 7-15. See also Mann's assessment of the reasons for anti-Semitism emerging at this time (p. 459): "Naturwissenschaft war Trumpf. Ihre Ueberlegenheit wurde auch von denen anerkannt, die nicht an ihr teilhatten, Philosophen und Historiker. Naturwissenschaft ist eine gewaltige Sache. . . ."

Major works in anti-Semitic theory from this period include: Wilhelm Marr, *Der Sieg des Judenthums Über das Germanentum* (1873) (on Marr, se Bein, "Modern Anti-Semitism," and Massing, pp. 6ff.); Eugen Dühring, *Die Judenfrage als Racen-, Sitten, und Culturfrage* (1881), which constituted the first and most important attempt to establish a scientific basis for anti-Semitism in biology, history, and philosophy; and Houston Stewart Chamberlain, *Die Grundlagen des XIX. Jahrhunderts* (1899).

Although our interest is focused on Germany, we must remember that racial anti-Semitism was an international movement at this time. Consider, e.g., Edouard Drumont (1844-1886), the leader of French anti-Semitism and author of *La France Juive* (1886). On French anti-Semitism, see Robert Francis Byrnes, *Antisemitism in Modern France* (New Brunswick, N.J., 1950); and on Austrian anti-Semitism, see Pulzer, pp. 127-188.

[72]Wilhelm Marr is generally credited with having coined the term "anti-Semitism." See Massing, pp. 211-212, n. 8; Bein, "Modern Anti-Semitism," p. 7, p. 8, n. 4. Strictly speaking, the term "anti-Semitism" should be reserved for antipathy against the Jew on the grounds of *racial* differences, and it is an anachronism to speak of anti-Semitism before the 1870s. Following general usage, however, we will use the term to refer to all forms of anti-Jewish expression in the period after 1870.

[73]Tal, "Ha-Anti-shemiut," pp. 76, 138, 145-146. Tal shows that Catholic and Protestant, as well as Jewish, contemporaries were aware that racial anti-Semitism contained this strong anti-Christian bias. Some anti-Semites, especially those of the Bayreuth stream associated with Wagner, claimed the Jews were interested in the growth of a deracinated proletariat as an instrument of Jewish domination. See p. 76.

[74]Bein, pp. 12-13; Pulzer, p. 70; Tal, "Ha-Anti-shemiut," p. 71.

[75]Cited by Tal, "Ha-Anti-shemiut," p. 92. The delegate was Ludwig Werner from Cassel, editor of an anti-Semitic paper, *Staatsbürger Zeitung*; the speech was given in 1893.

[76]Cited by Massing, p. 241, n. 12.

[77]Tal, "Ha-Anti-shemiut," p. 101.

[78]Cited by Bein, pp. 14, 19.

[79]Massing, *passim*, but especially pp. 85ff.; Pulzer, ch. X. Förster was Nietzsche's brother-in-law.

[80]Massing, pp. 84ff.

[81]Tal, "Ha-Anti-shemiut," p. 9.

[82]Massing, p. 107. On the general chauvinism of this period as expressed in German liberalism, see *supra*, p. 26f.

[83]*Ibid.*, pp. 100-101.

[84]Tal, "Ha-Anti-shemiut," p. 17. For a description of the agitation of 1880, see Massing, p. 40.

[85]Tal, "Ha-Anti-shemiut," pp. 61, 151. In 1905, one of the anti-Semitic parties dropped from its platform a call for the repeal of emancipation on the grounds that this would offend the German public (p. 95).

[86]*Ibid.*, pp. 82, 92, 94; Tal, "Conservative Protestantism," p. 107. Tal's

examination of the propaganda of the agitators shows that anti-Semitic charges remained mostly traditional (economic, social, partly religious), and, as a relatively new motif, also political. The modern racial charges were rather rare, and when concepts such as *Stamm* and *Rasse* were used, they were not endowed with associations drawn from scientific theories of race or from Social Darwinism. See Tal, "Ha-Anti-shemiut," p. 89.

[87]Tal, "Ha-Anti-shemiut," p. 133.

[88]*Ibid.*, p. 113.

[89]*Ibid.*, pp. 74, 80-81. Tal points out that this synthesis was a distortion of Chamberlain's concept by publicists for racial anti-Semitism. Chamberlain himself did not identify the Aryan race with the *Mittelstand*. For an example of the way in which racial concepts were mingled with those of romantic nationalism, note the following excerpt from an article which appeared in the *Freimaürer Zeitung* in 1876 under the title "Die Gründe der Abneigung gegen die Juden": "The Jew is equipped with all the virtues but also with all the vices of the Semitic race. . . . A deep abyss separates them from the German tribes with regard to racial fitness and ability in certain patterns of ideas, thought processes, and *Weltanschauung*. . . . Perhaps some brother or other is now, for the first time, becoming aware of the immutable nature of national spirit and still doubts the permanence of the social phenomena it creates. . . . We feel almost instinctively that the Jew is a son of alien seed." Cited by Katz, *Jews and Freemasons*, p. 146.

[90]Bein, p. 11; Pulzer, p. 24; Massing, pp. 87, 102, where he notes that, especially in rural districts, voting for anti-Semites did not mean bad relations obtained with the Jews one knew.

[91]On the use by Bismarck of Stöcker's anti-Semitic movement as a means of blunting the appeal of Social Democracy, see Massing, pp. xvi, 47, 105, and ch. III.

[92]This reversal was especially significant since earlier Freemasonry had been seen as one of the routes leading to Jewish social integration, or at least as an arena in which the struggle for it could be waged. See *supra*, n. 30, and Katz, *Jews and Freemasons*, p. 165. What the Protestant liberal Rudolf von Gneist called an "Umkehrung des Gesetzes [of emancipation] durch die Verwaltung" had taken place, and by 1914 Jews were shut out of almost all state institutions in every German Bundesstaat. Of 12,388 higher civil servants in 1907, only 244 (1.93 percent) were Jews. See Zechlin, pp. 49-50.

[93]Pulzer, p. 189.

[94]Katz, *Jews and Freemasons*, pp. 169-170. Note the decision by Ludwig Bamberger in 1893 not to stand for reelection after twenty-five years in the Reichstag. He declared the main reason was anti-Semitism, and he said he was repulsed less by the anti-Semitic agitation than by the fact that "three-fourths of my colleagues . . . are not at all disturbed thereby." See Hamburger, p. 24.

For contemporary assessments of the extent and depth of anti-Semitism, note the following reactions. The first is by a Jew, Jakob Wassermann, *Mein Weg als Deutscher und Jude* (Berlin, 1921), p. 39; and the second is by a Christian, Hermann Dachs, in a letter he wrote to Moritz Lazarus on August 27, 1892, cited by Toury, *Die politischen Orientierungen* p. 338:

(1) "Zum erstenmal begegnete ich jenem in den Volkskörper gedrungenen dumpfen, starren, fast sprachlosen Hass, von dem der Name Antisemitismus fast nichts aussagt, weil er weder die Art, noch die Quelle, noch die Tiefe, noch das Ziel zu erkennen gibt. Dieser Hass hat Züge des Aberglaubens ebenso wie der freiwilligen Verblendung, der

Dämonenfurcht wie der pfäffischen Verstocktheit, der Ranküne des Benachteiligten, Betrogenen ebenso wie der Unwissenheit, der Lüge und Gewissenlosigkeit wie der berechtigten Abwehr, affenhafter Bosheit wie des religiösen Fanatismus. Gier und Neugier sind in ihm, Blutdurst, Angst verführt, verlockt zu werden, Lust am Geheimnis und Niedrigkeit der Selbsteinschätzung. Er ist in solcher Verquickung und Hintergründigkeit ein besonderes deutsches Phänomen. Es ist ein deutscher Hass."

(2) "Der Antisemitismus steckt dem deutschen Volke viel tiefer im Blute, als es oberflächlich den Anschein hat, und wenn Spielhagen meint, in jedem Menschen steckte ein Stückchen von einem Sozialdemokraten, so kann man mit demselben Recht sagen, in jedem Deutschen steckt ein Stückchen von einem Antisemiten. Woher das? Eine bornierte Christlich-orthodoxe Clerisei hat uns diesen Widerhaken ins Fleisch gerannt. . . ."

See n. 34, *supra,* and Martin Philippson, *Neueste Geschichte des jüdischen Volkes,* II (Leipzig, 1910), p. 62.

[95]Toury, *Die politischen Orientierungen,* p. 159. Toury detects the first signs of a crisis as early as 1875 but argues that the real awareness of its existence came only from 1878 and after (pp. 170, 174).

CHAPTER TWO

[1]See Toury, *Die politischen Orientierungen,* p. 170, for press citations. See also Jacob Katz, "Jewry and Judaism in the Nineteenth Century," *Journal of World History,* IV:4 (1958), p. 889; Ismar Elbogen, *Geschichte der Juden in Deutschland* (Berlin, 1935), p. 190; Martin Philippson, *Neueste Geschichte des jüdischen Volkes,* II (Leipzig, 1910), p. 6; Eugen Fuchs, *Um Deutschtum und Judentum* (Frankfurt a.M., 1919), p. 90.

[2]Bernstein, pp. 187, 190. In describing the generation before 1878, Toury said, "Im Herzen einer überwiegenden Zahl deutscher Juden [war] kein Raum und keine Vitalität mehr fur positiv jüdische Empfindungen." In *Die politischen Orientierungen,* p. 153.

[3]Franz Kobler, ed., *Juden und Judentum in deutschen Briefen aus drei Jahrhunderten* (Vienna, 1935), pp. 351-352. See also Elbogen, *Geschichte der Juden in Deutschland,* p. 191, and the remarks of Dr. Samuel Kristeller, president of the Deutsch-Israelitische Gemeindebund, who, in 1883, expressed full confidence in the triumph of reason which would be achieved by elevating the general level of the populace. Kristeller's remarks are discussed by Tal, "Ha-Anti-shemiut," p. 266, n. 156.

[4]E.g., the reaction of the Viennese *Neue Freie Presse* to Treitschke's articles: "With its leading thought we see him place himself on a standpoint which absolves any liberal-minded and educated person in the future from concerning himself with him." Cited by Pulzer, p. 299. See also Steinschneider's reaction to Bruno Bauer's anti-Semitism: "Upon reading this essay of Bauer, one is struck and depressed by the experience of watching a basically gifted man and an outstanding liberal at that, stoop to such a low level and indulge in such gibberish." Cited by Rotenstreich, "For and Against Emancipation," p. 36. On the passivity of the bulk of Jewry who remained unconvinced by the argument of some communal leaders that a struggle against anti-Semitism was necessary, see Tal, "Ha-Anti-shemiut," p. 264, n. 142.

[5]On liberalism, see Hayes, pp. 46, 75; Pulzer, p. 32; Werner E. Mosse, "The Conflict of Liberalism and Nationalism and its Effect on Germany Jewry," *YBLBI,* IX (1970), 126.

[6]Cited by Rinott, p. 31.

[7]See Leonard Krieger, *The German Idea of Freedom* (Boston, 1957). Consider his comment (p. 65) on Thomasius (1655-1728), a jurist and publicist influenced by Grotius: "With Thomasius modern individualism in the explicit sense of an emphasis upon the inalienable rights which men possessed as individuals entered into German political theory, and Thomasius' use of these rights to intensify rather than to challenge the power of the absolutely ruling state set a pattern which was to be characteristic of a whole school of future German liberal thought. The general basis of rulership was strengthened, for all kinds of concrete social and political action by the ruler were justified in the name of individual rights." On p. 45, Krieger discusses "that remarkable process in which both the agents of political authoritarianism and the social hierarchy in Germany absorbed what was inevitable in innovation and adapted themselves to it in such wise as to leave the fundamental relationships of their position unimpaired."

[8]Pinson, ch. II.

[9]Cited in *ibid.*, p. 152.

[10]On this topic, see *ibid.*, pp. 106-107, and Mosse, "Conflict of Liberalism and Nationalism," pp. 125ff. Mosse emphasizes the lack of a necessary historical or logical connection between the ideologies of liberalism and nationalism. On the weakness of German liberalism, see Massing, p. 81, and on the illiberality of the liberals of 1848 on questions of national rights for nationalities they did not recognize, see Louis Namier, *1848: The Revolution of the Intellectuals* (Garden City, N.Y., 1964).

[11]Leopold Sonnemann and his paper, *Die Frankfurter Zeitung*, were representative of that small group of dissident liberals who opposed Bismarck on these issues in the name of principle. Ludwig Bamberger, on the other hand, supported the anti-Socialist law (as did Eduard Lasker), the annexation and, in part, the Kulturkampf. See Mosse, "Conflict of Liberalism and Nationalism," p. 132, and Massing, p. 35.

[12]Toury, *Die politischen Orientierungen*, p. 158. For those who cared to look for them, disturbing analogies could be found, and it would not have been difficult to imagine the possibility of laws restricting the Jews justified on their similarity to the Roman Catholics (an international religion with trans-national loyalties), to the Poles (a foreign nation within German borders, with a distinct cultural and linguistic tradition), or to the Social Democrats (an oppositional group engaged in activity subversive of the public order).

Note also Mann's assessment of liberalism by the end of the century (pp. 454-455): "So war der Liberalismus nicht mehr, was er in den vierziger Jahren gewesen war; ein Liberalismus der Interessen, nicht mehr der humanen Idee. . . . Die national-liberalen Historiker, die Droysen, Sybel, Treitschke hatten noch als Rebellen angefangen, wenn auch also ziemlich zahme. Jetzt wurde ihr Kult der Geschichte zum Kult des Erfolges, und hörten sie nicht auf zu besingen, wie wir es doch herrlich weit gebracht, Lobredner der neuen Ordnung; hatten sie noch etwas Kritisches zu sagen, so ging's gegen den Franzmann, gegen das liberale England, gegen die Sozialdemokratie oder gegen die eigene Vergangenheit. . . . Die Literatur wird dann zur Festrednerei. . . ."

[13]Pulzer, p. 100; Massing, p. 35; A. J. P. Taylor, *The Course of German History* (New York, 1962), pp. 126ff.; Veit Valentin, *The German People: Their History and Civilization from the Holy Roman Empire to the Third Reich* (New York, 1945), pp. 492ff.

[14]On the meaning of the term *"freisinnig,"* see Pulzer, p. 95, n.: "There is no exact equivalent for 'freisinnig' in English. It is sometimes rendered as liberal. . . . It really implies a mixture of social radicalism and anti-clericalism, with the emphasis on a rationalist intellectual attitude."

[15]Massing, p. 36.

[16]At the height of the Kulturkampf, the Center had adopted an anti-Semitic posture as a tactic against its liberal oppressors. That stance had now been largely abandoned, and hence—for some Jews—affiliation with the Center became attractive. See Pulzer, pp. 273ff.

[17]*Ibid.*, pp. 174ff., 177ff., 182-183, 189; Liebeschütz, "Problems of Diaspora History," p. 108.

[18]In the election of 1878 there was a tendency away from Jewish candidates both on the part of the parties and the voters; from 1881 on, no Jew sat in the Reichstag from the National Liberal Party. Toury, *Die politischen Orientierungen*, p. 193.

[19]*Ibid.*, p. 177.

[20]*Ibid.*, pp. 176-177; Leopold Auerbach, *Das Judenthum und seine Bekenner in Preussen* (Berlin, 1890), p. 100.

[21]The organ of the Reform movement was the *Allegemeine Zeitung des Judenthums;* of the Conservatives, *Die Israelitische Wochenschrift;* of the moderate Orthodox, *Die Jüdische Presse;* and of the ultra-Orthodox, *Der Israelit.*

[22]*Jewish Encyclopedia*, V, pp. 592-593; Elbogen and Sterling, p. 247; Kurt Wilhelm, "The Jewish Community in the Post-Emancipation Period," *YBLBI*, II (1957), p. 62. Although the Gemeindebund had declared in 1875 that it recognized its duty to defend Jews against attacks in the press by initiating court action or petitioning state agencies, it actually did so only in one case (in 1876). In that instance it obtained a prison sentence for the author of an anti-Semitic booklet and also confiscation of the pamphlet. See Auerbach, pp. 107-108.

[23]Examples of the Christian reaction include the resolution condemning restrictions on the rights of Jews passed by the Protestant Reformverein in Berlin in October 1880, the declaration against the anti-Semitic agitation by seventy-three prominent Berliners published the following month, and the rebuttal to Treitschke by the respected historian, Theodor Mommsen. See Meyer, "Great Debate," pp. 167-168; Pulzer, p. 337.

[24]Toury, *Die politischen Orientierungen*, p. 148; Elbogen, *Geschichte der Juden in Deutschland*, pp. 294-295.

[25]The text of the lecture appears in Moritz Lazarus, *Treu und Frei: Gesammelte Reden und Vorträge über Juden und Judenthum* (Leipzig, 1887), pp. 57-110.

[26]*Ibid.*, pp. 65-66.

[27]*Ibid.*, pp. 70-71.

[28]*Ibid.*, p. 74.

[29]*Ibid.*, p. 77. (Emphasis in original.) On Treitschke's response to this argument, see *supra*, p. 15f.

[30]*Ibid.*, pp. 88-89.

[31]*Ibid.*, p. 91.

[32]Cited by Massing, p. 38.

[33]Meyer, "Great Debate," p. 168; Auerbach, pp. 104-105; Fuchs, pp. 89-90. For information on earlier, similar, and equally unsuccessful efforts to elicit an official response favorable to the Jews, see Auerbach, pp. 101-102, 104. The Jewish leadership had tried and failed to have Prussian Judge Wilmanns

censored for writing *Die goldene Internationale* (1876). Likewise, an attempt in September 1878 to take legal action against the author of an anti-Semitic article calling for violence against Jews had ended with the dismissal of the charges.

[34]Pinson, pp. 167-168; Pulzer, pp. 97ff.

[35]Massing, p. 39.

[36]Massing, p. 40, cites Eduard Bernstein's recollection of this period:

"It was like a breaker of anti-Jewish reaction. A whole press sprang up which fed it. Anti-Semitic leaflets and libels against everything Jewish or suspect of Jewish sympathies were spread on a large scale; they advocated social and economic ostracism of the Jews and this ostracism was occasionally also carried out in a most insulting manner. . . .

"With scenes of rowdyism the like of which Berlin had never known before, the New Year of 1881 was rung in, after B. Förster, E. Henrici, Ruppel, Liebermann von Sonnenberg and other speakers had gone to work on an anti-Semitic mass meeting the night before. Organized bands roamed through the Friedrichstadt section, took positions in front of the popular cafes and, after listening to all kinds of insulting speeches, kept yelling: '*Juden raus!*' They stopped Jews or Jewish-looking people from entering and provoked brawls, window smashing and other savageries. All this, of course, in the name of defending German idealism against Jewish materialism and protecting honest German workers from Jewish exploitation."

[37]Massing, pp. 39-40.

[38]*Ibid.*, p. 40; Pulzer, p. 96; Wanda Kampmann, *Deutsche und Juden* (Heidelberg, 1963), pp. 253ff. The expression "cool and correct to the core" was used at the time by Virchow, the freisinnig delegate who had posed the interpellation. The debate took place on November 20 and 22, 1880.

[39]Cited by Klinkenberg, p. 340. See also Toury, *Die politischen Orientierungen*, p. 177. On the sense of powerlessness, see Auerbach, p. 107.

[40]Lazarus, pp. 118-119.

[41]*Ibid.*, p. 117.

[42]*Ibid.*, p. 121; see also p. 127.

[43]In the background of this concern was the incident centered on the response of the historian Heinrich Graetz to Treitschke. Graetz had written a counterattack in harsh and insulting tones, matching Treitschke's arrogance with his own hauteur. Graetz had been condemned by the great bulk of the Jewish press, which sought to dissociate itself from his tone and attitude. The texts of Graetz's replies to Treitschke are reproduced by Boehlich, pp. 25-31, 45-52. Meyer discusses the Jewish response to Graetz and his isolation in "Great Debate," pp. 154-159. See also Reuwen Michael, "Graetz contra Treitschke," *Bulletin of the Leo Baeck Institute*, December 1961, p. 317.

[44]Lazarus, pp. 119, 122.

[45]*Ibid.*, pp. 125-216. Note that the target of *Verbesserung* has now shifted, in part, from Jews who were insufficiently Germanized to those who were too Germanized.

[46]In addition to Lazarus, who was chairman, the group consisted of the following: Sal. Lachmann, Dr. Berthold Auerbach, Prof. Dr. Barth, Julius Bleichröder, Prof. Emil Breslauer, Prof. Breslau, Dr. Burg, *Gen.-Consul* Eisenmann, L. Friedländer, H. Goldschmidt, W. Hagelberg, *Bankdirector* Hermann, Dr. Herrlich, Prof. Hirschberg, Dr. Kalischer, Dr. Kirstein, Dr. Kristeller, M. G. Lewy, *Geh. Comm.-Rath* Liebermann, Ludwig Loewe, Dr. Mendel, Dr. Neumann, *Comm.-Rath* Simon, Prof. Steinthal, attorney Stern and Dr. Strassman. Listed in *ibid.*, p. 130, n.

[47]*Ibid.*, p. 155. See also Meyer, "Great Debate," p. 169.

[48]The December Committee continued to exist for another ten years, up to 1891; however, its only public meetings were those held in the first months of its existence. See Fuchs, p. 90, and *IDR*, January 1898, p. 3.

[49]The anti-Semites were Adolf Wagner, Liebermann von Sonnenberg, Joseph Cremer and Stöcker himself, who stood for election against Rudolf Virchow, the pathologist and leader of the Freisinnig Party, whose interpellation had sparked the *Judendebatte* the previous fall.

[50]Pinson, p. 572.

[51]Massing, pp. 44-45; Pulzer, pp. 98-99.

[52]Cited by Pulzer, p. 106. See also the manifesto of Jewish students at the University of Breslau in 1886 which began: "Anti-Semitism seems to be dying. This movement which for almost a decade has been stirring up the passions of the masses to an unprecedented degree, spreading a new ferment of hatred, envy and discontent among the people, seems to be weakening and gradually coming to an end. The time of high tides is over, when no newspaper appeared without dealing with the problem of defense or attack. The reckless baiting has stopped. That apostle of intolerance [Adolf Stöcker], applauded by the mob, has discontinued preaching racial hatred at public meetings. They no longer shamelessly try to abolish by legislation the rights which the Constitution guaranteed to us. The leaders of this movement are now silent; one after the other they have retired from the battlefield and from public life. . . ." The manifesto, however, went on to argue that the decline of anti-Semitic agitation had been accompanied by growth of hostility within the ranks of the student population. Cited by Adolf Asch and Johanna Philippson in "Self-Defence at the Turn of the Century: The Emergence of the K.C.," *YBLBI*, III (1958), p. 122.

[53]Elbogen, *Geschichte der Juden in Deutschland*, p. 295; Elbogen and Sterling, p. 272; Auerbach, pp. 109-110. See also p. 29, *supra* on the apologetic work commissioned by the Gemeindebund during this period.

[54]Tal, *"Ha-Anti-shemiut,"* pp. 89-90.

[55]Ahlwardt's writings were: *Der Verzweiflungskampf der arischen Völker mit dem Judenthum* (1890); *Der Eid eines Juden* (an attack upon Bleichröder for which Ahlwardt was sentenced to four months' imprisonment); and *Judenflinten* (1892; in this work he charged that a Jewish arms manufacturer had delivered defective rifles to the German army as part of a French plot to weaken German military strength). See Pulzer, pp. 112ff.; Massing, pp. 91-92.

[56]Massing, p. 91. The quotation is from the *Antisemitische Correspondenz*, the publication of the German Social Party.

[57]*AZJ*, July 22, 1892. See also *ibid.*, July 15, 1892, p. 338: "Aber wir vertrauen trotz alledem und alledem dem fortschreitenden Geiste der Menschheit. Unverwüstlich wie unsere religiöse Existenz, ist auch unser Optimismus. Selbst die trübsten Erfahrungen vermögen ihn nicht zu beugen . . . es kommt sicher der Tag, wo der fortschreitende Menschengeist sich auch dieses Märchens, wie so vieler anderer, schämen wird. . . . Auf diesen Tag aber hoffen wir!"

[58]Excerpts from the debate are reprinted by Massing, pp. 288-294. See also *AZJ*, July 11, 1890, for a letter from M. Ascher; May 30, 1890, p. 279; November 13, 1890, pp. 1-2 of *Gemeindebote*, citing a paper from Darmstadt calling for energetic Jewish activity to refute the anti-Semitic press; November 9, 1890, p. 239, on the Berlin city council praising the action of Justizrath Meyer,

presiding officer of the Berlin Jewish community for having been the first to speak out in defense of his co-religionists; March 28, 1890, pp. 165-167, where a letter is published which notes the weak defense of the Jews made by the liberal Christian Virchow. Virchow, the writer of the letter claimed, had made a statement with anti-Semitic overtones by implying that since the Jews had only recently come out of the ghetto, they needed to be brought closer to the Germans. The letter writer resented the implication that Jews were not fully Germanized and called attention to the fact that in the hearts of many liberals there was an antipathy toward Jews. He concluded: "Sie sehen, wir haben Feinde hüben wie Feinde drüben, wir müssen daher unsere Verteidigung selber in die Hand nehmen . . . und diese Verteidigung erachte ich als die Hauptaufgabe des *AZJ.*"

Much of the program of the Centralverein was foreshadowed at this time, though, significantly, only in minor notes buried in the back pages of the Jewish press: e.g., a call for overcoming Jewish fragmentation by forming a voluntary union (*AZJ*, May 23, 1890, p. 1, of the *Gemeindebote*); a proposal to send Jewish representatives to follow along after agitators and refute their statements and their published declarations (*ibid.*, April 18, 1890, p. 3, of the *Gemeindebote*); and recognition of the importance of legal action through established courts as a means of fighting anti-Semitism which promised to be far more successful than published refutations of calumny (*ibid.*, August 22, 1890, p. 2 of *Gemeindebote*).

[59]*JP*, May 12, 1892, p. 221.

[60]*Ibid.*, May 19, 1892, pp. 231ff. The same themes of distrust of official action and the need for concerted, unified Jewish self-defense were expressed in *IWOS*, May 20, 1892, pp. 161-162.

[61]See *IDR*, September 1899, p. 461, which recalls that in addition to the Committee there were, at the same time, "eine Unmenge kleinerer lokaler Komites zu dem selbem Zwecke."

[62]*JP*, February 16, 1893, p. 63, where the members of the Committee are listed; see Lazarus, p. 130, n., for the members of the December Committee.

[63]For a further discussion of Hildesheimer and his role in defense, see *infra*, p. 000.

[64]On the Committee, see Klinkenberg, p. 322; Elbogen, *Geschichte der Juden in Deutschland*, p. 297; Fuchs, pp. 55, 271; *AZJ*, April 13, 1894, p. 170; *IDR*, April 1898, p. 177. On James Simon, see "James Simon—Industrialist, Art Collector, Philanthropist," *YBLBI*, XI (1965), pp. 3-23, and Ulrich Steinman, "Some Notes on James Simon," *ibid.*, XIII (1968), pp. 277-282.

[65]These investigations were published as *Der jüdische Blutmord und der Freiherr von Wackerbarth-Linderode, Mitglied des Preussischen Abgeordnetenhauses, Ein antisemitisch-parlamentarisches.Kulturbild* (1892; on Tisza-Eszlar); and *Betrachtungen zum Prozess Buschhoff* (1892). See also the defense pamphlet by the third leader of the Committee, Edmund Friedemann, *Jüdische Moral und christlicher Staat* (Berlin, 1893).

[66]These works were *Die Kriminalität der Juden in Deutschland* (1896) and *Die Juden als Soldaten* (1896). Note that Willy Bambus, later active in the Zionist movement for a time, participated in the preparation of both these works (see *JP*, November 11, 1904, p. 468). Cf. Nathan's work on criminality to a similar effort in 1793 by David Friedländer, who, in an appendix to an essay urging reform, adduced evidence to show how low the crime rate was among Jews (see Meyer, *Origins of the Modern Jew*, p. 69). On the implications and methods

of the Jewish efforts to refute anti-Semitic charges regarding high criminality among Jews, see Tal, "Ha-Anti-shemiut," pp. 119-120, 124-125.

[67]At most the Committee was willing to accept contributions to help with its work (see *JP*, February 16, 1893, p. 63). On Nathan, see Fuchs, p. 55; Ernst Feder, *Paul Nathan: Ein Lebensbild* (Berlin, 1929); *idem*, "Paul Nathan, the Man and His Work," *YBLBI*, III (1958), 60-80. Later, Nathan and his associate in the Committee, James Simon, were active in the leadership of the Hilfsverein der deutschen Juden (founded in 1901), which worked on behalf of Jews in Europe and Palestine. The thrust of the Hilfsverein's work in East Europe illustrates the effect of the emancipation ideology to which Nathan and Simon were committed; the organization worked to improve the economic and social position of Eastern Jews in order to facilitate their absorption into the economic structure of their mother countries. Although Nathan advocated the introduction of Hebrew as the language of instruction in the organization's institutions in Palestine, he did this for purely pedagogic reasons. See Feder, "Paul Nathan," pp. 71-72.

[68]For an expression of Jewish support for the establishment of a non-Jewish defense organization before the creation of the Verein, see *AZJ*, June 27, 1890, p. 324: "Weshalb jedoch sollten wir nicht zur Bildung eines *Philosemiten-Bundes* schreiten? Wir haben die Pflicht, unsere Freunde zu sammeln, einen Bund zu gründen unter den Angehörigen unserer Rasse nicht allein, sondern auch in Gemeinschaft mit allen Uebrigen, welche sich mit uns in Menschenliebe, wetteifernd in edelster Plichterfüllung, verbinden wollen. Der Philosemiten sind, dessen dürfen wir gewiss sein, recht viele. Gelingt es uns, sie zu sammeln, so werden wir in erster Linie den Antisemitismus besiegen." (Emphasis in original.)

[69]Klinkenberg, p. 382, n. 10; S[imon] M. Dubnow, *Die neueste Geschichte des jüdischen Volkes*, II (Berlin, 1923), p. 44; and *Antisemiten-Spiegel* (Danzig, 1892), p. 358.

[70]By the end of the Weimar Republic, the majority of the membership was Jewish, although non-Jews were still prominent in positions of leadership. A great part of its funds were donated by Jews, and the Verein worked closely with the Centralverein. See Arnold Paucker, "Der jüdische Abwehrkampf," *Entscheidungsjahr 1932 (Zur Judenfrage in der Endphase der Weimarer Republik)* (Tübingen, 1965), p. 411, n. 18.

[71]*AZJ*, January 22, 1891, pp. 37-38; *ibid.*, January 29, 1891, pp. 49-50; *ibid.*, February 5, 1891, p. 1 of the *Gemeindebote*; *ibid.*, February 26, 1891, p. 2 of the *Gemeindebote*; *ibid.*, January 15, 1892, pp. 26-27; *ibid.*, January 22, 1892, p. 38. Cf. *IWOS*, March 5, 1891, p. 75.

The Verein published a journal, *Mittheilung*, and it established branches in various German cities. On an Austrian society with the same name, see Chaim Bloch, "Herzl's First Years of Struggle," *Herzl Year Book*, III (New York, 1960), pp. 82ff., and Simon Dubnow, *Weltgeschichte des jüdischen Volkes, Die neueste Geschichte des jüdischen Volkes*, X (Berlin, 1929), p. 88. The leadership of that body was made up of eminent members of the educated classes, including Baron Ferdinand Leitenberger, an industrialist and the president of the group; Baroness von Suttner, an author and pacifist who received the first Nobel Peace Prize in 1905; and Dr. Hermann Nothnagel, a physician who conceived the idea for the organization. On the relationship between this group and Theodor Herzl, see *infra*, pp. 108f.

[72]*AZJ*, January 22, 1891, p. 38.

[73]Elbogen, *Geschichte der Juden in Deutschland*, pp. 192, 295; Katz, *Freemasons*, p. 165.

[74]Asch and Philippson, p. 122. (This article contains the complete text of the manifesto in translation.)

[75]Walter Gross, "The Zionist Students' Movement," *YBLBI*, IV (1959); comment by R. Weltsch in *ibid.*, III, p. xxiii; George L. Mosse, *The Crisis of the German Ideology* (New York, 1964), p. 197. The following Kartell Convent song illustrates their position and tone (cited by Hermann Berlak in *Der Kartellconvent der Verbindungen deutscher Studenten jüdischen Glaubens* [Berlin, 1927], p. 17):

> "Wer unser Recht bestreitet,
> Als Jude Deutsche zu sein,
> Dem sei der Kampf bereitet,
> Dem unsre Kraft wir weih'n!
> Solang' man unsre Ehre
> Aus Rassenhass bedräut,
> Solang' der Väter Ehre
> Man Schimpf und Schande breut,
> Solang' von unsren Söhnen
> Noch lebt ein stark Geschlecht
> Solange soll ertönen
> Der Ruf: Für Ehr und Recht!"

The same tone is manifest in the motto of the Kartell Convent affiliate, Licaria, at the University of Munich: "Nemo me impune lacessit" ("None may harm me with impunity"). Cited by Alfred Hirschberg, "Ludwig Hollaender, Director of the C. V.," *YBLBI*, VII (1962), pp. 41-42. On Benno Jacob, see Kurt Wilhelm, "Benno Jacob, a Militant Rabbi," *ibid.*, pp. 75ff. For recognition by the Centralverein of the innovative character of student self-defense, see *IDR*, January 1898, p. 5.

[76]Kartell Convent members were later among the founders of the Centralverein. See Asch and Philippson, p. 138.

[77]Cited in *ibid.*, p. 124.

[78]*Ibid.*, p. 125.

[79]This pamphlet was reviewed briefly, and favorably, in *AZJ*, August 15, 1891. Jacobowski later wrote a critique of Friedrich Julius Stahl from the point of view of liberalism: *Der christliche Staat und seine Zukunft* (Berlin, 1894). See Robert A. Kann, "Friedrich Julius Stahl: A Re-examination of his Conservativism," *YBLBI*, XII, p. 71.

[80]Jacobowski, *op. cit.*, p. 5 (emphasis in original). As an example of the kind of defense literature that was more usual at that time see E. Friedemann, *op cit.*; Friedemann, a leader in the Committee, began his work with a quotation from Lessing: "Denn was mich Euch zum Christen macht, das macht Euch mir zum Juden." He sought to defend Judaism by citing extensively from the traditional religious literature to show the high moral values of the faith. The tone throughout is calm and academic.

[81]*Ibid.*, p. 31.

CHAPTER THREE

[1]Cited by Massing, p. 66.

[2]Cited in *ibid.*, p. 66.

[3]Cited in *ibid.* On the Tivoli conference see *ibid.*, pp. 60-68; Pinson, pp. 167ff.;

Pulzer, pp. 118ff. I am indebted to Dr. Ernst Hamburger who first called my attention to the significance of these events.

See also the observation of the *Preussische Jahrbücher* on the Tivoli Conference: "Basically the Conservatives have always been anti-Semitic. . . . By becoming anti-Semitic, the Conservative Party has turned into nothing new in its content, but it has become demagogic." Cited by Pulzer, p. 120. For a Jewish view of the relationship of anti-Semitism and the Conservative Party before Tivoli, see *AZJ*, December 11, 1891, pp. 589-590; the anti-Semites in the party were then dismissed as insignificant "hotheads," and possibilities of Jewish support for Conservative candidates was stressed, so long as the Conservatives would support the constitution and extricate itself from its flirtation with anti-Semitism.

⁴*AZJ*, December 30, 1892, pp. 627-628.

⁵The text appears, with a strong editorial endorsement, in *JP*, January 19, 1893, pp. 21ff., and in *IWOS*, January 27, 1893, pp. 36-37. Of the signers, fourteen had been active in the December Committee or the Committee or both; they included Hirsch Hildesheimer, Simon, Steinthal, Kristeller, Friedemann, and Nathan.

⁶F. Simon, *Wehrt Euch!* (Berlin, 1893). I have been unable to identify the actual name of the author.

⁷*Ibid.*, pp. 19, 21, 22-23, 24. In the last quotation, the wording in the original is: "Deutschtum und Judenthum soll sich in uns harmonisch verschmelzen; wir wollen *Deutsche* sein und *Juden* bleiben, *des neuen Reiches treue Bürger, des alten Gottes ehrfürchtige Bekenner*" (emphasis in original). The pamphlet was discussed and endorsed by *JP*, February 2, 1893, p. 49.; and by *IWOS*, January 27, 1893, p. 35, and February 3, 1893, pp. 41-42.

⁸On the pre-emancipation tradition of seeking government protection for the Jewish community, see Elbogen and Sterling, p. 274, and Sterling, "Jewish Reaction to Jew-Hatred," p. 120.

⁹*AZJ*, January 6, 1893, p. 1. On the disunity in the community, *AZJ* commented: "*Jene vielgerühmte und vielgescholtene jüdische Einigkeit existirt eigentlich nur in der erhitzten Phantasie unserer Gegner.* Denn so verschieden wie die politische und soziale, wie die religöse und geistige Weltanschauung der Juden, so verschieden wie ihre Anlagen und Temperamente, so verschieden sind auch die Ansichten und die Rathschläge, die jetzt von allen Seiten auftauchen, um die antisemitische Hetze zu bekämpfen." (Emphasis in original.) See also *AZJ*, January 20, 1893, p. 25. The proposal was attacked by *IWOS* (January 14, 1893, pp. 19-20), which questioned both the wisdom of the act and the right of the Berlin *Vorstand* to speak in the name of all Jewry.

¹⁰Löwenfeld was a student of Slavic languages and had already published *Gespräche über und mit Tolstoj* (1891) and *Tolstoj, sein Leben, seine Werke, seine Weltanschauung* (1892). He became the first authorized translator of Tolstoi's works into German and then founder of the first German Volkstheater. After World War I, when he was no longer alive, he was regarded by the ultra-patriotic Naumann Partei as its spiritual father. Löwenfeld was the uncle of Rahel Straus (her mother's brother), who notes the irony that the grandson of his twin brother, Samuel, was an enthusiastic supporter of Adolf Hitler. Rahel Straus, *Wir lebten in Deutschland* (Stuttgart, 1961), pp. 60-61.

¹¹Raphael Löwenfeld, *Schutzjuden oder Staatsbürger* (Berlin, 1893), p. 8.

¹²*Ibid.*, p. 12.

¹³*Ibid.*, pp. 6, 10. As an example of the phenomenon which concerned

Löwenfeld, see *JP*, February 18, 1892, p. 81, where the concept of "Jewish national feeling" is explored sympathetically.

[14]*Ibid.*, p. 9.

[15]*Ibid.*, p. 10.

[16]*Ibid.*, pp. 11, 12.

[17]*Ibid.*, pp. 15, 24-25.

[18]*Ibid.*, pp. 26-27.

[19]For a negative reaction to Löwenfeld's pamphlet for sowing disunity, see *AZJ*, January 13, 1893, p. 13, and January 20, 1893, p. 25; but see also *ibid.*, March 24, 1893, where the founding of the Centralverein was reported extensively, without comment. Included in that report was a discussion agreeing with many of the points made by Löwenfeld. See also the anonymous pamphlet *Volks-oder Salon-Judenthum* which defends Hildesheimer; this work was discussed in *IWOS*, February 10, 1893, pp. 51-52. The reaction of the Orthodox is discussed on p. 91, infra.

[20][Paul] Rieger, *Ein Vierteljahrhundert im Kampf um das Recht* (Berlin, 1918), p. 18.

[21]*Ibid.*, p. 19; M[artin] Mendelsohn, *Die Pflicht der Selbstvertheidigung* (Berlin, 1894), p. 12.

[22]Others were: Dr. J. Ginsberg, Dr. Grelling (an attorney), L. Kalisch (a city councilman), Dr. Martin Mendelsohn, *Sanitätsrat* Dr. Oldendorf, *Privatdozent* Dr. Hugo Preuss, Adolf Salomon, and *Maurermeister* Weile.

[23]Rieger, p. 19. Rieger points out that the term "jüdischen Glaubens" was chosen because it described the category under which Jewry in Germany was placed by the government.

[24]See Toury, *Die politischen Orientierungen*, pp. 200-202, and Massing, p. 71. Note especially Toury's assessment of the significance of the schism: "Für die inner deutschen Verhältnisse zwar von geringer Bedeutung, erschütterte dieser Vorgang doch in besorgniserregender Weise die Fundamente der jüdisch-politischen Ausrichtung. Denn 'ihre' Partei war es, die da auseinanderbrach, und daher mochte den Juden durchaus scheinen, als ob nun *alle* politischen Rahmen gesprengt seien." Note also, however, that Toury qualifies this comment by pointing out that a few Jews continued to remain loyal to the National Liberals and even to the Conservatives (*ibid.*, pp. 261ff.).

[25]One anti-Semitic leader calculated that since many Conservative candidates were known to be anti-Semites, the total number of anti-Semitic votes was closer to 400,000; he also pointed out that seven additional seats were won by anti-Semites who joined the Conservatives only after they had been elected. Pulzer, p. 122. See Massing, p. 229, n. 20.

[26]Pulzer, p. 122.

[27]Consider the election figures for Saxony, a region in which there were few Jews but where, nonetheless, political anti-Semitism had great appeal as a means for the *Mittelstand* to express a protest against the traditional parties of the right and the left. (The figures are taken from Pulzer, p. 123.)

	Conservatives	Nat'l. Lib.	Freisinn.	Anti-Semites	Social Democrats
1890	160,407	112,514	52,766	4,708	241,187
1893	135,709	35,741	30,439	116,013	273,000

[28]E.g., Prof. Hasse (later first president of the Pan-German League), who,

when faced with the competition of an anti-Semitic candidate in his district in 1893, agreed to support a ban of Jewish immigration, the expulsion of Jewish aliens, and a prohibition on ritual slaughtering. Though not an official candidate of the National Liberals, Hasse was a parliamentary affiliate of that party. See Pulzer, p. 195.

[29]*AZJ*, July 7, 1893, p. 1 of *Gemeindebote;* see *AZJ*, December 23, 1892, pp. 614-615, where the tendency of those friendly to the Jews to refer to a "justifiable kernel" in anti-Semitism is discussed. Full Freisinnig collaboration with the anti-Semites did not take place, however, until after 1900; see Toury, *Die politischen Orientierungen*, pp. 209, 211, and the discussion on p. 65, *infra*.

[30]*AZJ*, July 1, 1892, p. 313.

[31]*Ibid.*, March 24, 1893, p. 134; June 16, 1893, p. 277 (emphasis in original). See also *ibid.*, June 30, 1893, p. 301, and July 7, 1893, p. 315.

[32]For expression of this call for unification, see *IDR*, July 1895, p. 3: "Erstreben wir es mit heissem Bemühen, dass unsere Vereinigung zur ausnahmslosen Gesamtheit aller deutschen Juden werde. Darum ergeht nun auf's Neue der Ruf zum Sammeln; und als eine neue Fanfare soll diese Zeitschrift dienen, die deutschen Juden zusammenzurufen zu gemeinsamen Schutz und Trutz, zur Selbstvertheidigung, zur Selbsthülfe."

[33]*IDR*, September 1899, p. 458.

[34]Fuchs, pp. 51-52. See also the statement in *IDR*, August 1895, p. 45, by G. Stein: "Hier sind wir und bieten Euch die Hand! Der Mensch dem Menschen! Wir wollen Euch nicht beherrschen, wir wollen mit Euch leben, kein Staat im Staate, kein Sonderinteresse gegen das Allgemeine, aufgehend im Ganzen, nur für das Ganze wollen wir arbeiten am Heil der Menschheit. Wir hatten ein Vaterland, und wir haben dafür geblutet; wir haben Verwundete und Kranke gepflegt, erhobenen Herzens Danklieder gesungen . . . lasset Deutschland in wahrem Sinne unser Vaterland sein!"

[35]*IDR*, November 1895, p. 206. See also the statement by J. Rülf in 1890: "Everywhere this anti-Semitic fury signifies nothing more and nothing less than the beginnings of the social revolution. Let it be clearly understood by all who support anti-Semitism openly or secretly, or who merely tolerate it; it is not a question of the Jews at all, it is a question of subverting the entire order of life, society, and the state! Let no one believe that one can throw the Jews as meat to the revolutionary beast and thus meanwhile be saved oneself." Cited by Pulzer, p. 109.

[36]*IDR*, February 1901, p. 87. See Egmont Zechlin, *Die deutsche Politik und die Juden im Ersten Weltkriege* (Göttingen, 1969), pp. 53-54; statements by E. Fuchs in *AZJ*, April 19, 1895, p. 183, and by Maximilian Parmod [pseudonym for Dr. Apt] in *ibid.*, November 2, 1894, p. 520. Parmod wrote: "Indem die Juden für ihre *Rechtsgleichheit* kämpfen, kämpfen sie zugleich für die Befestigung der *staatlichen* Grundlage—*per aspera ad astra*." (Emphasis in original.)

[37]Cited by Tal, "Ha-Anti-shemiut," p. 116.

[38]As an example of one of the numerous expressions of optimism, see the letter from "Ein deutscher Jude" in *AZJ*, October 13, 1894, p. 504, which declared: "Aber der Tag wird und muss kommen, wo der Deutsche seine Augen öffnet und mit einem kräftigen Fusstoss all' jenes Gewürm von sich schleudert, wo seine wahre Natur, die herrliche deutsche Treue und Gerechtigkeit zum Durchbruche gelangt, und er fest die Hand seines deutschen Bruders jüdischen Glaubens zum ewigen Bunde fasst."

[39]E.g., *AZJ* August 14, 1896, pp. 385-386; *ibid.*, May 30, 1890, pp. 273-277; Rieger, p. 43; and articles by Ernst Tuch in *IDR*, October 1899, pp. 570-575, and in *OUW*, 1901, Heft 1, sp. 55-58. On Tuch, see pp. 70f., *infra.*

[40]See Massing, pt. 4, pp. 151-206, and the documents on pp. 311-320.

[41]An exception to this generalization was the circle gathered around Friedrich Naumann (*ibid.*, pp. 117-118).

[42]On this development, see p. 65, *infra.*

[43]The Zionists also, of course, offered a structural analysis of anti-Semitism which was, like that of the Social Democrats, rejected by the Jewish liberals. The Zionist view will be considered at length in the next chapter.

[44]See *AZJ*, February 2, 1894, p. 52, which recognized that while the agitators were beyond reach by Jewish argumentation, the indifferent masses were not.

[45]Fuchs, p. 87. See Hayes, pp. 176ff., for a discussion of the development of mechanical means of printing and of cheap wood-pulp paper, and the spread of general literacy in the late nineteenth century; the result was a boom in journal circulation throughout Western Europe.

[46]*IDR*, January 1902, p. 7. On the clear recognition by the Jews that anti-Semitism was demagogic in nature and that this fact had the deepest implications for its acceptance by the Conservatives, see Pulzer, pp. 120-125.

[47]Fuchs, pp. 58-59.

[48]As an example of the apologetic publications of the time, see *JP*, January 8, 1896, which carried a special four-page supplement listing the names of Jews who were wounded or killed in action defending Germany. Each was identified by his military unit, and the place where the casualty was suffered was listed as well. See also the remarks of Robert Weltsch in *YBLBI*, IV (1959), pp. xiii-xiv.

[49]See *AZJ*, February 21, 1902, and Rieger, p. 47. Among the other publications of the Centralverein which were disseminated widely were the following: Paul Rieger, *Zur Jahrhundertfeier des Judenedikts vom 11. März 1812* (distributed to 20,000 Jewish schoolchildren); Gustav Freytag, *Pfingstbetrachtung;* Cornill, *Das Alte Testament und die Humanität;* Hoffmann, *Der Schulchan Aruch und das Verhältnis der Rabinen zu den Andersgläubigen;* Gustav Levinstein, *Gesammelte Schriften;* Ismar Freund, *Die Emanzipation der Juden in Preussen;* and Jakob Neubauer, *Bibelwissenschaftliche Irrungen. ibid.*, pp. 49-50.

[50]*Ibid.*, pp. 48-49.

[51]Steinthal spoke to this point in 1894 (see Tal, "Ha-Anti-Shemiut," p. 49). On the special concern of some leaders of the Centralverein about the impact of Chamberlain, see *ibid.*, p. 72.

[52]As examples of such articles from *IDR*, see the following: Ludwig Rosenthal, "Deutsche und Juden" (on racial, "scientific" anti-Semitism), September 1895, pp. 115ff; Alphonse Lewy on the attack on the Bible, June 1897, pp. 295-310; and Paul Rieger, "Antisemitismus und Wissenschaft," September 1902 and October 1902. See also *AZJ*, December 14, 1894, pp. 589ff., for the lead article, "Der Kampf gegen die Bibel."

[53]Rieger, pp. 49-50.

[54]See *ibid.*, p. 29: "Der Verein erkannte im Rechtsschutz das beste Mittel, rohe Gewalt niederzuhalten, unlautere Kampfesweise zu entkräften und der Aufreizung der Massen entgegenzuarbeiten."

[55]*Ibid.*, p. 26.

[56]Later, with the development of local and regional affiliates, this surveillance was extended throughout Germany (*ibid.*, p. 48). See also *IDR*, Sep-

tember 1896, p. 459, which appealed to friends of the Centralverein in larger cities to keep it posted on local anti-Semitism. Note also the column "Briefkasten der Redaktion," a regular feature of the *IDR* which published reports sent in by individual members of the Centralverein reporting on anti-Semitic activites in their areas.

[57]*AZJ*, November 2, 1894, p. 519; the report of E. Fuchs on the first year's work of the Rechtsschutzkommission, delivered on April 16, 1894, and reprinted by Fuchs, pp. 6ff.

[58]Rieger, p. 28.

[59]E. Fuchs, in *AZJ*, April 19, 1895, p. 183.

[60]On the use of the term "Denunziantenverein" by the anti-Semites, see the statement by Willi Buch cited by Massing, p. 96, and *Antisemitisches Jahrbuch* (Berlin, 1898), p. 72. On Jewish criticism of the legal defense work, see the article by Emil Lehmann in *AZJ*, April 5, 1895, pp. 160-161.

[61]*AZJ*, April 19, 1895, p. 183. The reference to adulteration of foodstuffs alludes to the case of a Jewish butcher, Bonn, who had been convicted in Cleve of selling soiled meat to gentiles; it was charged that he had done so for religious reasons. See Rieger, p. 30.

[62]Fuchs, p. 184. See also his remarks in *AZJ*, April 19, 1895, p. 184: "Ja, wenn ich glaubte, das es der deutschen Staatsanwaltschaft an Gerechtigkeits- und Rechtssinn fehle, dann würde ich dem Kampfe widerrathen. . . . Aber da ich der felsenfesten Ueberzeugung bin, dass unsere Behörden unparteiisch und gewissenhaft nach bestem Wissen und Gewissen entscheiden. . . ." See also *AZJ*, October 26, 1894, pp. 506ff., for a discussion of the legal issues involved in bringing anti-Semites to trial and an expression of the hope that, through the courts, Jews could force the anti-Semites to recognize the equality of the law.

[63]Rieger, p. 29.

[64]Cited by Massing, pp. 96-97.

[65]*Ibid.*, pp. 94-95.

[66]From an interview with Walter Laqueur.

[67]Rieger, p. 27. Cf. the assessment by the *Antisemitisches Jahrbuch*, 1898, p. 71: "Diese sämtlichen Schutzvereine sind für den Antisemitismus . . . von Nutzen . . . dass sie einen jeden von uns zwingen, auf äusserste Vorsicht in der Form und auf unbedingte Richtigkeit in allen tatsächlichen Angaben bedachtzusein. . . ."

[68]Fuchs, p. 94; see Rieger, p. 27.

[69]See Toury, *Die politischen Orientierungen* pp. 204-205, 246-247 and "Mediniut yehudit b'germania, 1893-1918," (Hebrew), *Zion*, XXVIII: 3-4 (1963), p. 170. On the democratic elements in the Catholic political tradition and the failure of the liberals to recognize their existence, see Pinson, p. 153.

[70]Fuchs, pp. 66, 83; Rieger, p. 39. In the election of 1898 the Centralverein also urged its members to follow these guidelines: (1) no one should refrain from voting; (2) no one should vote for any party which has declared itself in favor of any sort of "*Ausnahmegesetz*"; and (3) no one should vote for a candidate who, even if only in the heat of the campaign, has expressed anti-Semitic opinions. See *IDR*, May 1898, p. 240.

[71]See Klinkenberg, p. 325. See also the text of the Centralverein's declaration in Rieger, p. 40; *IDR*, 1903, p. 327, which published a call to work against anti-Semitic candidates.

[72]*AZJ*, January 13, 1893, pp. 14-15; *ibid.*, March 31, 1893, pp. 148f., where the recantation appears. See also *ibid.*, May 26, 1893, pp. 241-243, for a lead article

dealing with the myth of a Jewish Center party, and the discussion by Toury, "Mediniut yehudit," pp. 169-170.

[73]Toury, "Mediniut yehudit," pp. 166-167. These efforts had the blessing of the Centralverein; see Fuchs, pp. 275-276 (where the idea of the Verband was broached in 1898); *IDR*, August 1902, pp. 430-431 (where the *Judentag* was endorsed); and *ibid.*, February 1904, pp. 73ff., and May 1904, pp. 255-256 (where support for the Verband is expressed). See also Jacob Toury, "Organizational Problems of German Jewry, *YBLBI*, XIII (1968), pp. 59ff.

Philippson's proposal was published in *AZJ*, September 28, 1900, pp. 459-461, and it created extensive debate, some of which is reflected in *ibid.*, October 12, 1900, pp. 485-486; November 9, 1900, p. 533; November 16, 1900, p. 548; October 19, 1900, pp. 495-497; April 5, 1901, p. 158; and May 31, 1901, p. 264. For the Orthodox reaction, see *JP*, January 4, 1901, pp. 1-2 and *ISR*, October 4, 1900, and October 25, 1900, pp. 1723-1726.

[74]*IDR*, May 1904, p. 255. Cf. Martin Philippson's statement in *ibid.*, February 1904, p. 78: "Dass von den Nationalliberalen . . . nicht zu hoffen ist, darüber braucht man nicht zu reden; die freisinnigen Fraktionen aber halten nicht zusammen und sind leider arg geschwächt, so dass sie trotz bestem Willen ihrerseits uns nichts nützen können."

[75]Toury, *Die politischen Orientierungen*, p. 209.

[76]*Ibid.*, pp. 202-203, 210-212, 217, 219, 276. See Toury, "Mediniut Yehudit," pp. 171ff., on the limited success of efforts to mount independent Jewish political activity in Posen, where the Jews occupied a unique position between German and Polish national groupings.

[77]Toury, *Die politischen Orientierungen*, p. 276.

[78]On Herzl, see the discussion on pp. 106ff., *infra*. On Pinsker, see the text of his *Autoemancipation* in Arthur Hertzberg, *The Zionist Idea* (New York, 1959), especially pp. 181ff., 185.

[79]An exception to this generalization was Löwenfeld's attack on the offensiveness of Orthodox worship with its references to Zion and his criticism of the Talmud. The Centralverein, however, did not follow Löwenfeld's lead on these issues; see *infra*, pp. 92f.

[80]On the loyalism of the Orthodox, see *infra*, p. 94.

[81]Hartmann had made the proposal in his book *Das Judenthum in Gegenwart und Zukunft* (1885), cited by Asch and Philippson, p. 128.

[82]E.g., Rabbi J. Rülf in *AZJ*, January 18, 1895, p. 32: "Lasset die Menschen nur erst wieder zur Besinnung kommen und ohne Voreingenommenheit, ohne Misszeitung und Missdeutung zur vollen Würdigung des Handelsverkehrs hingelangt sein—dann, ja, dann wind auch die Judenfrage gelöst sein. Dann wird man auch in dem jüdischen Trödler ein eben solch' nützliches und brauchbares Glied der Gesellschaft erkennen, wie in dem jüdischen Dachdecker, und einen Jeden in der Wahl seines Berufes ruhig gewähren lassen." See *ibid.*, December 28, 1894, p. 624, and February 15, 1895, p. 75.

[83]See Meyer, *Origins of the Modern Jew*, p. 169, on the proposal by the Verein für Wissenschaft des Judenthums to establish vocational training for Jews, c. 1819; and E. G. Lowenthal, "The Ahlem Experiment," *YBLBI*, XIV (1969), p. 166, on the formation of the Gesellschaft zur Verbreitung der Handwerke und des Ackerbaus unter den Juden des preussischen Staates in 1812. The Gesellschaft continued to exist into the period of Nazi rule.

[84]S. Meyer in *AZJ*, November 16, 1894, p. 546. Note the nuance added by Maximilian Stein in arguing for pursuit of manual labor among Jews, in *ibid.*,

April 19, 1895, p. 192: "Die Uebung des Handwerks wurde auch dem Antisemitismus am erfolgreichsten entgegenwirken, schon weil in dem Handwerkerstand kameradschaftliche Berührungs- und Annäherungspunkte zwischen Juden und Nichtjuden gegeben sind." Cf. also Tal, *Ha-Anti-shemiut*, p. 126, on the efforts of the German Jewish community to assist Polish and Russian Jews to emigrate to North America in order to avoid a concentration of East Europeans in German cities.

[85]*AZJ*, August 23, 1901, p. 408.

[86]In 1886 the name of the organization was changed to the Verein zur Verbreitung und Förderung der Handwerke unter den Juden.

[87]Although the impulse for Simon's plan came from his observation of East European immigrants in the United States, the institution he established in Germany served largely German-born youth. See E. G. Lowenthal, *op. cit.*, p. 172.

[88]*Ibid.*, p. 167.

[89]*AZJ*, March 8, 1895, pp. 113-114. See also Simon's pamphlet *Soziales zur Judenfrage: Ein Beitrag zu ihrer Lösung* in which he argued on behalf of his proposals. Further information on Ahlem may be found in E.G. Lowenthal, *passim; Zweiter Bericht über die israelitische Erziehungsanstalt zu Ahlem bei Hannover* (Hannover, 1897); *Dritter Bericht über die israelitische Erziehungsanstalt zu Ahlem bei* Hannover (Hannover, 1899); and in Alphonse Levy, *Die Erziehung der jüdischen Jugend zum Handwerk und zur Bodenkultur* (Berlin, 1895). The last-named work was by the editor of *Im deutschen Reich,* and in that pamphlet Levy urged support of Ahlem. For an example of the way in which the Jewish press supported Simon's work, see *IWOS*, March 23, 1894, pp. 89-90, where Ahlem is discussed appreciatively and the following comment is added: "Hier wird eine Art der *Abwehr des Antisemitismus* betrieben, die *mehr wert* ist, als manche kostspielige Veranstaltung mit fraglichem Erfolg." (Emphasis in original.)

Simon was also motivated by strong feelings of German patriotism and argued that by helping to rear Jewish children in manual and rural occupations, he was making them into better defenders of the fatherland. See Mosse, *The Crisis of German Ideology,* p. 145, and Simon's will, printed by E. G. Lowenthal, *op. cit.*, p. 180 where occupational retraining was justified by him as being "im Interesse meiner Glaubensgenossen und des Vaterlands."

[90]*Ibid.*, p. 169, and *IDR*, May 1901, pp. 293-295. See also, *IDR*, January 1898, p. 106 (a report on a lecture given by Ludwig Cohn on behalf of the Bodenkulturverein at a meeting of the Centralverein in Berlin); *ibid.,* September 1899, p. 463 (an expression of support by the Centralverein for the Bodenkulturverein and similar enterprises); and *ibid.,* April 1897, pp. 191ff. (urging support of Ahlem). Concern with economic distribution of the Jews in Germany continued after World War I; see Rieger, p. 46.

[91]See the articles by Gustav Tuch in *IDR*, October 1897, pp. 485-497, and by his son, Ernst, in *ibid.,* October 1899, pp. 570-575. Gustav asserted that in light of the German need for agriculturalists, Jewish "Einordnung in die nationale Arbeit" was a "Pflicht gegen das Vaterland." Cf., however, the letter from a Jewish cattle dealer in Württemberg in *ibid.,* January 1898, pp. 65-68, warning that agricultural occupations were in decline, and concluding: "Die Juden werden sich deshalb hüten, nur um antisemitischen Vorwürfen die Spitze abzubrechen, den landwirthschaftlichen Beruf zu ergreifen."

[92]E. G. Lowenthal, p. 169, and *Jüdisches Lexikon*, IV: 2, Col. 1174.

[93]In "Die wirtschaftliche Aufgabe der deutschen Judenheit," *OUW,* Heft 1,

1901, sp. 55-58. It is significant that while the *IDR* had carried other, less radical articles by Ernst and his father, Gustav (see n. 91 supra), this one was published in *OUW*.

⁹⁴E. G. Lowenthal, *op. cit.*, p. 169.

⁹⁵*OUW*, Heft 1, 1901, sp. 56-57.

⁹⁶Lazarus, p. 143.

⁹⁷Löwenfeld, p. 14.

⁹⁸Philippson, p. 10. In his official history of the Centralverein, Rieger conceded that although the gates of the ghetto had been opened a century earlier, "the ghetto-Jew, with the awkward obsequiousness of the upstart, has lasted beyond ghetto." See Rieger, p. 51. See also the letter written by Theodor Herzl to his parents from Berlin in 1885: "Gestern war Grande Soiree bei Treitel. An die 30-40 kleine, hässliche Juden und Jüdinnen. Kein tröstender Anblick." Also his reaction to Dühring recorded in his diary: "Die Schiefe der Judenmoral und der Mangel an sittlichem Ernst der Juden sind schonungslos aufgedeckt und gekennzeichnet. Daraus ist viel zu lernen." (Cited by Leon Kellner, *Theodor Herzls Lehrjahre* (Vienna and Berlin, 1920), pp. 127-128. For other references to Jewish defects which needed correction, see *AZJ*, November 3, 1893, p. 1 of *Gemeindebote* (report of a meeting of the Centralverein where Jewish improprieties needing reform were discussed); *IWOS*, November 3, 1893, pp. 342-343 (calling for "Erziehung der Schule entwachsenen Jugend zu *würdigen* Staatsbürgern, Ausrottung der widerlichen Untugenden der 'Schnodderigkeit,' der schlechten Manieren, der Zuchtlosigkeit, besonders im Verkehr in öffentlichen Lokalen, der Frivolität, des geist- und gemütlosen Genusses.") (emphasis in original); and *IDR*, April 1897, p. 191 (a discussion of "das durch die historischen Schicksale unserer Glaubensgemeinschaft aufgedrunge übermässige Streben nach Geld und Geldeswerth. . . .").

⁹⁹Wassermann, p. 55.

¹⁰⁰*Ibid.*, p. 15.

¹⁰¹The expression "rent in the soul" is from Micah Joseph Berdichevski (1865-1921), cited by Hertzberg, *The Zionist Idea*, p. 291. The modes through which this identity problem was dealt with differed in East and West Europe, of course; for purposes of this study, only the German Jewish response is considered at length.

¹⁰²On the *Preussische Jahrbücher*, see Pinson, p. 115.

¹⁰³*Preussische Jahrbücher*, October 1900, p. 132.

¹⁰⁴*Ibid.*, p. 133.

¹⁰⁵*Ibid.*, pp. 133-134. (Emphasis in original). On a similar statement for Herzl, see Alex Bein, *Theodor Herzl* (Philadelphia, 1941), p. 249.

¹⁰⁶*Preussische Jahrbücher*, October 1900, pp. 133-136.

¹⁰⁷*Ibid.*, p. 137. (Emphasis in original).

¹⁰⁸*Ibid.*, p. 138.

¹⁰⁹*Ibid.*, p. 139. (Emphasis in original).

¹¹⁰*Ibid.*, pp. 139-140.

¹¹¹*Ibid.*, p. 140. On this argument as a common pattern early in the emancipation, see Rinott, p. 16.

¹¹²*AZJ*, January 11, 1901, p. 4 of the *Gemeindebote*. In December 1900, the *Preussische Jahrbücher* carried a reply to Weisler by Rabbi Vogelstein. Vogelstein devoted himself largely to a defense of Judaism against the charge that Jewish morality is intrinsically inferior to Christian. See S. Lublinski's comments on

Vogelstein's essay in *Ost und West*, 1901, Heft 9, sp. 652; Lublinski rebuked the liberal Jews for imagining that "they have refuted the weighty arguments of a Benediktus Levita with the twaddle of a Rabbi Vogelstein."

[113]Meyer, *Origins of the Modern Jew*, ch. III; *Jewish Encyclopedia*, V, and Carl Cohen, "The Road to Conversion," *YBLBI*, VI (1961), pp. 263, 265.

[114]Rathenau published the essay under the pseudonym W. Hartenau. See Toury, *Die politischen Orientierungen*, p. 269.

[115]Massing, p. 146; Rosenberg, p. 40; Erich Gottgetreu, "Maximilian Harden," *YBLBI*, VII (1962) pp. 215-246.

[116]Rathenau pp. 134ff., "Höre Israel," pp. 3-4.

[117]*Ibid.*, pp. 5-6.

[118]*Ibid.*, p. 7.

[119]*Ibid.*, pp. 7-9.

[120]*Ibid.*, p. 10.

[121]*Ibid.*, p. 11.

[122]*Ibid.*, p. 12. On the völkisch ideology which forms the background for these judgments, see *infra*, pp. 134ff.

[123]*Ibid.*, pp. 12-16.

[124]*Ibid.*, pp. 16ff.

[125]*Ibid.*, pp. 19-20.

[126]*Ibid.*, p. 20.

[127]*Ibid.*, p. 13.

[128]Cited by Count Harry Kessler, *Walter Rathenau, His Life and Work* (New York, 1930), p. 37.

[129]*Ibid.*, p. 38.

[130]Walter Rathenau, *Briefe*, I (Dresden, 1926), 203-204. This letter was addressed to Wilhelm Schwaner, an anti-Semitic writer and publisher (see Zechlin, p. 16). On another occasion Rathenau explained that he remained a Jew because he thought it dishonorable to gain personal advantage by conversion and thus, implicitly, sanction the injustice done to the Jews. He wrote to Frau von Hindenburg, who wanted him to become foreign minister: "Even though my ancestors and I myself have served our country to the best of our abilities, yet, as you know, I am a Jew, and as such a citizen of the second class. I could not become a higher civil servant, nor even, in time of peace, a sub-lieutenant. By changing my faith I should have escaped these disabilities, but by acting thus I should feel that I had countenanced the breach of justice committed by those in power." Cited by Kessler, pp. 51-52.

[131]From *Staat und Judenthum*, cited by Kessler, pp. 27-28.

[132]On the völkisch ideology, see the discussion on pp. 134ff., *infra*.

[133]Consider, e.g., the statement by P. Philippson in 1883: "What does disturb me is the term 'race' . . . this term penetrates into minds [the idea that] the occupational structure, in our opinion also unhealthy, cannot be changed because its source is not in the historical conditions in which we live, but in our blood." Cited by Tal, "Ha-Anti-shemiut," p. 88. In this regard, note the efforts for occupational reform discussed above which reflected the liberal faith that conditions can change the man and that Jewish nature was not racially fixed (*ibid.*, p. 63).

[134]Fuchs, p. 97.

[135]See, e.g. *AZJ*, March 7, 1890, pp. 114-115 (asserting that the racial purity of the Germans had been blurred as early as the twelfth century); *ibid.*, December 23, 1892, pp. 616-620 and December 30, 1892, pp. 628-630 (an article on "Die

anthropologische Stellung der Juden" which concluded that the Jews were not an unmixed group racially). Note, also, the following statement by a rabbi (Dr. Rothschild) writing in *IWOS*, July 10, 1890, p. 213: "Die Juden [bilden] . . . *weder* ein besonderes Volk, *noch* eine gesonderte Nation . . . Sie haben keine besondere politische Vereinigung, sie sind Deutsche unter Deutschen, wie Franzosen unter Franzosen; sie haben auch keine gleiche Abstammung, sondern haben verschiedene Volksstämme in sich aufgenommen; sie sind eine Mischung orientalischer und occidentalischer Volkeselemente, die ehedem sogar vielfach und *en masse* erzwungen wurde und heute noch durch freiwillige Mischehen andauert, von *gleicher* Rasse und *demselben* Blute sind die Juden demnach nicht. . . ." (Emphasis in original.)

[136]*JP*, April 5, 1895, p. 145.

[137]*Ibid.*, November 25, 1904, p. 487.

[138]*AZJ*, April 15, 1892, pp. 185ff. (Emphasis in original.)

[139]*Ibid.*, July 3, 1891, p. 319. (Emphasis in original.) See *IDR*, November 1904, pp. 577-582, for a lengthy discussion of the Jewish racial question. While claiming that the Jews were not pure Semites but a group with mixed racial characteristics, the author maintained that there were certain clearly recognizable physical and psychological features which defined the present racial nature of the Jews. For similar discussions assuming a racial component in Jewishness, see *AZJ*, December 25, 1980, p. 636; *OUW*, 1901, Heft 12, p. 896 (by Martin Philippson); and *AZJ*, November 30, 1900, p. 566. The latter warned those who contemplated conversion to Christianity that racial anti-Semitism would prevent them from finding full acceptance in the Christian world; it argued: "Even if we are not descended from Hermann, the Cherusker, we can still console ourselves with the knowledge that our family tree is much, much older. . . . No, we do not forget natural history and Darwin. We know very exactly that, when a Jew is baptized, he does not thereby become a member of the Aryan race, and we are cheered heartily when just this is always held up to all those receiving baptism . . . We know that the Jewish race is a primary one, that despite all influences, climatic and others, it has always reproduced itself in its integrity, and that the Jewish type has remained the same during the course of millenia. But we also know that this very indestructible and unmistakable type in its noblest representations (where it is scarcely to be distinguished from that of the ancient Greeks and, as great ethnologists maintain, far surpasses [the Greek type] in spiritual expression and moral earnestness) remains, for the objective observer, a clear seal impressed on the coat of arms of the oldest nobility of the world-historical peoples."

For a rare expression of Jewish racial thinking before 1848, see Sterling, "Jewish Reaction to Jew-Hatred," p. 114.

[140]Cited by Rieger, p. 34.

[141]*Jüdisches Lexicon*, I, p. 1292.

[142]Fuchs, p. 228. See also p. 253, on his deep affinity for Germans and Europeans, irrespective of religious faith, as opposed to Africans or Asiatics who might be Jews. For other liberal expressions of the religious character of Jewish identity vis-a-vis Zionist claims of Jewish nationhood, see *AZJ*, February 28, 1896 (a review of Herzl's *Der Judenstaat*); *ibid.*, December 14, 1894, pp. 591-593; and *IWOS*, July 10, 1890, pp. 213-214 (article entitled *"Sind die Juden ein 'Volk' oder eine 'Nation?'"*)

[143]Lazarus, p. 71.

[144]*IDR*, February 21, 1902, pp. 85-86; see also *supra*, p. 59.

[145]*Ibid.*, November 1897, p. 533. Cf. the views of Rabbi Benno Jacob, a leader in the Centralverein after World War I, who held that the Jews were a separate tribe not related to the German race but still part of the German nation. Jacob was passionately anti-Zionist. See Wilhelm, "Benno Jacob," p. 78. See also the statement by Alphonse Levy, editor of *IDR*, in the issue of January 1898, p. 12: "Das Judenthum um seine Bekenner nur ein religiöses *und geschichtliches, aber kein nationales Band schlingt!*" (The emphasis under "und geschichtliches" is mine; the rest is in the original.)

[146]E.g., the statement on the events of 1893 by Martin Philippson in *Neueste Geschichte des jüdischen Volkes* (Leipzig, 1910), pp. 50-51: "Sogar Tausende von bisher Gleichgültigen und Lauen wurden sich ihrer Eigenschaft als Juden bewusst und traten mit Entschiedenheit, ja mit Begeisterung für Religion und Glaubensgenossenschaft in den Kampf. Der Antisemitismus . . . ist aber sonst—gegen seinen Willen—ein Element [of Judaism's] Wiederbelebung, Einigung und innerer Kraftigung geworden." Cf. the statement by Martin Mendelsohn, the Centralverein leader, on *Die Pflicht der Selbstvertheidigung*, p. 17: "Die Wiederkehr des Selbstbewusstseins unter uns Juden, das Verschwinden der jetzt leider noch so allgemeinen Scheu, offen zu bekennen, dass man Jude sei." Note also Fuchs's remark, in the context of a discussion of "inner mission": "Wir wollen in jedem einzelnen Juden das niedergetretene Selbstbewusstsein wieder aufrichten." Fuchs, p. 164.

[147]Fuchs, p. 164. For similar statements by Fuchs see p. 271 (a speech given on October 16, 1898), and *AZJ*, April 19, 1895, p. 185.

[148]Fuchs, p. 252. See also *IDR*, December 1904, p. 647, for an unsigned article praising the effect of the Centralverein in strengthening Jewish self-consciousness and enhancing a sense of solidarity among German Jews. It also attacked those Jews who converted to Christianity without religious conviction in order to escape anti-Semitism, and urged that Jews should ostracize these "Fahnenflüchtigen." Also see *AZJ*, February 2, 1894, pp. 51-52, noting that "Eine Menge gleich-giltiger, indifferenter Elemente, welche mit dem Judenthum nur noch lose verbunden sich fühlten, sehen sich plötzlich gezwungen, Farbe zu bekennen und Stellung zu nehmen gegenüber den Angriffen, welchen sie in ihrer Eigenschaft als Juden ausgesetzt sind."

Consider also the following poem written by Gustav Levinstein to commemorate the tenth anniversary of the founding of the Centralverein; it illustrates the mixture of German patriotism and Jewish pride that characterized the spirit of the Centralverein's leadership. From Gustav Levinstein, *Zur Ehre des Judenthums* (Berlin, 1911), pp. xiii-xv.

> So seid gegrüsst, die Ihr aus Deutschlands Gauen
> Gekommen hier vom Osten und vom West,
> Von Nord und Süd, Ihr Männer und Ihr Frauen,
> Zu feiern mit uns unser Stiftungsfest.
> Aus tausend Blicken seh'n wir leuchtend strahlen
> Der Liebe Zug, der aus dem Herzen steigt,
> Und hingegeben allen Idealen
> Zum Göttlichen, zum Ewigen sich neigt.
>
> Zehn Jahre sind es an dem heut'gen Tage,
> Da sich die Ueberzeugung laut brach Bahn,
> Dass nicht mit Schweigen, nicht mit leerer Klage
> Der Kampf zu führen gegen Trug und Wahn,

Dass wir vereinet nicht mit Furcht und Bangen
Den Nacken beugen, dass der Blick nicht fleht,
Dass wir nicht bitten, nein, dass wir verlangen,
Dass man uns wahr' des Rechtes Majestät.

Denn Deutsche sind wir, und dem Vaterlande,
Ihm dienen wir mit unserem Herz und Blut,
Mit ihm verknüpft sind aller Liebe Bande,
Was einst uns lieb in seiner Erde ruht,
In Deutschlands Munde leben Zions Lieder,
Der Harfe Klang durch seine Fluren weht,
In seine ärmsten Hütten steigt hernieder
Der Trost des Weltalls—Israels Gebet.

Verlanget doch, was nur das Herz kann geben,
Verlanget doch, was nur in unserer Macht,
Verlanget es und wär es unser Leben
Wir habens oft dem Vaterland gebracht.
Nur eins verlanget nicht, lasst uns den Glauben,
Der leuchtend drang einst durch die dunkle Nacht,
Ihr könnet ihn, Ihr dürft ihn uns nicht rauben,
Der die Erlösung dieser Welt gebracht.

Von ihm, von unserem Rechte tief durchdrungen,
So stehen alle hier für einen ein,
Und ist der volle Sieg noch nicht errungen,
Zum Siege führet der Central-Verein.
Denn für das Höchste streben wir auf Erden,
Und ein Bewusstsein giebt uns stete Kraft,
Nicht für uns selbst, im Dienste der Gemeinde,
So stehen wir gerüstet vor dem Feinde.

Denn dieser Glaube ist die ewige Quelle,
Aus der die Welt des Herzens Hoffnung nimmt.
Im stolzen Dome, in der Bergkapelle
Sein Echo in der Menschheit Seele dringt;
Vom dumpfen Aberglauben nicht getrübet,
An keine Wunderlehre fest gebannt,
So tönt er aus des Herzens Tiefen wieder
Und bringt den Himmel zu der Erde nieder.

Für jenen Glauben haben wir gelitten,
Wie noch kein Volk auf dem Planetenrund,
Verfolgt, zerstreut in der Nationen Mitten,
Schwor nicht zum falschen Eide unser Mund.
Noch stehen wir hier für alle Zeit als Zeugen,
Vertrauend auf des ewigen Gottes Wort,
Dass Berge mögen weichen und die Höhen,
Doch Israel, es wird nicht untergehen.

See the assessment of this development by the Verein zur Abwehr des Antisemitismus' *Antisemiten-Spiegel* (Danzig, 1892), p. 367: "Eine andere Folge der antisemitischen Bewegung ist die, dass sie den langsam, aber sicher fortschreitenden Process der Annäherung und Verschmelzung von Juden und Christen gestört hat. Die Juden haben sich, wie das natürlich und begreiflich ist, wieder enger aneinander geschlossen. Sie werden manche ihrer Besonderheiten, welche dem bürgerlichen Zusammenleben mit ihren christlichen Nachbarn nicht förderlich sind, um so zäher festhalten, je mehr sie bedrängt werden."

[149]See, e.g., the statement by Fuchs, p. 65: "Wer in der Bewegung steht, wird mit freudiger Genugtuung es empfinden, wie die Gemeinsamkeit der Abwehrbestrebungen und das Bewusstsein der erfüllten Pflicht das Judentum verinnerlicht, die Charactere stählt, die bangen Gemüter erhebt und mit neuer Hoffnung erfüllt. Selbstvertrauen und Selbstbewusstsein, Selbstachtung und Selbstkritik kehren ein. *Die Taufe gilt wieder als Ehrlosigkeit, als Fahnenflucht.* Der Gedanke, dass er nicht allein steht, dass Genossen für ihn und mit ihm kämpfen, hilft ihm die Unbillen leichter ertragen und nimmt seinem Herzen die Bitterkeit des Verlassenseins. Der einzelne Jude fühlt sich wieder als Mitglied der Gesamtheit, der er angehört." (Emphasis in original.) For similar expressions by Fuchs, see *AZJ*, April 19, 1895, p. 185, and *IDR*, March, 1901, p. 132.

[150]*IDR*, November 1895, pp. 229-230. However the suggestion to disavow the activities of the "bad Jews" was criticized by *JP*, February 9, 1893, pp. 53-55 (perhaps in reaction to Löwenfeld's attack on the Orthodox). See *ibid.*, August 8, 1895, pp. 321f.

[151]An example would be the statement by Georg Minden in *AZJ*, December 30, 1892, p. 627: "Der einzige wirksame Schutz gegen den Antisemitismus ist doch der, das die Juden streben, sittlich über dem Durchschnitt zu stehen und nicht zu einer religions-und vaterlandslosen Horde auszuarten."

[152]*IDR*, July 1895, p. 5.

[153]Mendelsohn, p. 19.

[154]*Ibid.*, p. 20.

[155]Cited in *IWOS*, November, 10, 1893, p. 352.

[156]For the general background in German affairs against which this development occurred, see Mann, pp. 493-494. Mann notes there ". . . enstanden seit den achtziger Jahren noch die grossen Interessenverbände, welche durch die Parteien, durch höfische Einflusse, durch direkte demagogische Propaganda, zu wirken suchten: Zentralverband deutscher Industrieller, Bund der Landwirte, Kolonialgesellschaft, Deutscher Bauernbund. . . . Auch geht es mit rechten Dingen zu, wenn sie sich organisieren, und es ist nur gut, wenn sie es in aller Oeffentlichkeit tun, anstatt heimlich." The last comment is especially interesting in view of the Centralverein's emphasis on both organized and public defense against anti-Semitism.

[157]*IDR*, November 1895, pp. 229f.

[158]Fuchs, p. 56. Mendelsohn (p. 7) states that unlike the Committee, the Centralverein was to be "der Zusammenschluss einer grossen Zahl, womoglich sodar äller Deutschen jüdischen Glaubens in einer imposanten Organization und deren Hinaustreten in die Breite Oeffentlichkeit." For response to this proposal by *JP* in the wake of Löwenfeld's pamphlet, see the lead article in the January 12, 1893 issue.

[159]*IDR*, September 1896, pp. 459-460 and *IWOS*, November 13, 1893, p. 243.

[160]For an example of earlier appeals for unity within the Jewish community in the face of anti-Semitism, see *AZJ*, March 27, 1891, pp. 145-146.

[161]Endorsements of the Centralverein by the *AZJ* may be found in issues for

May 26, 1893 (pp. 242-243) and December 28, 1894 (p. 613). Grudging support was expressed by *IWOS* in its issue for November 3, 1893 (pp. 342-343) after an attack on the organization by Rabbi Singer in the October 20, 1893 issue (pp. 325-326).

[162]On Hirsch's impact in spiritualizing Jewish existence in order to make acceptance of civil rights and political equality possible, see Toury, *Die politischen Orientierungen*, p. 71, n. 18. See also pp. 140 and 142 on the Germanism of the *ISR*, even in the period before 1870. For an assessment of the "new Orthodoxy" by a Zionist historian, see Adolf Böhm, *Die zionistische Bewegung bis zum Ende des Weltkrieges* (2d ed.; Tel Aviv, 1935) p. 77. See also Dubnow, *Weltgeschichte des jüdischen Volkes*, p. 68: "Doch war die Einstellung dieser beiden Gruppen [Reform and Orthodox] zu nationalen Fragen im Grossen und Ganzen die Gleiche. Die einen wie die anderen betrachteten sich als Deutsche jüdischen Glaubens, und der Unterschied zwischen Orthodoxen und Liberalen bestand nur darin, dass jene, gesetztreu wie sie waren, wenigstens den schlimmsten Auswüchsen der Assimilation, dem Renegatentum, Einhalt taten." To cite but a few of the many examples in the *ISR* in which the same attitudes toward Germany that informed the Centralverein are expressed, see issues for January 19, 1891, p. 90, asserting that Reform Jews and Orthodox are one in their devotion to Germany; October 11, 1898, p. 1457, declaring attachment to the fatherland; January 24, 1895, p. 123, affirming: "We would rather remain Germans of Jewish faith . . . than non-Jewish Jews who have their fatherland in Palestine. . . . *The true Jew in Germany is a genuine German, a faithful son of his German fatherland.* . . . We Jews constitute only a religious community. [We] do not deviate one step from this ancestral religion, but in all else we are loyal citizens of our fatherland" (emphasis in original); and January 26, 1891, p. 129, swearing fealty to the Kaiser on the occasion of his birthday, and declaring: "We swear to you that in time of need we will faithfully flock to your banner and battle with you and conquer for Germany's fame, and for the honor of the fatherland."

[163]Cited in *Jewish Encyclopedia*, VI, 396.

[164]Dubnow, *Weltgeschichte des jüdischen Volkes*, p. 70; Toury, *Die politischen Orientierungen*, p. 249, n. 25; Elbogen and Sterling, *Die Geschichte der Juden in Deutschland*, p. 248; Joseph Walk, "The Torah va'Avodah Movement in Germany," *YBLBI*, VI (1961) p. 238; Saul Raphael Landau, *Sturm und Drang im Zionismus* (Vienna, 1937), p. 210. See also the comment by the East European Zionist Shmarya Levin on his meeting with Azriel Hildesheimer: "Before me stood a representative of an old order, which had become petrified in ancient forms, and had little understanding of the problems of a living, suffering, and struggling Jewry." Shmarya Levin, *Youth in Revolt*, trans. by Maurice Samuel (New York, 1930), p. 228.

[165]*ISR*, May 14, 1890, p. 796; June 9, 1890, pp. 805ff; December 18, 1890, pp. 1780, 1787-1789; and March 2, 1893, p. 331. Likewise, with regard to "inner mission," the *ISR* argued that internal reforms must be carried out along with self-defense. The "Semitic fathers of anti-Semitism"—"all Jews whose manner of living provokes justifiable anger"—must be corrected, it argued; Jews were urged to "drive the spirit of odious self-interest out of our midst" and show their Christian neighbors that "the bad elements among us" were not representative of Jewry, something that would be accomplished by giving positions of honor in the Jewish community only to those of blameless character, loyalty and patriotism. See issue for December 28, 1892, p. 1964.

[166]*Ibid.*, March 2, 1893, p. 331.

[167]*Ibid.*, July 6, 1893, p. 1030.

[168]Löwenfeld, p. 24.

[169]Rahel Straus, *Wir lebten in Deutschland* (Stuttgart, 1961), p. 155.

[170]*JP*, January 12, 1893, pp. 13-14, and January 19, 1893, pp. 22-23. On the response of the *ISR*, see issues for January 16, 1893, pp. 77-79; January 23, 1893, pp. 117-119; and March 13, 1893, pp. 394-395. The *ISR* charged Löwenfeld's pamphlet with "pour[ing] oil upon the very fires which it purports to want to extinguish," and declared that the assertion that Jews who were loyal to Talmudic law were incapable of German patriotism was a "totally monstrous defamation."

[171]Mendelsohn, pp. 10-11; and Fuchs, pp. 56-57. See also p. 165, where Fuchs praised Maximilian Horwitz for refusing to share Löwenfeld's position toward the Orthodox and for rejecting his call for "Gewissenszwang" against them. The Centralverein's theses were closely patterned after those of Löwenfeld, but as Rieger notes: "Die Erörterung religiöser Fragen war mit ihnen [the theses] ausgeschlossen. Der Verein sollte die freiestdenkenden wie die strenggläubigen Juden zur Verteidigung ihrer staatsbürgerlichen Rechte zusammenfassen. Von diesen Grundsätzen ist er niemals abgegangen." See Rieger, pp. 21-22, and Klinkenberg, p. 325.

[172]Tal, "Ha-Anti-shemiut," pp. 116-117. Tal shows that this campaign was not carried on for economic reasons alone (i.e., to protect Christian butchers against competition), but was motivated by ideological factors as well, as shown by the fact that the campaign was carried on in areas where there were no Jews. The first successful prohibition of Jewish ritual slaughter was established in Switzerland in 1892 by a popular vote; in Germany the first petition of the Tierschutzvereine was submitted in 1887, and the second in 1889, but both were unsuccessful.

[173]Fuchs, p. 49. On the Centralverein's sensitivity to the charge that it disparaged the Talmud, see *AZJ*, October 6, 1893, p. 470, which reported on a meeting of the organization in which, the report claimed, the Talmud had been attacked. In the next issue (October 13, 1893, p. 492), Emil Lehmann corrected this account by publishing the text of the remarks which were actually made on that occasion.

[174]Tal, "Ha-Anti-shemiut," p. 118, and Rieger, pp. 32ff. See Paul Nathan, *Über das jüdische rituelle Schächtverfahren* (1894), for another defense of Orthodox ritual slaughter by a liberal Jew.

[175]*IDR*, October 1900, p. 505 (an article entitled "Anti-semitischer Tierschutz"). See *AZJ*, June 7, 1901, pp. 269-270, for another warning in a liberal Jewish journal that *"Gewissenszwang"* was being practiced under the guise of *"Tierschutz."* For Orthodox recognition of the liberal support on this issue, see *ISR*, October 16, 1893, p. 1549, and January 2, 1902, p. 2.

[176]Rieger, p. 34.

[177]E.G., *JP*, February 13, 1903, pp. 71-73, and *ibid.*, February 20, 1903, pp. 91-93, where the text of a lecture by Fuchs ("Rückblick auf die zehnjährige Tätigkeit des Centralvereins") is reprinted.

[178]On *Abwehr* and the *Rechtsstaat*, see *JP*, May 24, 1894, p. 212: *"Noch seid Ihr vollberechtigte deutsche Staatsbürger, solange Ihr Euch selbst dafür haltet! Noch lebt Ihr in einem geordneten Kulturstaate, wo die Verfassung nicht blosse tote Buchstaben darstellt, noch existiert das Gesetz, auf das Ihr pochen könnt. Es ist eine ernste Zeit, in der wir leben, aber durch feige Untätigkeit werden wir den Jammer der Gegenwart nie und nimmer überwinden. So nehmet tapfer den*

Kampf auf, der Euch von gewissenlosen Feinden aufgedrängt worden ist! Ehrlich und gerecht, offen und mutig soll dieser Kampf geführt werden, und wer an den Sieg der Gerechtigkeit glaubt, der kann auch an dem Sieg unserer guten Sache nicht verzweifeln." (Emphasis in original.)

On German patriotism, see *ibid.*, January 15, 1896, p. 22, an article on the twenty-fifth anniversary of the victory in the Franco-Prussian War. The article concluded: "Als *deutsche Juden,* eins mit *allen* seinen Gliedern in dem Gefühle *tiefsinniger* Liebe zum theuren Vaterlande, stimmen wir aus vollem Herzen ein in den Jubelruf, der heute wie Donnerhall die Gaue Germanien's durchbraust: *Heil unserem Kaiser! Heil dem deutschen Reich!"* (Emphasis in original.)

See also *ibid.*, August 1, 1901, p. 317 (for a representative expression of the *JP*'s optimism); April 23, 1896 pp. 193-194 (a review of Bernhard Cohn's *Vor dem Sturm,* expressing criticism of his advocacy of radical solutions to the Jewish question); and June 8, 1898, pp. 251ff. (on Zionism).

Hildesheimer's faction had long been supportive of Palestinian colonization through the Ezra circle, and *JP* had published material by S. R. Landau, one of Herzl's early co-workers, including his favorable review of *Der Judenstaat.* Hildesheimer, however, did not support political Zionism when it developed as an organized movement. See Landau, pp. 54, 211-212; Böhm, pp. 173-174; and Richard Lichtheim, *Toldot Ha-tsionut B'germania* (Jerusalem, 1951), p. 65.

[179]See *IDR*, December 1904, p. 647: "Die durch den Central-Verein bewirkte Kräftigung des Selbstbewusstseins und des Solidaritätsgefühls der deutschen Juden hat in erfreulicher Weise jede Kluft der politischen und religiösen Meinungsverschiedenheiten überbrückt, so dass jetzt viele Tausende zusammenstehen zur mannhaften Abwehr schnöder Angriffe und Verleumdungen."

[180]*ISR*, December 11, 1893, pp. 1863-1865.

[181]*Ibid.*, February 8, 1894, pp. 193-195.

[182]See the statement by Centralverein leader Emil Lehmann quoted from a leaflet by an anti-Semitic paper in Dresden and reprinted in the *ISR*, April 1, 1895. Lehmann reportedly had written: "We know nothing, and wish to know nothing, of the Talmud."

[183]*Ibid.*, March, 12, 1894, pp. 373-374.

[184]*Ibid.*, July 16, 1894, pp. 1043ff, and March 16, 1896, p. 458. The Centralverein statement had said: "Our God does not live in the fog of mysticism but rather in the heights of pure knowledge. We need no new gospel of love. . . ."

[185]*Ibid.*, March 23, 1896, p. 497. (Emphasis in original.)

[186]*Ibid.*

[187]*Ibid.*, March 16, 1896, p. 458.

[188]*Ibid.*, March 23, 1896, p. 497.

[189]E.g., *ibid.*, May 4, 1891, p. 645; January 4, 1893, p. 1; March 13, 1905.

[190]*Ibid.*, March 23, 1896, p. 497, and March 16, 1896, p. 458.

[191]*Ibid.*, June 7, 1894, pp. 831-832; cf. *ibid.*, January 1, 1891, p. 2.

[192]*Ibid.*, January 19, 1891, p. 90, and January 9, 1893, p. 42.

[193]*Ibid.*, May 4, 1891, pp. 644-645. (Emphasis in original.) See also *AZJ*, March 27, 1891, pp. 145-146.

[194]*ISR*, March 10, 1892, p. 379.

[195]*Ibid.*, May 25, 1891, pp. 755-756.

[196]*Ibid.*, February 20, 1893, pp. 269-270, and October 9, 1893, pp. 1508-1509. Note, however, the illogic of this line of argument which asserts but fails to

demonstrate a causal link between abandonment of traditional Judaism and the rise of racial anti-Semitism.

[197]*Ibid.*, June 28, 1894, p. 932. (Emphasis in original.) See also *AZJ*, June 15, 1894, pp. 277-278.

[198]*ISR*, June 12, 1890, p. 821.

[199]See also the articles by Dr. Ehrmann on "The Agitation against Ritual Slaughter" in which he lectured the Reformers for abandoning the tradition and saw the campaign against the practice of *shechita*, and the liberal Jewish response, as God's way of bringing the Jews back to *kashrut*. *Ibid.*, October 16, 1893, p. 1549, and November 2, 1893. See also *ibid.*, January 2, 1902, p. 2.

[200]*Ibid.*, January 1, 1891, p. 2; August 28, 1893, p. 1326; June 16, 1892, p. 867. See also *ibid.*, October 25, 1900, p. 1725.

[201]*Ibid.*, July 7, 1890, p. 954, (see also *ibid.*, March 3, 1890, p. 311); March 16, 1891, p. 413; February 20, 1893, pp. 269ff.

[202]*Ibid.*, February 23, 1893, p. 286.

[203]*Ibid.*, February 29, 1893, p. 271. For similar expressions of cynicism by the Orthodox about the efficacy of such liberal defense tactics as the declaration of the German rabbis on the Talmud, see *ibid.*, March 13, 1893, pp. 409-410. The text of the declaration appears in *AZJ*, February 17, 1893, pp. 73ff. Cf. also the Orthodox skepticism about the movement to further agricultural and manual labor among Jews, *ISR* June 22, 1896, pp. 947ff.

[204]*ISR*, January 2, 1893, pp. 3, 9, n.

[205]*Ibid.*, January 2, 1893, p. 3.

[206]*Ibid.*, July 7, 1890, p. 953.

[207]*Ibid.*, February 13, 1893, p. 235; January 23, 1890, p. 114.

CHAPTER FOUR

[1]On the history of Zionism, see Ben Halpern, *The Idea of the Jewish State* (Cambridge, 1961); Nahum Sokolow, *History of Zionism* (New York, 1969); Adolf Böhm, *Die Zionistische Bewegung* (Tel Aviv, 1935); and Alex Bein, *Theodore Herzl* (Philadelphia, 1941). Without questioning the profound significance for the Zionist movement of those Jewish nationalists who wrote in Hebrew or other languages, our consideration will be limited to the literature of the movement which appeared in the German.

[2]See Dubnow's assessment of the importance of anti-Semitism in the thinking of Herzl and Nordau: "Für Nordau wie für Herzl gab es nur die zwei Pole: Assimilation und politischer Zionismus; glaubten sie doch, dass das Judentum nur insofern eine Nation sei, als es 'einen gemeinsamen Feind' habe, eine Ansicht, die offenbar unter dem Drucke des Antisemitismus entstanden war. . . ." Dubnow, *Weltgeschichte des jüdischen Volkes*, p. 330. See also the claim by H.G. Adler that "Zionism was, indeed, the result of hatred against the Jews." H.G. Adler, *The Jews in Germany* (Notre Dame and London, 1969, p. 7.

[3]Of the figures discussed below, only Birnbaum departs significantly from this pattern. See also Lichtheim, p. 107.

[4]Ludwig Lewisohn, *Theodor Herzl: A Portrait for this Age* (Cleveland and New York, 1955), p. 36.

[5]See Bein, *Herzl*, chs. I, II; Lewisohn, pp. 34ff; and Leon Kellner, *Theodor*

Herzls Lehrjahre (Vienna and Berlin, 1920), *passim,* and especially pp. 27-30 on Herzl's encounter with anti-Semitism in the Burschenschaft.

[6]First published in the *Jewish Chronicle* of January 17, 1896, pp. 12-13, and reprinted in the *Herzl Year Book* (New York, 1960), III, p. 330. See also Bein, *Herzl,* pp. 34-35.

[7]Bein, *Herzl,* pp. 36, 38.

[8]Lewisohn, p. 39.

[9]Cited in *ibid.,* p. 20.

[10]Theodor Herzl, *Complete Diaries,* ed. by Raphael Patai, trans. by Harry Zohn, I (New York, 1960), p. 4.

[11]Bein, *Herzl,* p. 47.

[12]Herzl, *Diaries,* I, pp. 5-6; Bein, *Theodor Herzl,* ch. III.

[13]See Henry Cohn, "Theodor Herzl's Conversion to Zionism," *Jewish Social Studies,* XXXII:2 (April, 1970), 101-110, on the determinative role of Austrian anti-Semitism in the development of Herzl's Zionist consciousness.

[14]See Bein, *Herzl,* p. 89, for the background to this discussion. See also Kellner, p. 138.

[15]Cited in Bloch, "Herzl's First Years of Struggle," pp. 78-79.

[16]*Ibid.,* pp. 80-81. See also Herzl's later entries recalling this event, in *Diaries,* I, pp. 6-7.

[17]From this letter we also gain insight into Herzl's feud with Saul Raphael Landau over the role of *Abwehr* propaganda in the columns of *Die Welt.* Landau, the first editor of *Die Welt,* recalled Herzl's insistence that the Zionist publication must not be used for *Abwehr.* Landau had felt that it was the duty of a Jewish journal to refute all attacks against Jews and Judaism, but, he recalled: "Herzl had a different opinion. He emphasized with vigor that a Zionist paper must patiently and silently put up with anti-Semitic attacks, that is, attacks against the Jewish religion, against the Jewish population, [and] especially against Jewish equality. His explanation for this was: *'je ärger, desto besser'* [the worse, the better], that is: the worse it is with the Jews, the more numerously will they attach themselves to his movement." Landau continued to press for some defense work to be undertaken in the pages of *Die Welt,* but Herzl never yielded. For example, when Landau on one occasion wanted to draft a note protesting the action of an imperial commission which had required possession of a baptismal certificate for a certain job opening, Herzl refused him permission. Again, in suppressing a letter about an anti-Semitic proclamation which had been sent to *Die Welt* for publication, Herzl said: "It is not the task of this paper to engage in polemics against anti-Semitism." Landau, pp. 79-84.

See also Herzl's reference to the anti-Semites as "our best friends," (cited by Zechlin, p. 76), and also Lewisohn, p. 297, for Herzl's reaction to P. Nathan's *Criminality of the Jews in Germany:* "Of course, this pamphlet, which teems with figures, has been prompted, like many another 'defense,' by the error that anti-Semitism can be refuted by reason." Herzl considered the Verein an obstacle to his Zionist program and was annoyed when it invited the French critic of anti-Semitism, Leroy-Beulieu, to lecture in Vienna in answer to an attack on him by Herzl in *Die Welt.* The differences between Herzl and the Verein were aggravated when the Christian philo-Zionist Baron Manteuffel called the men of the Verein "numbskulls" and praised Herzl. See Bloch, "Herzl's First Years of Struggle," p. 88.

For later, more developed critiques of *Abwehr* along the lines mapped out by

Herzl, see the various articles published in *Die Welt:* against the Verein, June 1, 1897, pp. 4-5; against the Centralverein, July 11, 1902, pp. 4ff., and February 13, 1903, pp. 5-6; and against the Judentag as an *Abwehr* device, February 12, 1904, p. 3.

[18]Bloch, "Herzl's First Years of Struggle," p. 78.

[19]Herzl, *Diaries*, I, p. 7. See also Lewisohn, p. 52, and Bein, *Herzl*, p. 94.

[20]Bein, *Herzl*, p. 95.

[21]Lewisohn, pp. 249-250.

[22]Zechlin, p. 66.

[23]Lewisohn, pp. 242, 246-250.

[24]*Ibid.*, p. 238.

[25]*Ibid.*, p. 247. For evidence of similar attention to structural factors in Herzl's discussion of the peasantry, see p. 249.

[26]For similar structural analysis in *Die Welt*, see the article by D. Farbstein, July 2, 1897, pp. 3-4.

[27]Lewisohn, p. 247.

[28]*Ibid.*, p. 314.

[29]*Ibid.*, pp. 302-303. See also p. 244: "The outflow will be gradual, without any disturbance, and its very inception means the end of anti-Semitism. The Jews will leave as honored friends, and if some of them later return they will receive the same favorable welcome and treatment at the hands of civilized nations as is accorded all foreign visitors. Nor will their exodus in any way be a flight, but it will be a well-regulated movement under the constant check of public opinion. The movement will not only be inaugurated in absolute accordance with the law, but it can nowise be carried out without the friendly cooperation of the interested governments, who will derive substantial benefits."

[30]*Die Welt*, September 3, 1897, p. 5. See also Halpern, *Jewish State*, p. 141.

[31]Lewisohn, p. 234.

[32]Lichtheim, p. 82; on p. 83 Lichtheim discusses the manner in which the daily press, and especially the liberal papers with their highly Jewish readership, ignored the publication of *Der Judenstaat.*

[33]*AZJ*, July 2, 1897, pp. 316-317. (Emphasis in original.) See *Die Welt*, July 16, 1897, p. 1, for text of declaration by the *Protestrabbiner.*

[34]Chaim Bloch, "Theodor Herzl and Joseph S. Bloch," *Herzl Year Book*, I (New York, 1958), p. 155.

[35]N[athan] M[ichael] Gelber, "Herzl's Polish Contacts," *Herzl Year Book* (New York, 1958), I, pp. 216-217.

[36]Lewisohn, pp. 241-242.

[37]*Die Welt*, July 16, 1897, p. 2.

[38]Herzl did occasionally express some of the anti-Enlightenment cliches of his decade. In the conclusion to *Der Judenstaat* he wrote: "Universal brotherhood is not even a beautiful dream. Conflict is essential to man's highest efforts." Earlier in the same work he referred to the belief in the perfectability of man as "sentimental drivel," and added: "He who would peg the improvement of conditions on the goodness of all mankind would indeed be writing a utopia." See Lewisohn, pp. 251, 300.

[39]*Die Welt*, September 3, 1897, p. 5.

[40]Lewisohn, p. 237.

[41]*Ibid.*, p. 321. See p. 216 for Herzl's article welcoming the vindication of

Dreyfuss. Herzl greeted this early decision (later reversed) with enthusiasm and saw it as proof that most men were basically just.

[42]*Die Welt,* July 21, 1899, p. 3.

[43]Cited by Bein, *Herzl,* p. 526. See the peroration to *Der Judenstaat* in Lewisohn, p. 303: "The world will be liberated by our freedom, enriched by our wealth, magnified by our greatness. And whatever we attempt there [in the Jewish state] for our own benefit, will redound mightily and beneficially to the good of all mankind."

[44]Cited by Adler, *The Jews in Germany,* p. 146.

[45]Cited by Bein, *Herzl,* p. 162, n.

[46]See Meir Ben-Horin, *Max Nordau: Philosopher of Human Solidarity* (New York, 1956), pp. 65-66 for the anti-racial views of Herzl's associate, Nordau. Also see pp. 126-127 for Nordau's opposition to the racial ideas of Gobineau, Wagner, and Chamberlain.

[47]Bloch, "Herzl's First Years of Struggle," p. 79; Bein, *Herzl,* p. 91.

[48]See Ben Halpern, "Herzl's Historic Gift: The Sense of Sovereignty," *Herzl Year Book,* III (New York, 1960), pp. 32-33; Adler, *Herzl Paradox,* pp. 28, 31-33; and Bein, *Herzl,* pp. 279, 295. See also Halpern, *Jewish State,* p. 142.

[49]Cited by Lewisohn, p. 244.

[50]Lichtheim, p. 70. See Bodenheimer's pamphlet, *Wohin mit den russischen Juden?* (Hamburg, 1891), and his published memoirs, *So wurde Israel* (Frankfurt a.M., 1958), pp. 5, 18.

[51]For details on Bodenheimer's early organizational work and first statements, see Klinkenberg, pp. 343ff.

[52]Bodenheimer, *So wurde Israel,* pp. 23-24.

[53]*Ibid.,* pp. 21-22, 26, 31.

[54]*Ibid.,* p. 33. Note that this plan occurred to him before the first Jewish fraternities were founded in Breslau and Heidelberg (p. 34).

[55]*Ibid.,* pp. 44, 46, 48.

[56]Bodenheimer, *Wohin mit den russischen Juden?,* pp. 19, 31.

[57]Bodenheimer, *So wurde Israel,* p. 54; Lichtheim, p. 18.

[58]Bodenheimer, *So wurde Israel,* p. 61. On Wolffsohn, see Klinkenberg, p. 345.

[59]Bodenheimer, *So wurde Israel,* pp. 61-62; Lichtheim, pp. 70-71. Such links between early Zionism and *Abwehr* were not infrequent; e.g., Fabius Schach, one of the early members of the Nationaljüdische Vereinigung was also secretary of the Cologne branch of the Verein zur Abwehr des Antisemitismus. See Klinkenberg, p. 345.

[60]The theses appear in Henriette Hannah Bodenheimer, *Toldot Tochnit Bazel* (Jerusalem, 1947), p. 11, and in Lichtheim, after p. 96. See also *Die Welt,* June 11, 1897, p. 11.

[61]I am indebted to Halpern, *The Idea of the Jewish State,* pp. 139-141, for this discussion of the background to the Cologne theses.

[62]Halpern, p. 139.

[63]The program of the Berlin Zionist organization published the next year (1898) also advocated elevation of Jewish self-consciousness through education in Hebrew literature and culture but passed over the question of *Abwehr* in silence. See *Statuten der Berliner Zionistischen Vereinigung* (Berlin, 1898). See also Klinkenberg, p. 346.

[64]The correspondence is published in Bodenheimer, *Toldot Tochnit Bazel,* pp.

v, xxxiv. See also Halpern, *Idea of the Jewish State*, pp. 136-137.

[65]The leaflet is published in Lichtheim, after p. 88. All citations below are from that text.

[66]*Flugblatt #6* issued by Bodenheimer's organization said: "We suffer only because we are of another *Stamm* than the *Volk* around us." Published in Henriette Hannah Bodenheimer, *Im Anfang der zionistischen Bewegung*, (Frankfurt a.M., 1965), p. 63.

[67]Bein, *Herzl*, pp. 401-402, 458-459, 463.

[68]Toury, *Die politischen Orientierungen*, p. 183.

[69]Oppenheimer, p. 58.

[70]*Ibid.*, p. 32; Adolf Lowe, "In Memoriam Franz Oppenheimer," *YBLBI*, X (1965), pp. 138-139.

[71]Lowe, p. 138; Oppenheimer, p. 27. As a fifteen-year-old youth, when anti-Semitism was first emerging, Oppenheimer wrote this impassioned patriotic poem (p. 27):

> Meines Vaters Grossvater wohnte am Rhein,
> und vor ihm wohl zehn Geschlechter,
> und da sollt' ich kein Deutscher sein,
> kein eingeborener, echter?
> Meines Oheims Blut gab rote Spur
> bei Alsen an der Fähre,
> mein Vetter fiel bei Mars la Tour
> im Kampf für Deutschlands Ehre.
> Ich sah, wie im Aug' die Träne schwoll,
> als von Sedan die Kunde scholl,
> dem Vater er weinte selten:
> und Ihr wollt Fremde uns schelten?

[72]Toury, *Die politischen Orientierungen*, p. 274.

[73]Lowe, p. 138-139. See also Gross, p. 144. Oppenheimer participated actively in the Freie Wissenschaftliche Vereinigung, the student organization with many Jewish members which was most outspoken in its defense of *"bürgerlichem"* liberalism against the Verein deutscher Studenten, an aggressive nationalistic group inspired by Treitschke. (See Gross, p. 144, and Oppenheimer, p. 70).

In 1914 Oppenheimer wrote: "I do not strive for assimilation, but I am assimilated. I am a German, and I am as proud of this as I am of my Jewish antecedents. I am happy to have been born and educated in this country of Kant and Goethe, to speak their language, and to have absorbed their culture, art, science, and philosophy. To be a German is as sacred to me as is my Jewish heritage. . . . I combine within myself the Jewish and the German national consciousness. I and my friends stand firmly on the Basel program, and our good German sentiments do not hinder us from being good Zionists." (Cited by Adler, p. 109.)

[74]Oppenheimer, pp. 32, 33, 116.

[75]*Ibid.*, p. 33.

[76]*Ibid.*, p. 218. Although firmly opposed to "the excesses of fanatically enthusiastic youth" who espoused Jewish racism, Oppenheimer conceded that he had been unsuccessful: "Here, as everywhere, the extremists must gain the upper hand for the simple reason that they think and do nothing other than their movement, while we moderates have to further our own life work." *Ibid.* See also the article in *AZJ*, November 14, 1902, pp. 541-542, which reports on

Oppenheimer's article in *Ernstes Wollen*; there Oppenheimer had criticized both Chamberlain and the Zionist racists for this "unscientific" reasoning.

[77]Oppenheimer, p. 214.

[78]See the discussion by Robert Weltsch, "Introduction," *YBLBI*, IX (1964), pp. xxvf.

[79]Nathan Birnbaum, *The Bridge*, ed. by Solomon A. Birnbaum (London, 1956), p. 11.

[80]Leo Hermann, *Nathan Birnbaum: Sein Werk und seine Wandlung* (Berlin, 1914), pp. 8, 24. See Birnbaum's self-testimony (p. 23): "Im tiefsten Grunde ist der Zionismus die westjüdische Form und Phase der national-jüdischen Bewegung. Nicht nur Herzl hat aus seiner west-jüdischen Seele heraus geschrieben, sondern auch Pinsker und ich haben das in uns westjüdisch Gewordene in unseren zionistischen Schriften niedergelegt. . . ."

[81]Weltsch, pp. xxviiff.

[82]See Solomon Birnbaum, "Nathan Birnbaum," *Men of the Spirit*, ed. by Leo Jung (New York, 1964), p. 523.

[83]For a general discussion of Birnbaum's ideas on Jewish nationalism, see Werner J. Cahnman, "Adolf Fischhof and his Jewish Followers," *YBLBI*, IV (1959), pp. 132-133.

[84]*OUW*, August 1902, pp. 517-518.

[85]Nathan Birnbaum, *Ausgewählte Schriften zur jüdischen Frage* (Czernowitz, 1910), I, pp. 7-8, 41, 43.

[86]*Ibid.*, p. 42. See Pinsker's *Autoemancipation*, which influenced Birnbaum's formulation of the Jewish problem.

[87]*Ibid.*, p. 30.

[88]*OUW*, P. 519.

[89]Birnbaum, *Ausgewählte Schriften*, I, p. 26.

[90]*Ibid.*, p. 8. (Emphasis in original.)

[91]*Ibid.*, pp. 9-10.

[92]*Ibid.*, p. 18.

[93]*Ibid.*, pp. 15, 18-20.

[94]*Ibid.*, pp. 14-16. See the interesting discussion in *JT* of June 1902, pp. 49-51, where it was argued that the anti-Semites recognized the Zionists as their strongest enemies and only praised the Zionist movement publicly in order to weaken its appeal in the Jewish community.

[95]Such confrontations were rather frequent in Eastern Europe. See, for example, Sanford Ragins, "A Critical Analysis of Ber Borochov's Socialist Zionism" Hebrew Union College (unpublished Master's thesis, 1962), and Marie Syrkin, *Nachman Syrkin, Socialist Zionist* (New York, 1961).

[96]Birnbaum, *Ausgewählte Schriften*, I, p. 34.

[97]*Ibid.*, pp. 35, 39.

[98]*Ibid.*, pp. 38-39.

[99]*Ibid.*, pp. 12, 49.

CHAPTER FIVE

[1]Cited by Mann, p. 536.

[2]For the sections that follow, I have consulted Golo Mann, *Deutsche Geschichte des 19. und 20. Jahrhunderts* (Frankfurt, 1958); Gerhard Masur, *Prophets of Yesterday* (New York, 1966); Veit Valentin, *The German People* (New York, 1945); George L. Mosse, *The Crisis of the German Ideology* (New York,

1964); *idem,* "The Influence of the Völkisch Idea on German Jewry," *Studies of the Leo Baeck Institute* (New York, 1967), pp. 83-114; Walter Laqueur, *Young Germany, A History of the German Youth Movement* (New York, 1962); and *idem,* "The German Youth Movement and the 'Jewish Question'—A Preliminary Survey," *YBLBI,* VI (1961), pp. 193-205.

3Cited by Masur, p. 356.

4Laqueur, "The German Youth Movement," p. 203; Valentin, p. 542; Mosse, "The Influence of the Völkisch Idea," p. 86.

5Laqueur, *Young Germany,* p. 5.

6On the Youth Movement, see *ibid.;* on the völkisch ideology, see Mosse and Stern.

On the pan-European Character of the Youth Movement and the specific features which marked it in Germany, see Masur, pp. 353, 366. See also, Robert A. Kann, *The Hapsburg Empire, A Study in Integration and Disintegration* (New York, 1957), pp. 121-122, where a similar development in Czech politics is discussed. Kann describes the emergence there of a "far more aggressive ethnic nationalism."

7Masur, pp. 354, 357-358, 360; Laqueur, *Young Germany,* p. 4; Laqueur, "The German Youth Movement," p. 203; Mann, p. 541; Mosse, "The influence of the Völkisch Idea," *passim.*

8Mosse, *German Ideology,* p. 4.

9For extensive exposition of the thought of Lagarde and Langbehn, see Stern, *passim.*

10Mosse, "The influence of the Völkisch Idea," pp. 92, 114. For the manner in which university students were particularly prone to the influence of the völkisch ideology, see Norman Cohn, *Warrant for Genocide* (London, 1967), p. 173.

11Mosse, *German Ideology,* p. 301.

12On Langbehn's "incredibly ferocious anti-Semitism," see Stern, p. 61.

13Mosse, "The influence of the Völkisch Idea," p. 87.

14Laqueur, "The German Youth Movement," p. 194.

15Mosse, *German Ideology,* p. 182. For material on the discussion within the Wandervögel about Jewish participation, see Laqueur, "The German Youth Movement," pp. 195ff.

16Cited by Massing, p. 144. Ernest Hamburger recalled that his father was surprised to learn (c. 1906) that Jewish children in the gymnasium sat separately from non-Jews. From an interview with Hamburger, March 20, 1968.

17*Die Welt,* January 4, 1901, p. 2.

18Mosse, *German Ideology,* pp. 135, 197. Lichtheim (p. 66) notes that "anti-Semitism . . . was felt mainly in the universities of Germany . . . at the beginning of the 1890's.

19See *supra,* pp. 41ff.

20Herbert Strauss, "The Jugendverband: A Social and Intellectual History," *YBLBI,* VI (New York, 1961), p. 213.

21Gustav Mayer, *Erinnerungen* (Zurich and Vienna, 1949), p. 38; *Die Welt,* August 27, 1897, p. 5. See also Pulzer, ch. 26.

22Benedictus Levita [Weisler], "Die Erlösung des Judenthums," *Preussische Jahrbücher,* October 1900, p. 132. For a discussion of Weisler's ideas, see *supra,* pp. 73ff.

23Straus, pp. 76-77, recalls the impact which the Xanten ritual murder trial had upon her as a girl of twelve: "Dar war eine tiefe seelische Erschütterung for unsere Kinderherzen." See also Schlomo Rülf, *Ströme im dürren Land* (Stuttgart, 1964), pp. 20-21.

[24]Mayer, pp. 36, 38.

[25]*Ibid.*, p. 7. See also, p. 37.

[26]*Ibid.*, pp. 37, 155.

[27]*JT*, March 1901, p. 35.

[28]*Die Welt*, January 11, 1901, p. 3.

[29]Kurt Blumenfeld, "Ursprünge und Art einer zionistischen Bewegung,' *Bulletin of the Leo Baeck Institute*, IV (July, 1958), p. 131.

[30]Mosse, "The influence of the Völkisch Idea," p. 86.

[31]See Bernstein's assessment cited on p. 24, *supra*. See also *AZJ*, 1902, pp. 178-180, for a long fictional account by R. Brainin of a student who suffers from alienation and, despairing over the state of Judaism, longs for a positive faith which he might affirm. On the way in which liberal Judaism failed to appeal to the imagination of the youth, see Michael A. Meyer, "Caesar Seligmann and the Development of Liberal Judaism," *Hebrew Union College Annual*, XL-XLI, (1969-70), p. 552.

[32]Toury, *Die politischen Orientierungen*, p. 219.

[33]Israel Klausner, *Ha-oppozitsia l'Hertzl* (Jerusalem, 1960), p. 7.

[34]S[halom] Adler-Rudel, *Ostjuden in Deutschland, 1880-1940* (Tübingen, 1959), p. 14.

[35]Levin, p. 281. See also Adler-Rudel, pp. 14, 18, and Toury, "Nisyionot L'nihul Mediniut Yehudit B'germania, 1893-1918," *Zion*, XXVIII: 3-4 (1963), p. 177.

[36]Lichtheim, p. 65.

[37]E.g., Heinrich's brother Richard, Selig Soskin, Theodor Zlocisti, Willi Bambus, Nathan Birnbaum, and Samuel Lublinski. See Max Jungmann, *Erinnerungen eines Zionisten* (Jerusalem, 1959), pp. 18, 20.

[38]Gross, p. 143. On Loewe, see Bein, *Herzl*, p. 215; Lichtheim, pp. 71-74, 91; and Jungmann, p. 26. As an example of Loewe's publicist work on behalf of Zionism, see his *Antisemitismus und Zionismus* (1895), published under his pseudonym, Heinrich Sachse.

See also *IWOS*, November 30, 1894, p. 383, which quoted a report in a recent issue of *Deborah* on the role of the Russian students in fostering Jewish nationalism: "Die Nationalitätsbewegung nimmt besonders unter der akademischen Jugend der europäischen Universitäten zu (durch die dahin eingewanderten *russischen* Jünglinge)." (Emphasis in original.) *IWOS* added: "Freilich befürchten wir nicht, dass dieser *moderne Wahnsinn* dauerndes Unheil stiften werde. . . ." (Emphasis in original.)

[39]Straus, p. 154.

[40]Jungmann, pp. 12, 16. For Jungmann this movement was also accompanied by the resolution of his religious doubts through Zionism; he testified that when he became a Zionist, he abandoned Orthodoxy.

[41]Gross, pp. 147ff.

[42]Blumenfeld, "Ursprünge," p. 129. See also p. 138.

[43]Kurt Blumenfeld, *Erlebte Judenfrage* (Stuttgart, 1962), p. 39. See also Straus, pp. 99-100.

[44]Blumenfeld, *Erlebte Judenfrage*, p. 43.

[45]Blumenfeld, "Ursprünge," p. 131. See also *JP*, June 8, 1898, p. 252.

[46]Blumenfeld, *Erlebte Judenfrage*, pp. 69-70. In the debate within Zionism in 1914, Blumenfeld was arrayed against Bodenheimer and Oppenheimer, both

of whom opposed the proposal that *aliyah* be made a part of the German Zionist program.

[47]See Blumenfeld, "Ursprünge," p. 131: "Das erste Zeichen des Selbstbewusstseins war ein neues Gefühl der Distanz gegenüber der deutschen Welt. . . ."

[48]*Ibid.*, pp. 135-136. See p. 134 for a discussion of the opposition of the German Zionists to the apologetics of the assimilationists: "Wir legten aber keinen Wert darauf, uns gegenüber einer antisemitischen Welt zu rechtfertigen." See also Zechlin, p. 74.

[49]Blumenfeld, *Erlebte Judenfrage*, p. 53. Note also his comment in "Ursprünge," p. 137: "Der deutsche Zionismus hatte eine starke Anziehungskraft auf junge Menschen, für den die Tatsache, dass sie Zionisten wurden, die Rückkehr zum Judenthum bedeutete. Der deutsche Zionismus war und blieb eine Jugendbewegung. . . ."

[50]Blumenfeld, "Ursprünge," p. 130.

[51]Blumenfeld, *Erlebte Judenfrage*, p. 115. See also Moritz Goldstein's (b. 1880) reflections in "German Jewry's Dilemma Before 1914," *YBLBI,* II (1957), pp. 241-243.

[52]Blumenfeld, "Ursprünge," p. 134; see also his *Erlebte Judenfrage*, pp. 69-70, and Zechlin, p. 74.

[53]Blumenfeld, *Erlebte Judenfrage*, p. 115.

[54]Lewisohn, pp. 235, 245.

[55]Hans Kohn, *Martin Buber, Sein Werk und seine Zeit* (Cologne, 1961), pp. 23-24.

[56]Jungmann, pp. 17-18. For an example of recognition by the consensus press of the predominantly youth character of the Zionist movement, see *ISR,* March 16, 1896, p. 450.

[57]On the Kartell Convent and its ideology, see *supra,* pp. 41-43.

[58]Gross, p. 144.

[59]Straus, p. 92.

[60]Asch and Philippson, p. 134.

[61]Gross, p. 144; Oppenheimer, p. 70.

[62]Lichtheim, p. 74.

[63]*Ibid.,* p. 75; Gross, pp. 144-145; Jungmann, pp. 34-36. In time the Vereinigung Jüdischer Studierenden groups joined together to form the Bund Jüdischer Corporationen. A series of openly Zionist clubs was then founded outside the framework of that Bund, all bearing explicitly nationalistic names like Jordania, Hasmonaea, and Ivria. The latter were united in the Kartell Zionistischer Verbindungen, an openly Zionist umbrella organization. For further information on these organizations, see Gross, *passim;* Zechlin, pp. 63ff.; and Blumenfeld, *Erlebte Judenfrage,* p. 43.

[64]*JS,* December 1902, p. 130.

[65]See Lichtheim, pp. 75-76.

[66]*Die Welt,* January 6, 1899, p. 3. In a similar assessment Jonas Wolfsohn claimed that the Centralverein had failed to compete with the Zionists for student loyalties and that "die Jugend . . . ins Lager der Zionisten geht." *OUW,* March 1903, sp. 151.

[67]Mosse, *German Ideology,* p. 183.

[68]See Strauss, p. 214, on the activity of Alfred Apfel who worked to develop the Jugend Verband of the Unabhängiger Orden B'nai B'rith. Apfel stressed

the neutrality of his organization as a tactic to de-Zionize young Zionists. Apfel later became a Zionist (*ibid.*, n. 33).

[69]See Strauss, p. 212, where he cites from a response to a questionnaire describing the situation in Hannover about 1908: "Young Zionists like these [Klee and Gronemann] strongly worried the leaders of the Jewish community, especially as they fast increased in numbers, being strengthened by Eastern Jews. . . . The foremost opponent of the Zionist party was the Centralverein, a powerful organization in Hannover at that time. . . ." The same respondent noted that the Unabhängiger Orden B'nai B'rith founded their own organizations for Jewish youth at this time in order to keep them out of the bitter Zionist-anti-Zionist conflict that was developing.

Note also a characteristic attitude of the liberal consensus toward the ferment in the youth, expressed in *AZJ*, March 18, 1898: "Die neuen Gedanken unserer Jugend sind gewiss freudig zu begrüssen, aber sie müssen in die rechte Bahn gelenkt, und immer und immer muss es wiederholt werden, ein gottloses, ein religionsloses Judenthum giebt es nicht, das Judenthum steht und fällt mit der Thora."

[70]See Lichtheim, p. 97, who notes the energetic struggle between the Kartell Convent organizations allied with the Centralverein and the Zionist student groups for the affiliation of the Füchsen.

[71]Reported by Richard Treitel in "Der Student und der Antisemitismus, *AZJ*, July 5, 1901, pp. 315-316.

[72]For an Orthodox critique of the Kartell Convent, see *ISR*, October 27, 1902, p. 1791.

[73]His figure was based on corporate membership, i.e., the fact that whole communities had been enrolled in the Centralverein. For example, the entire Bavarian Landesverein had become affiliated.

[74]*IDR*, August 1901, pp. 379-392.

[75]See *ibid.*, August 1902, pp. 359-360. See also *ibid.*, 1901, pp. 426ff., and 1903, p. 243, where reports on the Centralverein meetings in which Zionists (especially Heinrich Loewe) participated in the debate are printed.

[76]See Toury, "Organizational Problems of German Jewry," pp. 57-90, who discusses the organizational interplay between the Zionists and the Centralverein in the period before World War I.

[77]D. Farbstein (b. 1868), in *Die Welt*, July 2, 1897, p. 4.

[78]*Die Welt*, January 20, 1899, p. 1.

[79]*Ibid.*, March 1, 1901, p. 4. See Toury, *Die politischen Orientierungen*, p. 210, for a discussion of a later article by Friedemann in which he argued against Jewish adherence to the Freisinnig parties. See also Theodor Zlocisti's comment in *OUW*, March 1904, sp. 149: "Der Traum der bürgerlichen Gleichberechtigung ist zerschlagen. Er verdiente nichts besseres. Er war der Lüge voll."

[80]Wilhelm Goldbaum's article on the fiftieth anniversary of the Revolution of 1848 (written under the pseudonym O. Erter) argued that 1848 had marked the death of *Weltbürgertum* and the birth of the national idea which was more progressive. *Die Welt*, March 25, 1898. See also *Der jüdische Student*, October 1902, p. 67, and Meyer, "Caesar Seligmann," pp. 552-553.

[81]Mosse, "The Influence of the Völkisch Idea," pp. 86-87.

[82]Mosse fails to realize that racial conceptions were also used by the Jewish youth. His claim about "the very absence of racism both from that ideology

which such Jews accepted and from their own" is not borne out by the evidence, *Ibid.*, p. 113. See *infra* pp. 148ff.

⁸³See Zechlin, p. 73: "Tatsächlich arbeiteten der Rassenantisemitismus als einer ihrer Bestandteile und der jüdische Nationalismus weitgehend mit dem gleichen Begriffsinstrumentarium, den gleichen Denkmodellen und Wertmasstäben. Beide formulierten die sogenannte Judenfrage mit ganz anderen Kategorien und auf einer anderen Ebene als die konfessionsorientierte Mehrheit der deutschen Juden, so dass eine Verständigungsmöglichkeit kaum offen blieb. . . ."

⁸⁴Cited by Tal, *Ha-Anti-shemiut,* p. 253, n. 46. The positive assessment of Buber's ideas by the German völkisch writer Karl Bückmann is noted in Mosse, *German Ideology,* p. 182.

⁸⁵E.g., *AZJ,* June 2, 1905, p. 260, where an article by Dr. J. Lewy (Danzig) noted: "Wie kann man eine infolge unendlich langer Religionsverfolgung durch Länder und Weltteile gehetzte und bunt durcheinandergewürfelte Menge, die überall von dem Milieu etwas angenommen hat, als ein Volk oder gar als eine Rasse bezeichnen?" *AZJ* of January 24, 1902, p. 38, reported on the Fifth Zionist Congress and noted: "Wir sind nun einmal keine Nation mehr, und wer die Rassenfrage in unser Kulturleben hinein trägt, der zeigt dadurch, dass er für die geschichtliche Entwickelung des Judenthums nicht das geringste Verständniss besitzt. . . ."

⁸⁶Moses Hess, *Rome and Jerusalem* (New York, 1958), pp. 26, 51.

⁸⁷Cited by Böhm, p. 84. See also Edmund Silberner, "Moses Hess," *Historia Judaica,* XIII:1 (April 1951) *passim,* esp. p. 17.

⁸⁸Hans Liebeschütz' assessment, in "German Radicalism and the Formation of Jewish Political Attitudes During the Earlier Part of the Nineteenth Century," *Studies in Nineteenth Century Jewish Intellectual History* (Cambridge, 1964), p. 167: "For a Jewish Burgher of the sixties Hess's Zionist ideas were almost as remote from his plan of life as the possibility of becoming an agitator for political revolution."

⁸⁹*Die Welt,* July 30, 1897, pp. 9f.

⁹⁰Although opposed to racial concepts and a critic of Gobineau and Houston Stewart Chamberlain, Max Nordau occasionally lapsed into rhetoric that helped give currency to the idea that the Jews were a race. He wrote of a *"jüdisches Naturell"*—a Jewish nature or disposition—made up of specific traits, and he argued: "Selbst der Jude, der bis über die Ohren assimiliert ist und dessen Mund von Betheuerungen überströmt, dass er mit seinen einstigen Volkgenossen nichts mehr zu schaffen habe, selbst er ist gegen seinen Willen ein Spross des alten Stammes, und ebenso wie er seine Gesichtszüge samt der Nase nicht umformen kann, so kann er auch seine jüdische Gemüthsart nicht ändern. Jeder, der eine feinere Empfindung und einen tieferen Blick hat, wird mit Leichtigkeit auch an diesen Leuten die Spuren des jüdischen Geistes erkennen. . . . Diese Geistesbeschaffenheit mag in einzelnen Fällen verzerrt oder getrübt in die Erscheinung treten, aber ganz verleugnen lässt sie sich nicht." *Die Welt,* January 18, 1901, p. 3. Also note his reference to "jüdischen Rasseneigenschaften" in his address at the opening of the First Zionist Congress in 1897, reprinted in *ibid.,* September 3, 1897, p. 6.

⁹¹*Ibid.,* January 2, 1903; the original had appeared in the periodical *Ernstes Wollen.*

⁹²*Ibid.,* December 12, 1902, pp. 5-6.

[93]See *Der jüdische Student*, September 1902, p. 85, which argued that in the time of Jacob in Egypt Jews were distinguished from other inhabitants of the land through "manifest werdende Verschiedenheit der Rasse."

[94]*Die Welt*, July 5, 1901, pp. 10-11.

[95]"Folglich ist der Judenstamm in Hinsicht der Rasse rein geblieben." *Ibid.*, p. 11. He also observed: "Aus allen meinen Angaben können wir schliessen, dass die Juden seit etwa 4000 Jahren nicht bloss die Leiber, sondern auch die Geister in einem Stamme in einer bestimmten, nur ihnen eigenthümlichen Lebensweise fortsetzen. . . . Seit Abraham ist kein anderer Stamm gekommen und haben sich die vorelterlichen Eigenschaften, die körperlichen und die geistigen, von Geschlecht zu Geschlecht fortgepflanzt und gesteigert. Bei den Juden ist die geschlechtliche Zuchtwahl auf ein Minimum beschränkt." *Ibid.*, pp. 11-12. Note his conclusion to the second part of the lecture in a subsequent issue of *Die Welt*, July 10, 1901, p. 9: "Ich glaube durch meinen Vortrag Sie überzeugt zu haben, dass die Juden in anthropologischer, physiologischer und pathologischer Hinsicht Eigenthümlichkeiten haben, die ihnen angeboren sind und Folgen der Vererbung und Fortpflanzung in ihrem Stamme sind."

[96]*Ibid.*, November 11, 1898.

[97]*Ibid.*, June 14, 1902, pp. 3-4.

[98]*Ibid.*, April 19, 1901, pp. 3-5.

[99]Dr. med. Jeremias in *ibid.*, May 3, 1901. See also the article by Hermann Jalowicz in *JT*, May 1901, pp. 57-65, in which he argues that the degeneracy of the Jewish masses in the East is due to specific social and economic conditions in the ghetto and that physical rebirth is possible.

[100]*Die Welt*, June 15, 1900, p. 2, *JT*, May 1900, p. 4. See also Mosse, "The Influence of the Völkisch Idea," pp. 109-110. On earlier calls for Turner activity by pre-Zionist youth, see Asch and Phillippson, p. 124. Note George Joachim's plea in 1894 for developed Jewish physical prowess as a response to anti-Semitism in "Der Antisemitismus und der jüdische Student," *JP*, August 30, 1894, p. 356.

[101]*JT*, May, 1900, p. 8.

[102]*ISR*, October 13, 1904, p. 1703. Surveying the gymnastic movement in 1900, Nordau attacked the long-established pattern of mortification of the flesh by Jews, noting carefully that there had been skilled and powerful Jewish gladiators in ancient times and that the present deterioration of physique was the result of a pattern forced upon a basically sound people by others. He called for honoring "our oldest traditions" by becoming once again "deep-chested, robust-limbed, brave-visaged men." Moreover, vigorous exercise would create self-consciousness and character, as well as physical strength. He praised the existing Turnvereine, and especially the choice of the name Bar Kochba, who was "die letzte weltgeschichtliche Verkörperung des kriegsharten, waffenfrohen Judenthums." *Die Welt*, June 15, 1900, pp. 2-3. Note the attempt by A. Berliner to root Turner activity in the Bible: "Turnerisches in der Heiligen Schrift," *JT*, April, 1902, pp. 57-63.

[103]*JT*, May 1900, p. 1.

[104]See *ibid.*, p. 4, which describes the struggle between Zionists and non-Zionists over the Vereinstendenz when the first club was organized. The compromise adopted was still clearly Zionist: "Der Verein bezweckt die Pflege des Turnens und der national-jüdischen Gesinnung unter seinen Mitgliedern."

[105]*Ibid.*, p. 4; *ibid.*, December 1900, p. 88. See *JS*, August 1902, p. 71, where a Jew is defined by "Abstammung," not by religion, and Jewry is declared not to be a "Religions-Gemeinschaft."

[106]See, e.g., the article by Georg Arndt, "Zur jüdischen Rassenfrage," *JT*, December 1902, p. 200, and the unsigned article "Jüdische Erziehungsprobleme," *ibid.*, January 1901, p. 508.

[107]E.g. Arndt, *op. cit.*, and *JT*, January 1901, pp. 5, 7. See the report on a speech by M. Zirker, editor of *JT*, in Cologne in 1904, in which Zirker listed a number of symptoms of degeneracy among Jews, including the declining marriage and birth rates, specific diseases such as diabetes, neurasthenia, deafness, and blindness (which occurred with greater frequency among Jews than non-Jews), and the smaller physical size and breast measurement and the weaker musculature of Jews. *ISR*, October 13, 1904, p. 1703. See also *JT*, November 1900, p. 74.

[108]*JT*, Nov. 1900, p. 74.

[109]*Ibid.*, January 1901, p. 7.

[110]*Ibid.*, November 1900, p. 75.

[111]*Ibid.*, p. 74.

[112]*Ibid.*, October 1901, p. 129.

[113]*Ibid.*, October 1900, p. 67. See the *Turnlied* by Auerbach in *ibid*, April 1901, p. 45, and the marching song by Theodor Zlocisti in *ibid*, June 1900, pp. 13-14. Note also Salo Baron's rather exaggerated assessment of the impact of these activities on anti-Semitism: "Another psychological factor of undeniable importance has always been the defenselessness of the Jewish minority which provoked hatred and maltreatment. All the sadistic impulses which go to make child- and wife-beaters arise at the sight of this defenseless object of hate. . . . In this sense, the post-emancipation regeneration of the Jewish physique and the Jewish participation in sports has certainly counteracted anti-Semitic feeling more than a flood of publicist apologies. . . ." Salo Wittmayer Baron, *A Social and Religious History of the Jews*, II (New York, 1937), p. 288.

[114]*JP*, June 16, 1904, pp. 243-244.

[115]*JT*, June 1901, pp. 73-74. (Emphasis in original.) See the report on a speech by M. Zirker in *ISR*, October 13, 1904, p. 1703, and also the recollection by Gustav Mayer that Jews were excluded from the academic Turnvereine. *Erinnerungen*, p. 38.

[116]*JT*, January 1901, p. 3.

[117]*Ibid.*, p. 5.

[118]Cited by Sterling, *Er ist wie du*, p. 164.

[119]Cited by Adler, *Jews in Germany*, p. 42.

[120]See Theobald Scholem, "Zur 50. Wiederkehr des Todestages von Friedrich Ludwig Jahn," *JT*, October 1902, pp. 166-167. For an example of the ways in which Jahn's writings were appropriated for Jewish gymnastics, see *ibid.*, July 1900, p. 21. For favorable references to Jahn pre-dating the establishment of the Jüdische Turnvereine, see Asch, p. 124 (in the platform of the Kartell Convent), and *Die Welt*, December 9, 1898, p. 9 (an article by Eli Samgar arguing for the establishment of Jewish gymnastic clubs).

[121]Mosse, "The Influence of the Völkisch Idea," p. 110.

[122]On Buber's use of this term, which, for him, signified the importance of Zionism, see Grete Schaeder, *Martin Buber: Hebräischer Humanismus* (Göttingen, 1966), p. 1.

[123]Kohn, p. 42. Buber's other associates were E. M. Lilien, Davis Trietsch,

and Chaim Weizmann. For more background on the "democratic fraction" of which Buber was a part, see Klausner, ch. 6. Further plans to publish a periodical entitled *Der Jude* did not materialize at this time, although a statement of intent did appear in the fall of 1903. See Kohn, p. 45. For a characteristic liberal reaction to völkisch thought, see the article by Leopold Auerbach in *AZJ*, July 1, 1898, pp. 305-308.

[124]*Jüdischer Almanach*, 1902, pp. 11-13.

[125]*Ibid.*, p. 16. See the article by Salomo Liebhardt, "Der organische Staat," *Die Welt*, October 22, 1897, pp. 4-5.

[126]Buber was called such by Ernst Simon; cited by Schaeder, p. 191. Cf. however, Birnbaum's assessment of Buber's Zionism as a "rhapsodic, philosophic intermezzo of all kinds of intellectual moods and whimseys." Cited by Baron, p. 342.

[127]Schaeder, p. 193.

[128]See Kohn, p. 51, who also notes the influence of the Hebrew essayist Berdyczewski and of the poet Tschernichowski, whose poetry Buber translated.

[129]Martin Buber, *Die jüdische Bewegung (1900-1914)* (Berlin, 1920), p. 69.

[130]"Das Zion der jüdischen Frau," *Die Welt*, April 26, 1901, p. 5. See Hermann Cohen's observation in 1880: "I confidentially assert, we [Jews] all wish we had an absolutely German-Germanic appearance of which we at present bear only the climatic side effects. . . ." Cited by Mayer, "Great Debate," p. 152.

[131]Buber, *Die jüdische Bewegung*, p. 245.

[132]*Ibid.*, p. 251.

[133]*Ibid.*, pp. 90-91, 245, 252. See the assessment of recent Jewish art by Robert Jaffee in *Die Welt*, April 3, 1901, p. 24: "So vereinigt eine *neue jüdische Kunst* die Zartheit und unendliche Differenziertheit eines kosmopolitischen europäischen Lebens mit dem dunklen Blute, das durch tausend Adern von den starken, gesunden Lebensvorgängen her in das Herz eines Volkes zusammenflutet. . . ."

[134]Buber, *Die jüdische Bewegung*, p. 85.

[135]*Ibid.*, pp. 90-91. Buber described one of the figures in an Ury painting: "Und aus dem Jungen, Wagemuthigen, Hoffnungstrunkenen neben ihm, durch dessen edlen Rassenkopf die frische Lebenskraft des Volkes wie ein Glutstrom fliesst, Visionen, Ideen, Pläne erregend. . . ." *Die Welt*, April 3, 1901, pp. 10, 12.

[136]*Ibid.*, p. 166. Similarly, the festivals of the Jewish tradition were not merely religious holidays but occasions "which tell the entire fate of a *Volksseele*." From *Die Welt*, March 1, 1901, p. 9, where he also writes: "Alles gilt mir meines Blutstammes Schönheit und Glück." See Buber's Purim poem with similar terminology, *ibid.*, March 8, 1901, p. 10.

[137]On Landauer, see Solomon Liptzin. *Germany's Stepchildren* (Cleveland, New York and Philadephia, 1961), pp. 229-238; Paul Breines, "The Jew as Revolutionary: the Case of Gustav Landauer," *YBLBI*, XII (1967), pp. 75-84; Mosse, "The Influence of the Völkisch Idea," pp. 93ff.; Zechlin, p. 78; and Schaeder, p. 189.

[138]As mentioned in the preface, for a number of reasons this study does not include a lengthy examination of the response of the Jewish left to anti-Semitism. There was no identifiable "Jewish left" in Germany at this time, although later, principally among Eastern Jews, Jewish socialism developed as

a movement that was self-consciously Marxist and Zionist. Those Jews who did participate in German socialism—and they were many—tended to treat the Jewish problem from a socialist perspective, without reference to their own background or origins. Eduard Bernstein, for example, recalled that the role of the Jewish press in the Kulturkampf and in the effort to suppress socialism, and the function of Jewish capital in the *Gründer* era made such an impression upon him that he "selbst zuweilen anti-jüdisch gestimmt wurde." He greeted the first signs of anti-Semitism in the late 1870s as an understandable reaction against undue Jewish pressures. He changed his attitude about anti-Semitism only when its intensity grew in the next years, but even then he maintained that the only way to combat it was through the Socialist International. (Bernstein, p. 195.) In his words, "Die Judenfrage als Frage eines besonderen nationalen Rechts oder Interesses von Juden aufzufassen, ist mir nicht in den Sinn gekommen" (p. 194). Bernstein never denied his Jewish origin, but he also never felt moved to express his solidarity with other Jews in response to anti-Semitism (p. 187).

Bernstein's attitude was shared by Rosa Luxemberg, who also denied the existence of a special Jewish problem requiring specific modes of response. In 1917 she wrote from her prison cell: "Was willst du mit dem speziellen Judenschmerz? Mir sind die armen Pofer der Gummiplantagen in Putumayo, die Neger in Afrika, mit deren Körper die Europäer Fangball spielen, ebenso nahe . . . diese erhabene Stille der Unendlichkeit, in der so viele Schreie ungehört verhallen, sie klingt in mir so stark, dass ich keinen Sonderwinkel im Herzen für das Ghetto habe: ich fühle mich in der ganzen Welt zu Hause, wo es Wolken und Vögel und Menschentränen gibt. . . ." (Cited by Zechlin, p. 18) For similar views by Karl Kautsky, see his *Are the Jews a Race?* (New York, 1926); see Toury, pp. 224-245.

On the long tradition of socialist hostility to Jews and Judaism, see Karl Marx, "On the Jewish Question," trans. by Helen Lederer (Cincinnati, 1955); the various articles by Edmund Silberner (see bibliography); Solomon F. Bloom, "Karl Marx and the Jews," *Jewish Social Studies* IV:1 (1942), pp. 3-16; Kampmann, pp. 322-349; and Dubnow, *Neueste Geschichte*, p. 47.

[139]Cited by Breines, p. 76. See also Mosse, "Influence of the Völkisch Idea," p. 94.

[140]Breines, p. 81.

[141]Cited in *ibid.*, p. 83.

[142]*Ibid.*, pp. 77, 82-83.

[143]Reprinted by Kohn, p. 298.

[144]Buber, pp. 7, 16. See Leo Winz' journal *Ost und West* for a similar union of völkisch ideas with universalism. Founded in 1901, *Ost und West* was critical of the dominant German Jewish leadership, friendly to the *Ostjuden*, and devoted to interpreting East European Jewish culture to the German Jewish community. The declaration of purpose for the new journal stated: "So wollen wir auch jüdisches Leben preisen, nicht wie es heute ist, sondern wie es sein soll und schon zu werden beginnt. Wir verstehen darunter ein selbstbewusstes, innerlich gefestigtes und geheiligtes, treues und fruchtbares jüdisches Leben, das auf dem Boden eines schönen Menschentums und einer stillen Arbeit für allgemeinen Kulturfortschritt die gute Eigenart unserer Rasse entfaltet." *OUW*, 1901, sp. 1-2.

[145]Zechlin, p. 79. See Mosse, p. 96: "The völkisch influence on German Zionism did not, in the end, transform the belief in a Jewish Volk into an

aggressive and exclusive ideology. But the German völkisch development led in precisely this direction, providing a deep, long-lasting difference between such Jewish and German thought. . . . For Jewish youth, the acceptance of this [völkisch] ideology never quite obliterated that belief in humanity to which their liberal parents held so ardently."

CONCLUSION

[1]Cited by Hirschberg, p. 45.

BIBLIOGRAPHY

PRIMARY SOURCES

Antisemiten-Spiegel. Danzig: A. W. Kasemann, 1892.

Antisemitisches Jahrbuch für 1898. Berlin: W. Geise, 1898.

Auerbach, Leopold. *Das Judenthum und seine Bekenner in Preussen.* Berlin: Sigmar Mehring, 1890.

Bernstein, Eduard. "Wie ich als Jude in der Diaspora aufwuchs." *Der Jude,* II (1917-1918), 186-195.

Birnbaum, Nathan. *Ausgewählte Schriften zur jüdischen Frage.* 2 vols. Czernowitz: Birnbaum and Kohut, 1910.

―――. *The Bridge.* Edited by Solomon A. Birnbaum. London: Jewish Post Publications, 1956.

Blumenfeld, Kurt. *Erlebte Judenfrage, Ein Vierteljahrhundert deutscher Zionismus.* Stuttgart: Deutsche Verlags-Anstalt, 1962.

―――. "Ursprünge und Art einer zionistischen Bewegung." *Bulletin of the Leo Baeck Institute,* IV (July, 1958), 129-140.

Bodenheimer, Max I. *So wurde Israel.* Frankfurt a. M.: Europäische Verlags-Anstalt, 1958.

―――. *Wohin mit den russischen Juden?* Hamburg: Verlag des Deutsch-Israelitischen Familienblatts "Die Menorah," 1891.

Boehlich, Walter, ed. *Der Berliner Antisemitismusstreit.* Frankfurt a. M.: Insel-Verlag, 1965.

Buber, Martin. *Die jüdische Bewegung,* vol. I. Berlin: Jüdischer Verlag, 1920.

Buber, Martin, Berthold Feiwel, and Chaim Weizmann. *Eine jüdische Hochschule,* Berlin: Jüdischer Verlag, 1902.

Dohm, Christian Wilhelm. "Concerning the Amelioration of the Civil Status of the Jews." Translated by Helen Lederer. Cincinnati: Hebrew Union College, 1957. (Mimeographed.)

Dritter Bericht über die israelitische Erziehungsanstalt zu Ahlem bei Hannover. Hannover, 1899.

Friedemann, Edmund. *Jüdische Moral und christlicher Staat.* Berlin: S. Cronbach, 1893.

Fuchs, Eugen. *Um Deutschtum und Judentum,* Frankfurt a.M.: J. Kauffmann, 1919.

Glatzer, Nahum N., ed. *Leopold and Adelheid Zunz: An Account in Letters (1815-1885).* London: East and West Library (for the Leo Baeck Institute), 1958.

Herzl, Theodor. "A Solution of the Jewish Question," republished as "Herzl's First Publication in the Jewish Cause from the *Jewish Chronicle,* January 17, 1896." *Herzl Year Book,* III (1960), 91-104.

―――. *Complete Diaries.* Edited by Raphael Patai. Translated by Harry Zohn. 5 vols. New York: Herzl Press, 1960.

―――. "From Herzl's Early Diary." *Herzl Year Book,* I (1958), 330-332.

Hess, Moses. *Rome and Jerusalem*. Translated and edited by Maurice J. Bloom. New York: Philosophical Library, 1958.

Jacobowski, Ludwig. *Offene Antwort eines Juden auf Herrn Ahlwardt's "Der Eid eines Juden."* Berlin: C. Küchenmeister, 1891.

Jüdischer Almanach. 5663. Edited by B. Feiwel and E. M. Lilien. Berlin: Jüdischer Verlag, [1902].

Jungmann, Max. *Erinnerungen eines Zionisten*. Jerusalem: Rubin, Mass, 1959.

Kobler, Franz, ed. *Juden und Judentum in deutschen Briefen aus drei Jahrhunderten*. Vienna: Saturn Verlag, 1935.

Landau, Saul Raphael. *Sturm und Drang im Zionismus*. Vienna: Verlag Neue National-Zeitung, 1937.

Lazarus, Moritz. *Treu und Frei: Gesammelte Reden und Vorträge über Juden und Judenthum*. Leipzig: C. F. Winter'sche Verlagshandlung, 1887.

Levita, Benedictus. "Die Erlösung des Judenthums." *Preussische Jahrbücher*, October, 1900.

Levin, Shmarya. *Youth in Revolt*. Translated by Maurice Samuel. New York: Harcourt, Brace and Co., 1930.

Levinstein, Gustav. *Zur Ehre des Judentums*. Berlin: Verein deutscher Staatsbürger jüdischen Glaubens, 1911.

Levy, Alphonse. *Die Erziehung der jüdischen Jugend zum Handwerk und zur Bodenkultur*. Berlin: E. Billig Nachf, 1895.

Lewisohn, Ludwig. *Theodor Herzl: A Portrait for this Age*. Cleveland and New York: World, 1955.

Loewenberg, Ernst L. "Jakob Loewenberg: Excerpts from His Diaries and Letters." *YBLBI*, XV (1970), 183-209.

[Loewenfeld, Raphael.] *Schutzjuden oder Staatsbürger?* 3rd ed. Berlin: Schweitzer and Mohr, 1893.

Lublinski, Samuel. *Nachgelassene Schriften*. Munich: Georg Müller, 1914.

Marx, Karl. "On the Jewish Question." Translated by Helen Lederer. Cincinnati: Hebrew Union College, 1955. (Mimeographed).

Mayer, Gustav. *Erinnerungen*. Zürich and Vienna: Europa Verlag, 1949.

Mendelsohn, M[artin]. *Die Pflicht der Selbstvertheidigung*. Berlin: Imberg & Lefson, 1894.

Oppenheimer, Franz. *Erlebtes, Erstrebtes, Erreichtes: Lebenserinnerungen*. Berlin: Welt-Verlag, 1931.

Plaut, W. Gunther. *The Rise of Reform Judaism: A Sourcebook of its European Origins*. New York: World Union For Progressive Judaism, 1963.

Rathenau, Walther. *Briefe*. 2 vols. Dresden: Carl Reissner Verlag, 1926.

———. "Höre Israel," in *Impressionen*. Leipzig: S. Hirzel, 1902. pp. 1-20.

Rückblick und Besinnung. Essays collected on the occasion of the 50th anniversary of the founding of the "Verbindung jüdischer Studenten 'Maccabaea' im K.J.Z." Tel Aviv, 1954.

Rülf, Schlomo. *Ströme im dürren Land*. Erinnerungen. Stuttgart: Deutsche Verlags-Anstalt, 1964.

Ruppin, Arthur. *Die Juden der Gegenwart: Eine sozialwissenschaftliche Studie*. Berlin: S. Calvary & Co., 1904.

Sachse, Heinrich [Heinrich Loewe]. *Zionisten-Kongress und Zionismus: eine Gefahr?* Berlin: Hugo Schildberger, 1897.

Schnitzler, Arthur. *The Road to the Open*. Translated by H. Samuel. New York: Alfred A. Knopf, 1923.

Selig. *Reflexionen zu Walther Rathenau's Impressionen: Höre Israel.* Eine Erwiderung. Worms: H. Krauter, 1902.
Simon, F. *Wehrt Euch! Ein Mahnwort an die Juden.* Berlin, 1893.
Statuten der Berliner Zionistischen Vereinigung. Berlin, 1898.
Straus, Rahel. *Wir lebten in Deutschland.* Stuttgart: Deutsche Verlags-Anstalt, 1961.
Treitschke, Heinrich von. *A Word About Our Jewry.* Translated by Helen Lederer. Cincinnati: Hebrew Union College, 1959. (Mimeographed.)
Wassermann, Jakob. *Mein Weg als Deutscher und Jude.* Berlin: S. Fischer Verlag, 1921.
Zweiter Bericht über die israelitische Erziehungsanstalt zu Ahlem bei Hannover. Hannover, 1897.

SECONDARY SOURCES

Adler, H. G. *The Jews in Germany.* Notre Dame and London: Notre Dame Press, 1969.
Adler, Joseph. *The Herzl Paradox.* New York: Hadrian Press and Herzl Press, 1962.
Adler-Rudel, S[halom]. *Ostjuden in Deutschland 1880-1940.* Tübingen: J.C.B. Mohr (Paul Siebeck), 1959.
Altmann, Alexander. "The New Style of Preaching in Nineteenth Century German Jewry." *Studies in Nineteenth Century Jewish Intellectual History.* Edited by Alexander Altmann. Cambridge: Harvard University Press, 1964, pp. 65-116.
Arendt, Hannah. *The Origins of Totalitarianism.* New York: Meridian Books, 1959.
Asch, Adolph, and Johanna Philippson. "Self-Defence at the Turn of the Century: The Emergence of the K.C." *YBLBI,* III (1958), 122-139.
Baron, Salo Wittmayer. *A Social and Religious History of the Jews.* Vol. II. New York: Columbia University Press, 1937.
Bein, Alex. "Halifat Michtavim beyn Herzl v'Rathenau." ("Correspondence between Herzl and Rathenau.") *Bitzaron,* VII (1942-43), 108-113, 188-189.
———. "Modern Anti-Semitism and its Effect on the Jewish Question." *Yad Washem Studies.* Vol. III. Jerusalem: Yad Washem, 1959. 7-15.
———. "Some Early Herzl Letters." *Herzl Year Book,* I (1958), 297-329.
———. *Theodor Herzl.* Philadelphia: Jewish Publication Society, 1941.
Ben-Horin, Meir. *Max Nordau: Philosopher of Human Solidarity.* New York: Conference on Jewish Social Studies, 1956.
Berlak, Hermann. *Der Kartellconvent der Verbindungen deutscher Studenten jüdischen Glaubens.* Berlin, 1927.
Bieber, Hugo, ed., and Moses Hadas, trans. *Heinrich Heine: A Biographical Anthology.* Philadelphia: Jewish Publication Society, 1956.
Birnbaum, Solomon. "Nathan Birnbaum." *Men of the Spirit.* Edited by Leo Jung. New York: Kymson Publishing Co., 1964, 519-549.
Bloch, Chaim. "Herzl's First Years of Struggle." *Herzl Year Book,* III (1960), 77-104.
———. "Theodor Herzl and Joseph S. Bloch." *Herzl Year Book,* I (1958), 154-164.
Bloom, Solomon F. "Karl Marx and the Jews." *Jewish Social Studies,* IV:1 (January, 1942), 3-16.
Bodenheimer, Henriette Hannah. *Im Anfang der zionistischen Bewegung.* Frankfurt a.M.: Europäische Verlagsanstalt, 1965.

————. *Toldot Tochnit Basel* ("The History of the Basel Program"). Jerusalem: Reuben Maas, 1947.

Böhm, Adolf. *Die zionistische Bewegung bis zum Ende des Weltkrieges.* 2d ed. Tel Aviv: Hotzaah Ivrit, Ltd., 1935.

Breines, Paul. "The Jew as Revolutionary: The Case of Gustav Landauer." *YBLBI,* XII (1967), 75-84.

Buber, Martin. "Moses Hess." *Jewish Social Studies,* VII:2 (April, 1945), 137-148.

Byrnes, Robert Francis. *Antisemitism in Modern France.* New Brunswick, New Jersey: Rutgers University Press, 1950.

Cahnman, Werner J. "Adolph Fischhof and His Jewish Followers." *YBLBI,* IV (1959), 111-139.

Cervinka, Frantisek. "The Hilsner Affair." *YBLBI,* XIII (1968), 142-157.

Cohen, Carl. "The Road to Conversion." *YBLBI,* VI (1961), 259-279.

Cohen, Henry J. "Theodor Herzl's Conversion to Zionism." *Jewish Social Studies,* XXXII:2 (April, 1970), 101-110.

Cohn, Norman. *Warrant for Genocide.* New York and Evanston: Harper & Row, 1966.

Dubnow, S[imon] M. *Die neueste Geschichte des jüdischen Volkes.* Vol. III. Berlin: Jüdischer Verlag, 1923.

————. *Weltgeschichte des jüdischen Volkes.* Vol. X. Translated from the Russian by A. Steinberg. Berlin: Jüdischer Verlag, 1929.

Edelheim-Muehsam, Margaret T. "The Jewish Press in Germany." *YBLBI,* I (1956), 163-176.

Elbogen, Ismar. *A Century of Jewish Life.* Philadelphia: Jewish Publication Society, 1953.

————. *Geschichte der Juden in Deutschland.* Berlin: Lichtenstein, 1935.

Elbogen, Ismar, and Eleonore Sterling. *Die Geschichte der Juden in Deutschland.* Frankfurt a.M.; Europäische Verlagsanstalt, 1966.

Feder, Ernst. *Paul Nathan: Ein Lebensbild.* Berlin: Deutsche Verlagsgesellschaft für Politik und Geschichte, 1929.

————. "Paul Nathan, the Man and His Work." *YBLBI,* III (1958), 60-80.

Friedlander, Fritz. *Das Leben Gabriel Riessers.* Berlin: Philo Verlag, 1926.

Gelber, N[athan] M[ichael]. "Herzl's Polish Contacts." *Herzl Year Book,* I (1958), 197-231.

Glatzer, Nahum N. "The Beginnings of Modern Jewish Studies." *Studies in Nineteenth Century Jewish Intellectual History.* Edited by Alexander Altmann. Cambridge: Harvard University Press, 1964, 27-46.

————. *Leopold Zunz: Jude-Deutscher-Europäer.* Tübingen: J.C.B. Mohr (Paul Siebeck), 1964.

Gold, Hugo. *Geschichte der Juden in Wien.* Tel Aviv: Olamenu, 1966.

Goldstein, Moritz. "German Jewry's Dilemma: The Story of a Provocative Essay." *YBLBI,* II, (1957), 236-254.

Gottgetreu, Erich. "Maximilian Harden." *YBLBI,* VII (1962), 215-246.

Graupe, Heinz Moshe. "Steinheim and Kant." *YBLBI,* V (1960), 140-175.

Gross, Walter. "The Zionist Students' Movement." *YBLBI,* IV (1959), 143-164.

Halpern, Ben. "Herzl's Historic Gift: The Sense of Sovereighty." *Herzl Year Book,* III (1960), 27-36.

————. *The Idea of the Jewish State.* Cambridge: Harvard University Press, 1961.

Hamburger, Ernest. "One Hundred Years of Emancipation." *YBLBI,* XIV (1969), 3-66.

Hamerow, Theodore S. *Restoration, Revolution, Reaction: Economics and Politics in Germany, 1815-1871*. Princeton, New Jersey: Princeton University Press, 1958.

Hayes, Carlton J.H. *A Generation of Materialism (1871-1900)*. New York, Evanston, and London: Harper and Brothers, 1941.

Hermann, Leo. *Nathan Birnbaum: Sein Werk und seine Wandlung*. Berlin: Jüdischer Verlag, 1914.

Hertzberg, Arthur. *The French Enlightenment and the Jews: The Origins of Modern Anti-Semitism*. New York: Schocken Books, 1970.

———. *The Zionist Idea*. New York: Meridan Books and The Jewish Publication Society, 1959.

Hirschberg, Alfred. "Ludwig Hollaender, Director of the C.V." *YBLBI*, VII (1962), 39-74.

Irvine, William. *Apes, Angels and Victorians: Darwin, Huxley, and Evolution*. New York: Meridian, 1959.

"James Simon: Industrialist, Art Collector, Philanthropist." *YBLBI*, X (1965), 3-23.

Jewish Encyclopedia. New York and London: Funk and Wagnalls, 1925.

Kampmann, Wanda. *Deutsche und Juden*. Heidelberg: Lambert Schneider, 1963.

Kann, Robert A. "Assimilation and Antisemitism in the German-French Orbit in the Nineteenth and Early Twentieth Century." *YBLBI*, XIV (1969), 92-115.

———. "Friedrich Julius Stahl: A Re-examination of his Conservatism." *YBLBI* XII (1967), 55-74.

———. *The Hapsburg Empire: A Study in Integration and Disintegration*. New York: Praeger, 1957.

Katz, Jacob. Review of *Er ist wie Du* by Eleonore Sterling. *Journal of Jewish Studies*, VIII:3, 4 (1957), 246.

———. "Jewry and Judaism in the Nineteenth Century." *Journal of World History*, IV:4 (1958), 881-900.

———. *Jews and Freemasons in Europe, 1723-1939*. Cambridge: Harvard University Press, 1970.

———. "The Term 'Jewish Emancipation': Its Origin and Historical Impact." *Studies in Nineteenth Century Jewish Intellectual History*. Edited by Alexander Altmann. Cambridge: Harvard University Press, 1964, 1-26.

———. *Tradition and Crisis: Jewish Society at the End of the Middle Ages*. New York: Free Press, 1961.

Kautsky, Karl. *Are the Jews a Race?* New York: International Publishers, 1926.

Kellner, Leon. *Theodor Herzls Lehrjahre*. Vienna and Berlin: R. Löwit, 1920.

Kessler, Count Harry. *Walter Rathenau, His Life and Work*. New York: Harcourt, Brace and Co., 1930.

Klausner, Israel, *Ha-oppozitsia l'Herzl* ("The Opposition to Herzl"). Jerusalem: Achiever, 1960.

Klinkenberg, Hans Martin. "Zwischen Liberalismus und Nationalismus im zweiten Kaiserreich (1870-1918)." *Monumenta Judaica*. Cologne: Konrad Schilling, 1963, 309-384.

Kohn, Hans. *Martin Buber, Sein Werk und seine Zeit*. Cologne: Joseph Melzer Verlag, 1961.

Krieger, Leonard. *The German Idea of Freedom*. Boston: Beacon Press, 1957.

Laqueur, Walter. "The German Youth Movement and the 'Jewish Question'—A Preliminary Survey," *YBLBI*, VI (1961) 193-205.

———. *Young Germany, A History of the German Youth Movement*. New York: Basic Books, 1962.

Leschnitzer, Adolf. *The Magic Background of Modern Anti-Semitism: An Analysis of the German-Jewish Relationship.* New York: International Universities Press, 1956.

Lessing, Theodor, *Der jüdische Selbsthass.* Berlin: Jüdischer Verlag, 1930.

Lichtheim, Richard. *Toldot Ha-tsionut B'germania* ("The History of Zionism in Germany"). Jerusalem: Hahistadrut Hatsionit, 1951.

Liebeschütz, Hans. "German Radicalism and the Formation of Jewish Political Attitudes During the Early Part of the Nineteenth Century." *Studies in Nineteenth Century Jewish Intellectual History.* Edited by Alexander Altmann. Cambridge: Harvard University Press, 1964, 141-170.

———. "Problems of Diaspora History in XIXth Century Germany." *Journal of Jewish Studies,* VIII:1, 2 (1957), 103-111.

———. "Treitschke and Mommsen on Jewry and Judaism." *YBLBI,* VII (1962), 153-182.

Liptzin, Solomon. *Germany's Stepchildren.* Cleveland, New York, and Philadelphia: Meridian and Jewish Publication Society, 1961.

Lowe, Adolph. "In Memoriam Franz Oppenheimer." *YBLBI,* X (1965), 137-149.

Lowenthal, E[rnst] G[ottfried]. "The Ahlem Experiment: A Brief Survey of the 'Jüdische Gartenbauschule.' " *YBLBI,* XIV (1969), 165-181.

Lowenthal, Marvin. *The Jews of Germany.* Philadelphia: Jewish Publication Society, 1936.

Mann, Golo. *Deutsche Geschichte des 19. und 20. Jahrhunderts.* Frankfurt a.M.: S. Fischer Verlag, 1958.

Marcus, Jacob. R. *The Rise and Destiny of the German Jew.* Cincinnati: Union of American Hebrew Congregations, 1934.

Masur, Gerhard. *Prophets of Yesterday: Studies in European Culture, 1890-1914.* New York: Harper and Row, 1966.

Massing, Paul W. *Rehearsal for Destruction.* New York: Harper and Brothers, 1949.

Meyer, Michael A. "Caesar Seligmann and the Development of Liberal Judaism in Germany at the Beginning of the Twentieth Century." *Hebrew Union College Annual,* XL-XLI (1969-1970), 529-554.

———. "Great Debate on Antisemitism: Jewish Reaction to New Hostility in Germany, 1879-1881." *YBLBI,* XI (1966), 137-170.

———. *The Origins of the Modern Jew: Jewish Identity and European Culture in Germany, 1749-1824.* Detroit: Wayne State University Press, 1967.

Michael, Reuwen. "Graetz contra Treitschke." *Bulletin of the Leo Baeck Institute,* IV:16 (December, 1961).

Morgenthau, Hans. J. "The Tragedy of Germany-Jewish Liberalism." *Leo Baeck Memorial Lecture,* 4. New York: Leo Baeck Institute, 1961.

Mosse, George L. *The Crisis of German Ideology: Intellectual Origins of the Third Reich.* New York: Grosset and Dunlap, 1964.

———. "The Influence of the Völkisch Idea on German Jewry." *Studies of the Leo Baeck Institute.* New York: Frederick Ungar Co., 1967, 83-114.

———. "The Conflict of Liberalism and Nationalism and its Effect on German Jewry." *YBLBI,* XV (1970), 125-139.

Namier, Louis. *1848: The Revolution of the Intellectuals.* Garden City, New York: Doubleday and Company, Anchor Books, 1964.

Paucker, Arnold. "Der jüdische Abwehrkampf." *Entscheidungsjahr 1932. Zur Judenfrage in der Endphase der Weimarer Republik.* Edited by Werner E. Mosse. Tübingen: Mohr, 1965, 405-499.

Petuchowski, Jakob J. "Manuals and Catechisms of the Jewish Religion in the Early Period of the Emancipation." *Studies in Nineteenth Century Jewish Intellectual History*. Edited by Alexander Altmann. Cambridge: Harvard University Press, 1964, 47-64.

Philippson, Martin. *Neueste Geschichte des jüdischen Volkes*. Vol. 2. Leipzig: Gustav Fock, 1910.

Philipson, David. *The Reform Movement in Judaism*. New York: Macmillan, 1907.

Pinson, Koppel S. *Modern Germany: Its History and Civilization*. New York: MacMillan, 1954.

Pois, Robert A. "Walter Rathenau's Jewish Quandry." *YBLBI*, XIII (1968), 120-131.

Prinz, Arthur. "New Perspectives on Marx as a Jew." *YBLBI*, XIII (1970), 107-124.

Pulzer, Peter G. J. *The Rise of Political Antisemitism in Germany and Austria*. New York, London, and Sydney: John Wiley and Sons, 1964.

Reichmann, Eva G. *Hostages of Civilization: A Study of the Social Causes of Antisemitism in Germany*. Boston: Beacon Press, 1951.

Reichmann, Hans. "Der Zentralverein deutscher Staatsbürger jüdischen Glaubens." *Festschrift zum 80. Geburtstag von Rabbiner Dr. Leo Baeck*. London: The Council for the Protection of the Rights and Interests of Jews from Germany, 1953.

Reinharz, Jehuda. *Fatherland or Promised Land: The Dilemma of the German Jew, 1893-1914*. Ann Arbor: University of Michigan Press, 1975.

Reiss, Hans Siegbert, ed. *The Political Thought of the German Romantics*. New York, Oxford, 1955.

Reissner, Hanns Günther. *Eduard Gans: Ein Leben im Vormärz*. Tübingen: J.C.B. Mohr (Paul Siebeck), 1965.

Rieger, [Paul]. *Ein Vierteljahrhundert im Kampf um das Recht*. Centralverein deutscher Staatsbürger jüdischen Glaubens, 1918.

Rinott, Moshe. "Gabriel Riesser: Fighter for Jewish Emancipation." *YBLBI*, VII (1962), 11-38.

Rosenbaum, Eduard. "Franz Oppenheimer: A Digression." *YBLBI*, XI (1966), 336-338.

―――. "Rathenau—A Supplementary Note." *YBLBI*, XIII (1968), 132-134.

―――. "Reflections on Walter Rathenau." *YBLBI*, IV (1959) 260-264.

Rosenberg, Arthur. *Imperial Germany: The Birth of the German Republic, 1871-1918*. Boston: Beacon Press, 1964.

Rotenstreich, Nathan. "On the Groundwork of Herzl's Ideas." *Herzl Year Book*, III (1960), 165-173.

―――. "For and Against Emancipation—The Bruno Bauer Controversy." *YBLBI*, IV (1959), 3-36.

―――. *The Recurring Pattern: Studies in Anti-Judaism in Modern Thought*. New York: Horizon Press, 1964.

Rürup, Reinhard. "Jewish Emancipation and Bourgeois Society." *YBLBI*, IV (1969), 67-91.

Sandler, Ahron. "The Struggle for Unification." *YBLBI*, II (1957), 76-84.

Schaeder, Grete. *Martin Buber: Hebräischer Humanismus*. Göttingen: Vondenhoeck and Ruprecht, 1966.

Schmidt, H.D. "Anti-Western and Anti-Jewish Tradition in German Historical Thought." *YBLBI*, I (1959), 37-60.

Schorsch, Ismar. *Jewish Reactions to German Anti-Semitism, 1870-1914.* New York, London and Philadelphia: Columbia University Press and Jewish Publication Society of America, 1972.

———. Review of *Christians and Jews in the Second Reich* by Uriel Tal. *Judaism,* XIX:3 (Summer, 1970), 373-377.

Schnabel, Franz. *Deutsche Geschichte im neunzehnten Jahrhundert.* 12 Vols. Freiburg: Herder-Bücherei, 1965.

Schwab, Hermann. *The History of Orthodox Jewry in Germany.* London: Mitre Press, n.d.

Shohet, Azriel. *Im Hilufei T'kufot: Reshit Ha-haskalah B'yahadut Germaniya* ("Beginnings of the Haskalah Among German Jewry"). Jerusalem: Bialik Institute, 1960.

Silberner, Edmund. "The Anti-Semitic Tradition in Modern Socialism." *Scripta Hierosolymitana,* III. Jerusalem: Magnes Press, 1956, 378-396.

———. "Antisemitism and Philosemitism in the Socialist International." *Judaism,* II:2 (April, 1953), 117-122.

———. "Friedrich Engels and the Jews." *Jewish Social Studies,* XI:4 (October, 1949), 323-342.

———. "German Social Democracy and the Jewish Problem prior to World War I." *Historia Judaica,* XV:1 (April, 1953), 3-48.

———. "Moses Hess." *Historia Judaica,* XIII:1 (April, 1951), 3-28.

———. "Was Marx an Anti-Semite?" *Historia Judaica,* XI:1 (April, 1949), 3-52.

Sokolow, Nahum. *History of Zionism.* New York: Ktav, 1969.

Steinman, Ulrich. "Some Notes on James Simon." *YBLBI,* XIII (1968), 277-282.

Sterling, Eleonore O. "Anti-Jewish Riots in Germany in 1819, a Displacement of Social Protest." *Historia Judaica,* XII:1 (April, 1950), 105-142.

———. *Er ist wie Du. Aus der Frühgeschichte des Antisemitismus in Deutschland (1815-1850).* Munich: Chr. Kaiser Verlag, 1956.

———. "Jewish Reaction to Jew-Hatred in the First Half of the Nineteenth Century." *YBLBI,* III (1958), 103-121.

Stern, Fritz. *The Politics of Cultural Despair: A Study in the Rise of the Germanic Ideology.* Berkeley and Los Angeles: University of California Press, 1961.

Stern-Taubler, Selma. "The German Jew in a Changing World." *YBLBI,* VII (1962), 3-10.

Strauss, Herbert. "The Jugendverband: A Social and Intellectual History." *YBLBI,* VI (1961), 206-235.

Susman, Margarete. *Ich habe viele Leben gelebt. Erinnerungen* 2d ed. Stuttgart: Deutsche Verlags-Anstalt, 1964.

Syrkin, Marie. *Nachman Syrkin, Socialist Zionist.* New York: Herzl Press, 1961.

Tal, Uriel. "Ha-Anti-shemiut B'reich Ha-germani Ha-sheyni, 1870-1914 ("Antisemitism in the Second German Reich, 1870-1914"). Unpublished Ph.D. dissertation, Hebrew University, Jerusalem, 1963.

———. "Conservative Protestantism and the Status of the Jews in the 'Second Reich,' 1870-1914." *Zion,* XXVII:1, 2 (1962), 87-111.

———. "Liberal Protestantism and the Jews in the Second Reich, 1870-1914." *Jewish Social Studies,* XXVI:1 (January, 1964), 23-41.

Taylor, A. J. P. *The Course of German History.* New York: Capricorn Books, 1962.

Theilhaber, Felix A. *Judenschicksal.* Tel Aviv: Olympia, n. d.

Toury, Jacob. "Jüdische Parteigänger des Antisemitismus." *Bulletin of the Leo Baeck Institute,* IV:16 (December, 1961), 323-335.

———. "Organizational Problems of German Jewry: Steps toward the Establishment of a Central Organization, 1893-1920." *YBLBI*, XIII (1968), 57-90.

———. *Die politischen Orientierungen der Juden in Deutschland.* Tübingen: J. C. B. Mohr (Paul Siebeck), 1966.

———. "Nisyionot L'nihul Mediniut Yehudit B'germaniya, 1893-1918" ("Attempts to Direct Jewish Politics in Germany, 1893-1918"). *Zion*, XXVIII:3-4 (1963), 165-205.

Tramer, Hans. "Vom Ungeist der Zeiten." *Bulletin of the Leo Baeck Institute,* IV:16 (December, 1961), 249-267.

Trevor-Roper, H. R., "Some of My Best Friends Are Philosophes." Review of *The French Enlightenment and the Jews* by Arthur Hertzberg. *New York Review of Books,* August 22, 1968, 11-14.

Valentin, Veit. *The German People: Their History and Civilization from the Holy Roman Empire to the Third Reich.* New York: Alfred Knopf, 1945.

Veblen, Thorstein. *Imperial Germany and the Industrial Revolution.* Ann Arbor Paperbacks. Ann Arbor: University of Michigan Press, 1966.

Viereck, Peter. *Meta-Politics: The Roots of the Nazi Mind.* New York: Capricorn Books, 1961.

Walk, Joseph. "The Torah va'Avodah Movement in Germany." *YBLBI*, VI (1961), 236-256.

Wawrzinek, Kurt. *Die Entstehung der deutschen Antisemitenparteien (1873-1890).* Berlin: E. Ebering, 1927.

Weltsch, Robert. "Introduction." *YBLBI*, IX (1964), ix-xxxii.

———. "Introduction." *YBLBI*, XIV (1969), ix-xxiii.

Wiener, Max. *Abraham Geiger and Liberal Judaism: The Challenge of the Nineteenth Century.* Philadelphia: Jewish Publication Society of America, 1962.

———. *Jüdische Religion im Zeitalter der Emanzipation.* Berlin: Philo Verlag, 1933.

Wilhelm, Kurt. "Benno Jacob, a Militant Rabbi." *YBLBI*, VII (1962), 75-94.

———. "The Jewish Community in the Post Emancipation Period." *YBLBI*, II (1957), 47-75.

Zechlin, Egmont. *Die deutsche Politik und die Juden im ersten Weltkrieg.* Göttingen: Vandenhoeck and Ruprecht, 1969.

INDEX

223